Science Fusion in Contemporary Mexican Literature

Bucknell Studies in Latin American Literature and Theory

Series editor: Aníbal González, Yale University

Dealing with far-reaching questions of history and modernity, language and self-hood, and power and ethics, Latin American literature sheds light on the many-faceted nature of Latin American life, as well as on the human condition as a whole. This highly successful series has published some of the best recent criticism on Latin American literature. Acknowledging the historical links and cultural affinities between Latin American and Iberian literatures, the series productively combines scholarship with theory and welcomes consideration of Spanish and Portuguese texts and topics, while also providing a space of convergence for scholars working in Romance studies, comparative literature, cultural studies, and literary theory.

Recent titles in the series:

Science Fusion in Contemporary Mexican Literature
Brian T. Chandler

Nature Fantasies: Decolonization and Biopolitics in Latin America
Gabriel Horowitz

The Aesthetic Border: Colombian Literature in the Face of Globalization
Brantley Nicholson

White Light: The Poetry of Alberto Blanco
Ronald J. Friis

Latin American Literature at the Millennium: Local Lives, Global Spaces
Cecily Raynor

Exemplary Violence: Rewriting History in Colonial Colombia
Alberto Villate-Isaza

Transpoetic Exchange: Haroldo de Campos, Octavio Paz, and Other Multiversal Dialogues
Marília Librandi, Jamille Pinheiro Dias, and Tom Winterbottom, eds.

Early Puerto Rican Cinema and Nation Building: National Sentiments, Transnational Realities, 1897–1940
Naida García-Crespo

Machado de Assis and Narrative Theory: Language, Imitation, Art, and Verisimilitude in the Last Six Novels
Earl E. Fitz

Beyond Human: Vital Materialisms in the Andean Avant-Gardes
Tara Daly

For more information about the series, please visit bucknelluniversitypress.org

Science Fusion in Contemporary Mexican Literature

Brian T. Chandler

LEWISBURG, PENNSYLVANIA

Library of Congress Cataloging-in-Publication Data

Names: Chandler, Brian T., author.
Title: Science fusion in contemporary Mexican literature / Brian T. Chandler.
Description: Lewisburg, Pennsylvania : Bucknell University Press, [2024] |
    Series: Bucknell studies in Latin American literature and theory |
    Includes bibliographical references and index.
Identifiers: LCCN 2023031269 | ISBN 9781684485208 (hardcover) |
    ISBN 9781684485192 (paperback) | ISBN 9781684485215 (epub) |
    ISBN 9781684485222 (pdf)
Subjects: LCSH: Mexican literature—20th century—History and criticism. |
    Science in literature. | BISAC: LITERARY CRITICISM / Modern /
    20th Century | LITERARY CRITICISM / Caribbean & Latin American
Classification: LCC PQ7155 .C43 2024 | DDC 860.9/9720905—dc23/eng/20231124
LC record available at https://lccn.loc.gov/2023031269

A British Cataloging-in-Publication record for this book is available from the British Library.

Copyright © 2024 by Brian T. Chandler

All rights reserved

No part of this book may be reproduced or utilized in any form or by any means, electronic or mechanical, or by any information storage and retrieval system, without written permission from the publisher. Please contact Bucknell University Press, Hildreth-Mirza Hall, Bucknell University, Lewisburg, PA 17837–2005. The only exception to this prohibition is "fair use" as defined by U.S. copyright law.

References to internet websites (URLs) were accurate at the time of writing. Neither the author nor Bucknell University Press is responsible for URLs that may have expired or changed since the manuscript was prepared.

♾ The paper used in this publication meets the requirements of the American National Standard for Information Sciences—Permanence of Paper for Printed Library Materials, ANSI Z39.48-1992.

bucknelluniversitypress.org

Printed and bound by CPI Group (UK) Ltd, Croydon, CR0 4YY

For Keri, Camille Gale, and Lily Lessie

Contents

Note on Translations   ix

Introduction: Entangling Science, Literature, and Culture in Mexico   1

1   Entangled Matter: The Science Poetry of Alberto Blanco   23

2   Quantum Mechanics, History, and the Question of Scale in Jorge Volpi's *En busca de Klingsor*   47

3   Automatons, Androids, and Androcentrism in Ignacio Padilla's *El androide y otras quimeras*   67

4   A Science of Good and Evil: Sabina Berman's Darwinian Ethical Turn   85

5   In Search of a New Language: Autopoiesis and the Anthropocene in Maricela Guerrero's *El sueño de toda célula*   109

6   Dimensions of Embodied Experience: Space and Time in Elisa Díaz Castelo's *Principia*   133

Conclusions: Knowing and Belonging in an Entangled Universe   161

Acknowledgments   167
Notes   169
Bibliography   197
Index   213

Note on Translations

Unless otherwise noted, translations are mine. When translating poetry, I have erred on the side of comprehensibility for non-Spanish readers, at times using additional verbiage to communicate polyvalent words and images over reproducing lyrical patterns and form in the original.

Science Fusion in Contemporary Mexican Literature

Introduction

ENTANGLING SCIENCE, LITERATURE, AND CULTURE IN MEXICO

Of the close to two hundred stations in the Mexico City metro system, La Raza stands out as one of the most fascinating as it houses the Túnel de la ciencia (Tunnel of Science), a scientific exhibition and museum designed to be experienced by passengers rushing along their commute. In addition to a library, interactive exhibits, and informative displays, the focal point of the tunnel is the *bóveda celeste*, an illuminated celestial vault depicting the autumn night sky. For countless commuters who daily pass through the darkened walkway only to rush to catch the next train or to walk outside into the evening where light pollution obscures but a handful of stars, those few minutes in the tunnel may be the one time in the day when science is explicitly on display. In addition to staking the claim of being the world's first scientific museum housed in a public transportation facility, it professes to be the world's most visited, with a staggering 1,884,607 "visitors" passing through it each month.[1] Its placement at the heart of a major point of transfer in Mexico City's metro system serves as a powerful symbol, for the passengers' journeys are made possible by the technological entanglement of the scientific and the human with electromagnetic and gravitational forces acting upon human-material assemblages of metal, glass, plastic, and flesh, all to facilitate movement and life in this modern metropolis.

Pausing for a moment to take in the Túnel's displays amid the hustle and bustle of people moving from one place to another—not for the faint of heart during rush hour—one perceives a clear connection between movement, interconnectivity, flow, and the happening of life in the museum's exhibits as well as their surroundings. Many of the displays explicitly address these themes such as the expansive exhibition titled "De las Redes Sociales a la Red Cósmica del Universo" (From Social Networks to the Cosmic Network of the Universe), where one infographic emphasizes that the universe is one vast network of "filamentos" (filaments), "huecos" (holes), and "nudos" (knots).[2] Using a composite infrared

1

image of the distribution of galaxies in the local universe, the cosmos appears in the display as a vast web of light with embedded pictures that zoom in to explain different structures within this greater reticular network. The images' accompanying text likewise uses metaphorical language that connects the human to the universe, describing, for example, how the different images portray aspects of space and time that scientists must put together like "piezas de un rompecabezas" (pieces of a puzzle). The text even bestows on the universe anthropomorphic qualities, as when it explains how darker areas in the image of the local universe show that "la red cósmica tiene un esqueleto constituido por partículas que no emiten luz" (the cosmic network has a skeleton made up of particles that do not emit light). From a universe "out there" waiting to be explored and explained through human ingenuity to a reality that, at least through human language, can be described only with metaphor, the exhibits of the Túnel de la ciencia convey humanity as part of a conceptually and physically entangled cosmos.

I begin with a slight detour through Mexico City's metro system, a space where Carlos Monsiváis sardonically noted that "se disuelven las fronteras entre un cuerpo y otro" (the limits between one body and another dissolve),[3] because I explore similar interconnectivities in works of contemporary Mexican authors who utilize scientific knowledge and conceptual analogues to reorient the human within more-than-human networks, entanglements, and intra-active relations. In doing so these authors purposefully highlight the ways in which the natural sciences and culture are enmeshed in order to reposition human bodies and subjectivity as both emerging from and constitutive to the same matter, forces, and phenomena that are the object of scientific study. I identify these works as examples of *ciencia-fusión* (science-fusion), extending Guillermo Cabrera-Infante's description of Jorge Volpi's *En busca de Klingsor* (*In Search of Klingsor*) to include many other contemporary works that similarly transpose and transculturate scientific discourse and concepts to address issues in biopolitics, historiography, metaphysics, ethics, and ecological crisis in the age of the Anthropocene. In classifying these works as ciencia-fusión, I put a special emphasis on the concept of fusion, the creative action of merging and emerging, while maintaining a distinction with works that use science through speculative fiction under the genre of *ciencia ficción* (science fiction). Reflecting Rafael Catalá's call for an integrated vision of reality that brings literature and science together in what he coins *cienciapoesía*,[4] works of ciencia-fusión appear across literary genres as diverse as the novel, poetry, short fiction, and theater. While they often take up disparate themes and utilize scientific knowledge and knowledge making in different ways, they all share a common characteristic of explicitly fusing science and literature together to problematize humanist dualisms such as subject-object, nature-culture, and human-nonhuman and, of course, the long-standing divide between science and literature. In this manner, these authors use science to

INTRODUCTION

reposition the human within an interconnected and material universe while at the same time continuing heterogenous legacies of conciliation in Mexican literature between artistic and scientific domains of knowledge.

Like the displays in the Túnel de la ciencia, works of ciencia-fusión use metaphor—a transference from one domain to another—to establish conceptual connections between the cosmos and the human.[5] The metaphor of entanglement features prominently in ciencia-fusión and, consequently, informs my analysis of these works. While in general usage the term conveys images of a knotting together, in quantum mechanics entanglement reveals an essential aspect of the universe unimaginable until only recently. Among the many strange phenomena that occur at subatomic scales, quantum entanglement describes how electrons, photons, and other particles can become linked so that the state observed in one particle will be correlated in the other. Even over unfathomably vast distances, these entangled particles will simultaneously reflect the system's quantum state, undermining our intuitive understanding of causality and the way even faraway objects interact with each other. Famously described by Albert Einstein as "spooky action at a distance," entanglement describes a specific physical phenomenon, yet its potential as metaphor has advanced our understanding of networks, assemblages, and systems far beyond its original application in quantum mechanics. Likewise, interconnectivity features throughout works of ciencia-fusión, as the authors entangle not only science and art but also the material with the human, portraying a reality that is intrinsically intermeshed and relational. As a result, these works reveal a deeper understanding of the universe and new conceptualizations with which to confront the sociocultural and environmental issues of the present.

INTERCONNECTIVITIES BETWEEN SCIENCE, LITERATURE, AND CULTURE

Perhaps more than any other public personality in Mexico today, José Gordon is the face of popularized science communication through his widespread journalistic work in television, print, radio, and online platforms. A novelist and translator himself, Gordon brings together topics related to science and the arts, seeking to find common points of departure and convergence between the two. In his book-length essay *El inconcebible universo* (*The Inconceivable Universe*), Gordon takes readers on a journey through moments in famous works of literature where, for fleeting instants, science and art seem to come together to express the dream of unity, the elusive theory of everything where all matter and forces in the universe are unified. While Gordon celebrates how these works express profound insights, he maintains that the dream remains unrealized: "El drama tanto en nuestras vidas, como en la literatura, como en la ciencia, es que cuando creemos tocar esa unidad se desvanece, parece ser tan sólo una ilusión en medio de la trágica fragmentación individual y colectiva" (The drama in our lives, as much in literature as in science, is that when we think we're touching that unity it vanishes, seeming to be just an illusion in the midst of our tragic individual and collective fragmentation).[6] The dream of bringing together natural science and art to better understand our universe is obviously not a new proposition. The distance between science and the humanities is often viewed through the lens of what C. P. Snow famously called the "two cultures," with both operating in different domains with their own sets of knowledge-making practices.[7] Like Snow, who argued for dialogue between the two cultures driven apart over the previous centuries, similar calls for consilience between what Edward Wilson terms various "branches of knowledge" frequently employ an arborescent metaphor that portrays the disciplines as sharing a unified foundation and goals in the pursuit of understanding our world.[8] Such rapprochements argue for the summative value of collaboration and reconciliation between science and art, each bringing to the table particular knowledge as when Volpi affirms how "la literatura es otra forma de aproximación al mundo, a la realidad y a los seres humanos, tan válida como la ciencia y por eso deberían estar mucho más cerca una de otra" (literature is another way of approaching the world, reality, and human beings, as valid as science and therefore the two should be much closer to each other).[9]

One of the most common ways that literature and science have been brought together is through the recognition that both are inherently discursive activities. Since language can never be a pure mediator of reality, both science and literature are human constructs and, as such, incorporate narrative patterns and inflections of society and culture.[10] Consequently, Victoria Carpenter states, "The boundaries of science and literature are permeable; they are continuously crossed and illuminated by a variety of narrative forms and their interpretation. Changes in our perception of the world are informed in equal measure by scientific and humanistic disciplines."[11] Science and culture are both discourses mediated by what Jerry Hoeg terms "the Social Imaginary," and therefore we can "expect to find mutual influences or reciprocal relations between the two discourses."[12] In addition to models of reciprocity, we often find science and literature explained in complementary terms. In this manner, Gerardo Herrera Corral, physicist and lead investigator for the Mexican research team at the Large Hadron Collider, sees the relations between literature and science as corresponding, explaining how, for example, José Emilio Pacheco's poetry actually illustrates many scientific models and concepts: "Los poetas tienen las palabras difuminadas para decir lo que los físicos delinean con precisión en ecuaciones y símbolos" (Poets have the indeterminate words to say what physicists delineate with precision in equations and symbols).[13] Herrera Corral argues for the creative potential through complementarities between both, asserting that "sólo los físicos y los poetas tienen el poder de atisbar lo eterno" (only physicists and poets have the power to glimpse the eternal).[14] Whether through reciprocity as a mutual movement through common language and culture or in a complementarity that holds science and literature like two sides of the same epistemic coin, fostering such connectivity dislodges literature and science from the tired metaphors of two distinct and irreconcilable cultures while establishing relationalities, both real and potential.[15]

Wittingly or not, to speak of arts and the natural sciences as two cultures is to dehistoricize their development mediated through Hoeg's Social Imaginary. Miguel de Asúa maintains that the separation between science—with its own object of study and methods—and literature—as an expressive and aesthetic activity—largely dates in Western cultures to the sixteenth century.[16] The eighteenth and nineteenth centuries brought a further intensification of the divide, establishing the two as separate domains, with literature becoming the aesthetic work of the belles lettres at the same time that the word "scientist" appears for the first time.[17] Bruno Latour classifies these separations modernity's obsessive work of "purification," which lends itself legitimacy through the very same ontological division that it creates, classifying all things as being either of Nature or of Culture.[18] That is to say, science as we understand it today is intrinsically entangled with early modernity from which it emerged, which, uncoincidentally, is entangled with European colonization and the need for exploration, explication, and classification of unknown plant and animal species as well as human societies. Antonio Barrera-Osorio observes that early European encounters with the Atlantic world fostered the development of empirical observation as a key element of modern epistemological practices, proposing that the Scientific Revolution started not with Copernicus or any other thinker but "in the 1520s, in Spain, when merchants, artisans, and royal officials confronted new entities coming from the New World and had to devise their own methods to collect information about those lands: there were no avocados in Pliny's pages."[19] Empiricism continued to play a key role in European colonial projects through the seventeenth and eighteenth centuries. Although scholars and writers of all stripes at the time would have shared a classical education in the arts and, therefore, would have spoken the "same language,"[20] scientific writing began to distinguish itself in many aspects from other forms of rhetoric. Mary Louise Pratt puts forth that writing and the divulgation of scientific knowledge through linguistic apparatuses during the early modern and modern periods "were central agents in legitimating scientific authority and its global project alongside Europe's other ways of the world, and being in it."[21] To speak of the two cultures in the context of Latin America, therefore, requires acknowledgment and continual awareness of coloniality's deployment of science as well as its heterogenous positioning throughout the region's history. María del Pilar Blanco and Joanna Page observe how the transfers of ideas, technologies, materials, and people that have shaped the history of science in Latin America necessarily are marked by asymmetries of power.[22] In examining the ways in which the region has historically been the locus of both the deployment and production of scientific knowledge, the elegant metaphoric simplicity of the two cultures as branches on the tree of knowledge obscures the true rhizomatic multiplicities that connect science and literature along lines of historicity, politics, race, religion, and language, to name but a few.[23]

Similarly, the presence of science and scientific themes in Latin American literature is often not readily identifiable as such because it is frequently enmeshed in topics such as medicine, race, technology, and biopolitics. Moreover, as Alicia Rivero explains, using an explicitly scientific perspective to study literature is much less common in approaching Spanish-language works than in Anglo-American, French, and other critical traditions.[24] This fact runs contrary to the sheer number of authors and works written in Spanish that overtly incorporate scientific thought into themes, structures, and language, as can be evidenced in Rafael Catalá's brief and admittedly inexhaustive overview of literature and science in Spanish-language works that lists over eighty authors ranging from the usual suspects in Jorge Luis Borges and Severo Sarduy to the poetry of José Martí and Lucila Velásquez.[25] Evelyn Fishburn and Eduardo Ortiz point out that Snow's contention of the two cultures "was never as pertinent in Latin America, where much closer links have always existed between the humanities and the sciences."[26] Urging that we frame these intersections beyond the study of literary works where science is treated in explicit ways, Victoria Carpenter proposes that, when approaching science in Latin American literature, we must take a step beyond the link between the writer and science and instead treat "both literary and scientific texts as products of human mind and therefore abiding by all the rules it creates, scientific and humanistic alike."[27] Noting the pervasiveness of science as being of culture itself, Carpenter ponders whether the transformational influence of scientific thought is "a privilege of the select few or is it indeed an all pervading experience in Latin American literary narrative from late modernism to the present day?"[28] Several recent studies in Latin American literature affirm this pervasiveness of science in society through many works that, at first glance, may not seem to explicitly deal with the topic.[29] For example, in *Medicine, Power, and the Authoritarian Regime in Hispanic Literature*, Oscar A. Pérez examines how "contemporary authors have articulated, challenged, and resignified authoritarian narratives of medicine and disease" in order to reexamine the role of science, technology, and medicine in the legacies of authoritarian regimes.[30] While none of the works that Pérez takes up would be explicitly identifiable as ciencia-fusión, they nonetheless engage the scientific underpinnings of gender, constructions of authority, subjectivity, and the differential values placed on ways of knowing. Similarly, David Dalton's *Mestizo Modernity: Race, Technology, and the Body in Postrevolutionary Mexico* uses an interdisciplinary approach to explore the portrayal of indigenous bodies in literature, film, and art to show how race formation in twentieth-century

INTRODUCTION

Mexico centers around science and modernity: "As it is tied to technology, *mestizaje* moves beyond an inherited, genetic construction and becomes a racialized articulation of Carlos Alonso's 'myth of modernity.'"[31] The same themes of modernity, (post)humanism, and different ways of knowing abound in the works of ciencia-fusión that I examine here, underscoring the connections between these works and others from Latin America and Mexico.

LITERATURE AND SCIENCE IN MEXICO

We do not have to go looking very far from this book's point of departure to find examples of how science, culture, and literature are entangled in Mexico. Commuters that emerge from the metro station that holds the Túnel de la ciencia can head southwest along the busy thoroughfare Avenida Insurgentes to take in the imposing Monumento de la Raza (Monument of the People/Race), for which the metro station gets its name and identifying pictogram. Located just a few minutes' walk from the entry to the metro, the Monumento de la Raza is a pre-Columbian styled pyramid adorned with Mexica-inspired sculptures and reliefs. Constructed in the 1930s to honor the past and present people of Mesoamerica, it is a powerful reminder of the centrality of *mestizaje* (miscegenation) in the formation of a post-Revolutionary national identity centered on the idea of Mexico being of one people, *la raza* (the race / the people). The reliefs that adorn the monument depict a past that is subsumed into a national futurity, reflected in the conceptual movement from the foundations of the pyramid to its zenith topped with an eagle that represents the modern state, the rising of a new Tenochtitlán for a new people. From this same historical and cultural milieu, José Vasconcelos articulated his utopic vision of a new "fifth race" of the future, *la raza cósmica* (the cosmic race), that would arise from the Americas. Itself a reaction to social Darwinism and the racist application of biological and sociological discoveries so influential in the first decades of the twentieth century,[32] Vasconcelos's *La raza cósmica* (*The Cosmic Race*, 1925) paradoxically refutes yet also incorporates scientific and technological discourse, reflecting what Brais Outes-León terms a "heterogeneidad conceptual" (conceptual heterogeneity) in which diverse registers coexist and complement each other.[33] Given that Vasconcelos frequently turned to scientific discourse to sustain his antipositivist ideas,[34] his writings feature a hybridity that simultaneously refutes the infiltration of positivistic thinking into the humanist domains of philosophy and culture while employing many of those same scientific methods and discourse to articulate his vision for humanity. Vasconcelos's writings, like the Monumento de la Raza, reflect the heterogeneous ways science infuses Latin American literature as well as the complex role it plays throughout Mexican history.[35]

Near the top of each side of the Monumento de la Raza's pyramid there are bronze castings that depict different Mesoamerican leaders. One of the sides

8   SCIENCE FUSION IN CONTEMPORARY MEXICAN LITERATURE

features Nezahualcoyotl, the fifteenth-century poet-philosopher and ruler of Tex-coco whose poetry incorporated science and technology as aesthetic expressions of beauty.[36] Michael Capobianco and Gloria Meléndez note how the linguistic structure of the Nahuatl language embraces complementary dualities, allowing poets such as Nezahualcoyotl to combine words and concepts to create new meanings through diphrases such as *in xochitl* (flower) / *in cuicatl* (song or poetry) as conveying "the only truth on earth."[37] In Nahua metaphysics, monistic dualities abound as we see in the supreme source of all cosmic energy, the godlike male-female unity *Ometeotl*, from which all things own their existence and con-tinued sustenance.[38] During the Conquest and colonial period, indigenous cos-movisions were subjugated, but as we will see not eliminated, by European matrices of power. The relationship between science and literature in post-Conquest Mexico is consequently heterogenous, both in the engagement between indigenous and Western cultures and in the already present heterogeneity in European thought itself that reflected the multiplicity of discourses and ideas cir-culating in early modern Spain.[39] At the same time as European coloniality was spreading across the planet, philosophers and thinkers were redefining the idea of science, what before had been known as "natural philosophy," drawing out the initial contours of the division between the arts and science that effectively per-sist until today.[40] In Mexico during the colonial and viceregal periods we find a heterogenous treatment of science with the first scientific text in the Americas in Alonso Gutiérrez's *Physica speculatio* in 1557 as well as the better-known scientific work of polymath Carlos de Sigüenza y Góngora, popularly known as the Mexi-can DaVinci.[41] Sigüenza y Góngora's documented friendship with Sor Juana Inés de la Cruz—she dedicating a sonnet to him, he delivering the eulogy at her funeral—was propelled by their intellectual pursuits in natural philosophy and poetry.[42] In Sor Juana's poetry we see how she framed art and science as mutually nurturing activities. David Galicia Lechuga observes that, for Sor Juana,

> la ciencia no era empleada únicamente como parte de los recursos expresivos que todo poeta debía utilizar para manifestar sus pensamientos, emociones e imágenes, sino que constituía también su propia y particular manera de vivir el mundo, ya que siempre manifestó un afán de conocimiento que buscaba abarcarlo todo.[43]

> science was not only used as part of the expressive resources that all poets used to express their thoughts, emotions, and images, but also constituted her own particular way of living the world, since she always expressed a desire for knowledge that sought to encompass everything.

From many lesser-known works to the magistral *Primero sueño* (*First Dream*, 1692), Sor Juana's poetics reflect theoretical frameworks circulating in scientific debates of the age.[44] In them, we see Classical philosophy, Ptolemian cosmology,

INTRODUCTION   9

and hermeticism all coexisting to express a universe of harmony through which the celestial orbs sojourn in sublime synchronicity. The conceptual heterogeneity of Sor Juana's verses echoes the concurrent transition of natural philosophy into science in Western thought as well as the cultural milieu of colonial Mexico in which the lettered class—almost exclusively male—engaged the discoveries of their day.

As science and literature continued their drift into separate spheres, Enlightenment-era Mexican scholars, like other non-European intellectuals, were not considered part of the Republic of Letters by many European scholars of the age.[45] However, this period also saw an emergence in Mexico of what José Francisco Robles calls "Enlightenments," heterogenous approaches to knowledge that included a reevaluation of Mexico's past, incorporating "the vision of the pre-Columbian past [that] had entered the viceregal present bearing Westernized aspects."[46] While Mexico's independence brought the country political autonomy, it also saw the closure of most scientific institutions including the Real y Pontificia Universidad de México (Royal and Pontifical University of Mexico) in 1833. Later in the nineteenth century, Gabino Barreda and other scholars would circulate Comtean positivism, which would have a profound impact in Mexico and extend far beyond the practice of science. In the final decades of the century Porfirio Díaz's advisory group of *científicos* (scientists), what Laura Suárez y López-Guazo calls "the Mexican positivist oligarchy," would become the "driving force for the continuity of Porfirio Díaz's dictatorship as a guarantee of their privileged social position."[47] While it is still of debate whether the científicos were positivists or not, the vast majority of the so-called scientists were not scientists at all but actually technocrats, highlighting the complex ways even the term "science" has historically moved in Mexican culture.[48] In the nineteenth century we also see how discoveries and theories posited by the likes of Gregor Mendel and Charles Darwin reverberate in literary texts throughout Latin America.[49] Given that the political and scientific establishment embraced and, at times, distorted positivistic thinking to maintain power and marginalize populations under the pretense of social Darwinism and eugenics, it comes as no surprise that during the decades after the Mexican Revolution we see a robust literary response to uses and abuses of science within society. In this atmosphere Vasconcelos's seminal *La raza cósmica* moves the idea of miscegenation away from scientific or sociological realms to create what Ignacio Sánchez Prado describes as an "anticolonial" text that communicates a mestizaje that evolves from representing diversity in ethnic and cultural terms toward a political ideal that creatively encompasses a more complex notion of spirit and history.[50]

If Vasconcelos is often cited as the face of anti-Darwinist thinking in Mexico, Alfonso Herrera is one of Darwin's greatest defenders in Latin America.[51] In 1904 Herrera published his book *Nociones de biología* (*Notions on Biology*), which announced the creation of *plasmogenia* (plasmogeny), a new science that studied the genesis and constitution of protoplasm with the ultimate goal of finding the chemical formula to create life.[52] Jorge Quintana-Navarrete explains how plasmogeny was both a scientific and philosophical discourse. Being part scientific theory, part project of biopolitical transformation, and part holistic philosophy of life and nature, it puts forth "una imagen potente del movimiento inmanente de la vida y su constante apertura al devenir" (a powerful image of the immanent movement of life and its constant opening toward becoming).[53] We will see similar conceptualizations in many works of ciencia-fusión nearly a century later such as Maricela Guerrero's *El sueño de toda célula* (*The Dream of Every Cell*, 2018), where the motif of cells that dream of becoming cells portrays an uncannily similar movement of life as continual becoming. We also see a similar coming together of spirituality, metaphysics, and science in the decades following the Mexican Revolution such as in chemist and Contemporáneo poet Jorge Cuesta's *Canto a un dios mineral* (*Song to a Material God*, 1942). It is perhaps not by chance that Jorge Volpi's first novel *A pesar del oscuro silencio* (*In Spite of the Dark Silence*, 1992) is an exploration of Cuesta's poetry and tragic life in which Jorge—this Jorge being the novel's protagonist—"endorses one of the poet's main obsessions: to abolish time."[54] As we will see in the following chapters, time, or rather the human-centered perception of time, is a fundamental insight that informs many of the works of ciencia-fusión.

The decades that follow see a flourishing of works that engage literature and science in innovative ways. In addition to themes of science and technology in many of his short stories, a large percentage of Alfonso Reyes's literary production possesses what Daniel Sifuentes Espinoza terms "una estructura metódica" (a methodical structure) that more closely approximates scientific rather than literary discourse.[55] These structures appear throughout his groundbreaking and influential 1944 work of literary theory *El deslinde* (*The Boundary*), where he establishes mutual influence among the methodologies of science, history, and literature. Reyes identifies various "contaminaciones" (contaminations) such as that of science by literature,[56] that, far from being detrimental, actually propel the work of science as it needs literature to break the limits it imposes on itself.[57] What is more, Reyes affirms that all intellectual activity is linguistic and therefore all minds operate literarily without even knowing it.[58] In his study on the Spanish American essay, John Skirius notes Reyes's characterization of the essay as the "centaur of the genres" given its propensity to merge together complementarities in a process not dissimilar to what Skirius identifies as Reyes's own particular centaur, "la literatura mitad lírica, mitad científica" (literature half lyrical, half scientific).[59] Similarly, Octavio Paz views complementarities between science and literature and lauds the former's capacity to solve many of the world's practical problems as well as its ability to "aclarar otras de orden ontológico: ¿De dónde surge el mundo que nos rodea? y ¿cuál es el destino de la vida en el universo?" (clarify others of an ontological order: Where does the

INTRODUCTION

world around us come from? And what is the destiny of life in the universe?).[60] Paz brought poetry and science together in *Corriente alterna* (*Alternating Current*), published in 1967, where he famously argued,

> Hay más de una semejanza entre la poesía moderna y la ciencia. Ambas son experimentos, en el sentido de "prueba de laboratorio": se trata de provocar un fenómeno, por la separación o combinación de ciertos elementos, sometidos a la presión de una energía exterior o dejados a la acción de su propia naturaleza.[61]

> There is more than one similarity between modern poetry and science. Both are experiments, in the sense of "laboratory test": it is about producing a phenomenon through the separation or combination of certain elements subjected to the pressure of an exterior energy or left to develop according to the laws of their own nature.

At that same time that he saw similarity in methods and objects, Paz warned of the extremities of reductive analogies, as can be perceived in his criticism of those who see in DNA a new religion, saying "el hombre es la boca que empaña el espejo de las semejanzas y las analogías" (man is the mouth that fogs up the mirror of similarities and analogies).[62] Here in the self-inflicted fogged reflection Paz is surely evoking Sor Juana's "hombres necios" (foolish men) who want things both ways, echoing similar warnings from Vasconcelos and Reyes of the danger of believing science somehow capable of simultaneously taking away and replacing the divine.

In the last half of the twentieth century, we see a number of works that take up questions like those that Paz ponders. In José Emilio Pacheco's poetry we find fires in the sky and waves crashing with the creative energy of the Big Bang as well as drops of water that become singularities, containing the entire universe as potentiality in a singular point.[63] Trained chemist turned poet Gerardo Deniz pushes the limits of language to bring science and art together as can be appreciated in his graphic poetry such as the calligram "Poema de Tristán," which consists of the musical notation of the Tristan chord and chemicals going into a chalice that are actually the poet's drawing of the structural formulas of estrogen and testosterone.[64] No less—or perhaps more—graphically portrayed is an entire chapter of Arturo Azuela's novel *El matemático* in which through his male gaze the mathematician-narrator describes, in great detail, a sexual encounter through the laws and theories of physics.[65] The limits between science and literature are explored in Salvador Elizondo's short story "Anapoyesis," where Professor Pierre Emile Aubanel posits and constructs the "anapoyetrón," a machine capable of extracting and transforming the thermodynamic energy that the poet has deposited in their verses. The Professor inputs several fragments of poetry to varying effect, but it is, of course, Mallarmé's verses that produce the most powerful explosion of energy. Aubanel's machine would wholly fuse art and

12   SCIENCE FUSION IN CONTEMPORARY MEXICAN LITERATURE

science, finally proving that both are subject to the same laws of the universe. Yet it is capable of providing only a brief and ultimately deadly glimpse of José Gordon's elusive dream of unity. The works of ciencia-fusión that I analyze in the following chapters continue on these and many other paths and foundations laid out over centuries by Mexican authors, blurring, transgressing, and often entangling the limits between science and literature.

ENTANGLING THE MATERIAL AND THE HUMAN THROUGH CIENCIA-FUSIÓN

While recent works of ciencia-fusión are a continuation of the heterogenous ways science and literature interface in Mexican culture, they also present novel perspectives primarily centered around the (re)orientation of humanity within the greater more-than-human universe. While there is a degree of variation in their application among authors and works, we can identify in form and theme three central characteristics that, when implemented together, distinguish ciencia-fusión from other subgenres. First, in addition to thematically incorporating scientific knowledge to enrich our understanding of the cosmos, life, and humanity's place in the world, authors of ciencia-fusión also transpose scientific discourse and concepts from the fields of biology, mathematics, physics, and chemistry to the realms of culture, religion, historiography, ethics, and even matters of human affect and social relationships. In particular, these authors utilize metaphor, both as it is readily employed in scientific thought and as a mapping from one experiential domain to another as a way of entangling the natural sciences and the arts. Second, ciencia-fusión questions and problematizes humanist paradigms and thinking as reflected in dualistic metaphors that divide science and literature, nature and culture, or even human and nonhuman. At the same time that these authors problematize many tenets of humanism, they embrace several others, reflecting the heterogeneity both in the employment of Western humanism in Spanish America as well as in notions or potentialities of subsequent posthumanist thinking. The final common characteristic of ciencia-fusión is the genre's depiction of a universe that is relational and interconnected, where all matter and phenomena are ultimately constitutively bound together. These works frequently depict life and phenomena and, in some cases, reality itself as emerging from the intra-action of matter and forces. As a result, the idea of a discrete and stable human subject gives way to perpetual intra-active and autopoietic processes, highlighting the entangled nature of reality.

It follows that works of ciencia-fusión prominently feature transposition and metaphor as both are the consequence of and the key to understanding a universe defined by the connectivity of all things. In their groundbreaking work on the conceptual processes at work through metaphor, George Lakoff and Mark Johnson establish that metaphor is not simply a device of poetic imagination or rhetorical flourish, but rather "our ordinary conceptual system, in terms of which we both think and act, is fundamentally metaphorical in nature."[66] The Greek etymology of the word *metapherein*, "to transfer," underscores the idea of movement from one domain to another implicit in any metaphorical arrangement. Seeing metaphor as a "matter of imaginative rationality,"[67] Lakoff and Johnson argue that metaphor offers a third way of understanding that vacillates between objectivism with its ordering principle of truth and subjectivism with the primacy of experience, uniting reason and imagination and offering insight into "the way we *understand* the world through our *interactions* with it."[68] Work in cognitive linguistic studies has long held metaphor as the mechanism through which one experiential domain is partially mapped or projected onto another recipient domain with the important constraint that such mapping never violate the basic structure of the recipient domain.[69] Yet recent research suggests that greater material interconnectivity is also at play in making metaphors given that they "emerge from world engagements in real time" and as such "are not necessarily standing ready in cognitive reserve but may be inspirations or outflows of sensations, environmental and embodied connections."[70] David R. Gruber asserts that "metaphors are always to some extent outside the head; their origination and success are connected to objects in unruly environments."[71] In a similar fashion, in ciencia-fusión metaphors and transposition between the human and the more-than-human underscore the materiality and intra-activity that constitutively bind together both source and recipient domains. In these works metaphors, much more than rhetorical flourishes or conceptual tools, reflect the connectivity and ceaseless movement of a universe in perpetual becoming.

In order to challenge an anthropocentric worldview that is the root of many of the sociopolitical and environmental issues of the present, authors of ciencia-fusión question and problematize dualisms such as science-literature, nature-culture, and human-nonhuman, challenging many, while not entirely discarding all, foundational principles of humanism. As we have seen how the reception and deployment of science differ greatly depending on geographic and political positions within matrices of power, the legacy of Western humanism likewise varies greatly across locations between center and periphery.[72] For this reason, Rosi Braidotti argues that we must treat humanism as equally heterogeneous, positioning humanist and posthumanist thought within politics of location, through situated and accountable knowledge practices.[73] Moreover, Sánchez Prado posits that Latin American intellectual figures such as Alfonso Reyes, Leopoldo Zea, and José Vasconcelos articulate different forms of humanism that utilize its varied traditions to "reivindicar la historicidad y cultura de América a contrapelo del eurocentrismo y la colonialidad" (vindicate the historicity and culture of the Americas against the current of Eurocentrism and coloniality).[74] Given the heterogenous experience of humanism in Latin America, it comes as no surprise that the concept of the posthuman would be equally diverse as we can see in its

14 SCIENCE FUSION IN CONTEMPORARY MEXICAN LITERATURE

varied treatment across works of ciencia-fusión. Pointing to the difficulty in speaking of posthumanism where humanism has always been contested and unevenly enacted, Sánchez Prado sees in Latin American posthumanism the opportunity to likewise articulate new forms of cultural subjectivity and critical assemblages before globalizing processes where "el posthumanismo no sustituye la tradición humanista latinoamericana, sino que se intersecta con ella" (posthumanism does not substitute the Latin American humanist tradition, but rather intersects with it).[75] Added to this regional heterogeneity, we see that what exactly constitutes posthumanism in theoretical terms is equally varied. Francesca Ferrando avers that the designation "posthumanism" actually stands for a multiplicity of worldviews that "share a common perception of the human as a non-fixed and mutable condition, but they generally do not share the same roots and perspectives."[76] Similarly, the authors of ciencia-fusión do not portray humanism, subjectivity, and the relationship that the two establish with the more-than-human world in a unified way. However, all utilize science to reorient humans and human conditions within greater frameworks of materiality, contesting the traditional culture-nature and human-nonhuman binaries that are a feature of humanism.

Aníbal Quijano argues that European and Cartesian epistemology provides a rational foundation for coloniality based on a Eurocentric perspective of knowledge while also functioning as a distorting mirror of reality.[77] Given that humanism is a fundamental part of coloniality,[78] countering its logic requires what Mabel Moraña identifies as a certain "impureza epistémica, resistente a cualquier hegemonía" (epistemic impurity, resistant to any hegemony).[79] Likewise, Walter Mignolo proposes that to carry out the work of decoloniality is to delink "from the traps of Western epistemic ontology and to open up to epistemic pluriversality."[80] In this manner, works of ciencia-fusión denaturalize scientific discourse and portray how it intersects with contrasting conceptualizations of the human, within what Lucy Bollington and Paul Merchant identify as a "zone of conflict and multiplicity at the edge of what is termed 'human' [that] can generate fresh assessments of the ways in which Latin American cultural production has confronted historical, ethical, political, and economic processes."[81] In bringing scientific discourse into contact with alternate knowledges and knowledge-making practices, both historical and potential, ciencia-fusión pushes the limits of such human-nonhuman relations and harnesses the possibilities for Latin American posthumanisms to open up "new dimensions in long-standing debates about identity and difference, the local and the global, and coloniality and power in Latin American culture."[82] Most writers of Mexican ciencia-fusión hail from Mexico City and other urban centers and typically tap into cosmopolitan aesthetics, employing what Sánchez Prado terms, in a more expansive context, "strategic Occidentalism" to co-opt and transculturate colonial knowledge.[83] Indeed we could argue that given their social, linguistic,

INTRODUCTION

and ethnic backgrounds as well as open embrace of both Western and non-Western knowledges, these writers reflect many, but certainly not all, of the common aspects of the "quasi-criollo subject position [that] has become characteristic of postcolonial writers."[84] As is explicitly made manifest in the ciencia-fusión genre, Latin American authors are uniquely positioned to bring together science and literature in novel ways given the region's "historical constitution of cultural fields as spaces of heightened discursive hybridity."[85]

To reorient questions of the human and materiality, we are reminded of Mignolo's assertion that "most of culture and civilizations on the planet see relations while in the West we are taught to see entities, things."[86] In this way, meaning is made through connectivity and process, an epistemic orientation featured overtly in ciencia-fusión. Perhaps more than any other theoretical term, "assemblage" has been the most associated with process- or relation-oriented epistemologies and ontologies. Growing out of the work of Gilles Deleuze and Félix Guattari, various thinkers in assemblage theory have modified the concept of "assemblage" (*agencement* in French) from its original meaning as a provisional iteration of Deleuze and Guattari's concept of the conditions of relations that they originally term the desiring machine.[87] For Deleuze and Guattari, an assemblage functions like "a constellation of singularities, prolongable by certain operations, which converge, and make the operations converge."[88] Frequently, the term "assemblage" is now employed to mean an apparatus or a collection of things that Manuel DeLanda describes as "wholes whose properties emerge from the interactions between parts."[89] While not strictly adherent to Deleuze and Guattari's original conceptualization, the idea of assemblage has informed actor-network theory, an approach to science and technology studies that posits that everything, both human and nonhuman, is organized in constantly changing assemblages, or networks of relations. In this book I use the assemblage as well as several other concepts like "multiplicities," "rhizome," and "territorialization" that Deleuze and Guattari employ in their works including *A Thousand Plateaus*. The emphasis on the assemblage as the model of relationality and interconnectivity between both human and nonhuman has also inspired what have been termed new materialist theories—distinct from other historical, dialectical, or mechanical materialisms—that see nonhuman and material processes in an "ontology that is very different from the substantialist Cartesian or mechanistic Newtonian accounts of matter."[90]

As we will see in the works of ciencia-fusión we explore, in these relational frameworks agency takes on distributive qualities, problematizing the dualistic conception of subjects that act upon objects. Jane Bennett argues that beyond living subjectivities, all matter has the capacity to be an actant and produce effects through processes,[91] and given that "matter itself is lively, then not only is the difference between subjects and objects minimized, but the status of shared materiality of all things is elevated. All bodies become more than mere objects, as the thing-powers of resistance and protean agency are brought into sharper relief."[92] The ability to affect, then, originates not from within "a human subject—posited in isolation from the nonhuman—but a material-semiotic network of human and nonhuman agents incessantly generating the world's embodiments and events."[93] Héctor Hoyos puts forth that reading Latin American literature through a new material lens provides novel insights where seeing things *in* history allows us to examine "the noninstrumental use of stories and literary language to upset the nature-culture divide, affect our rapport with things, and reassess our place in human-nonhuman history."[94] Likewise, Tara Daly highlights the vibrancy of matter in Latin American literature and, in particular, the unique ways that Andean avant-garde authors and artists represent matter, materiality, and humanity's place in the world. By combining notions of material vitality as proposed by Bennett to autochthonous concepts such as the *buen vivir* (good living) and *vincularidad* (connectedness), Daly demonstrates how "through their inventive language and forms" authors and artists "animate 'life' as an affective relationship between the human body, which includes the mind, and other materials."[95]

I build upon many of these same ideas and similarly utilize the theoretical lens of new materialism to examine works of Mexican ciencia-fusión. In particular, I structure much of my analysis on the concepts of intra-action and autopoiesis. While distinct concepts—the former comes from the field of theoretical physics and the latter from biology—both describe processes of mutual constitution from entangled matter. Intra-action is a concept proposed by physicist-philosopher Karen Barad that stands in contrast to interaction, which implies preexisting subjects and objects that interact with each other. Barad takes inspiration in Niels Bohr's interpretations of quantum mechanics including the implications of the fact that the experimenter's presence and participation necessarily make them part of the experiment. As such, knowledge-making practices are material enactments that are mutually constitutive to the phenomena they seek to describe.[96] Agency, then, is an enactment, as it does not precede but rather emerges through intra-action. Therefore, "'distinct' agencies are only distinct in relation to their mutual entanglement; they don't exist as individual elements."[97] Barad coins the neologism "intra-action" to signify this "mutual constitution of entangled agencies."[98] Barad's agential realism provides a framework that nullifies dualities such as human and nonhuman, material and discursive, and nature and culture to show that "knowing is a material practice of engagement as part of the world in its differential becoming."[99]

Like Barad's agential realism, the concept of autopoiesis is centered on material processes of becoming, a depiction of life that is reflected in several works of ciencia-fusión. First proposed by Chilean neurobiologists Humberto Maturana and Francisco Varela in 1972, autopoiesis, in the simplest terms, describes how a living system produces and maintains itself by creating its own parts or

INTRODUCTION   17

components. Maturana explains the literary origin of the name for the model of biological systems that he and his partner were developing:

> It was in these circumstances that one day, while talking with a friend (José Bulnes) about an essay of his on *Don Quixote de la Mancha*, in which he analyzed Don Quixote's dilemma of whether to follow the path of arms (*praxis*, action) or the path of letters (*poiesis*, creation, production), and his eventual choice of the path of *praxis* deferring any attempt at *poiesis*, I understood for the first time the power of the word "poiesis" and invented the word that we needed: *autopoiesis*. This was a word without a history, a word that could directly mean what takes place in the dynamics of the autonomy proper to living systems.[100]

Central to Maturana and Varela's conceptualization is the perpetual relationality among all living things—from single cells to complex organisms—and their environments. While reproduction is one feature of autopoiesis, creation here is principally centered on the act of self-production or self-making, explaining "how we living beings necessarily co-create our internal biology and external sociocultural ecosystems . . . these complex systems and dynamic, autopoietic processes by which an individual continually self-realizes at every living moment."[101] Autopoietic becoming is the product of countless interactions between a living system and its environment, what Maturana and Varela term "structural couplings," effectively the constitutive process of creating life from organic and inorganic matter.

In the following pages, I apply Barad's concept of intra-action and Maturana and Varela's autopoiesis to show how works of ciencia-fusión depict human bodies and subjectivity as emerging from networks, systems, and relations that are also the object of scientific study. In many respects, we can extend autopoiesis metaphorically to the works we will examine here, seeing how they engage with and become through coupling, contacts, and exchanges with outside materials. I cannot claim that any of these works realize José Gordon's dream of unity, but I do propose that they imagine and communicate transformative ways of seeing the universe and humanity. In engaging, interconnecting, transposing, and establishing analogues between science and literature, these works transculturate scientific knowledge and knowledge making to create texts that entangle the human and the nonhuman. Through these novel conceptualizations the authors put forth new ways of seeing, knowing, and becoming in a material universe.

Scientific-Literary Fusions in Contemporary Mexico

This book is organized into chapters in which I analyze one or more works by a single author to illustrate the breadth and variety of approaches to the practice of ciencia-fusión. I have ordered the chapters thematically, highlighting the binding concept of connectivity, with each chapter continuing themes raised in the preceding pages. While this introductory chapter provides a brief historical and theoretical contextualization for contemporary works of ciencia-fusión, in the chapter that follows, "Entangled Matter: The Science Poetry of Alberto Blanco," I examine how the science poetry of Alberto Blanco puts forth a vision of the entanglement between matter and human experience. Departing from the ideas that Blanco sets forth in his various "Theories" such as in "Newton's Theory," where the lyrical voice declares that "There is but one law / that equally governs / the mind of a physicist / as the verses of this poem,"[102] I apply the concept of intra-action articulated by Karen Barad to demonstrate how Blanco's poetry articulates an ontology where reality emerges through the mutual constitution of entangled agencies, an idea that is central to Blanco's work as well as that of the other authors that we take up here. In the poems human experience and metaphors of meaning find so many analogues in scientific discourse because both co-emerge from the same phenomena and mutually constitutive human-material agencies. While much of the chapter looks at Blanco's science poetry most recently compiled in *La raíz cuadrada del cielo* (*The Square Root of Heaven*, 2016), I show how this ontology underpins Blanco's oeuvre over the past five decades, including his many works that do not explicitly address scientific themes. This first chapter, therefore, introduces and establishes a theoretical framework for the overarching concept of the entanglement between the material and the human that will be developed further in the following chapters.

In the following chapter, "Quantum Mechanics, History, and the Question of Scale in Jorge Volpi's *En busca de Klingsor*," I examine Jorge Volpi's novel *En busca de Klingsor* (*In Search of Klingsor*, 1999), the best-known work of Mexican ciencia-fusión due to its commercial and critical success. I begin the chapter by explaining and expanding upon the idea of scale and how its application allows us to remap spatiotemporal and conceptual connectivity. I then demonstrate how Volpi's novel can be read as a metafictional meditation on the idea of scale in narrative, be that literary or historiographical. Through the transposition of discoveries about causality and chance in classical and quantum physics, Gustav Links, the narrator of the novel, seeks to find a greater meaning in history writ large by exploring the seemingly unpredictable actions, coincidences, and results of chance that undermine a deterministic view of history. By reading the novel through the lens of scalar theory, I conclude that, through a narration that focuses microscopically on the seemingly random nature of humanity, Volpi's novel explores how agential realism brings a seemingly stochastic element to history that, when considered at different scales, provides a deeper understanding of the concepts of uncertainty and disorder.

Subsequently, "Automatons, Androids, and Androcentrism in Ignacio Padilla's *El androide y otras quimeras*" delves into the work of Ignacio Padilla, who,

INTRODUCTION

like fellow Crack generation writer Jorge Volpi, takes up the relationship between science and literature in several of his works. In this third chapter, I begin by connecting the idea of scale in Volpi's novel to its application in Padilla's short fiction. I then focus on the collection *El androide y otras quimeras* (*The Android and Other Chimeras*, 2008) and how Padilla explores the themes of automation and autonomy, the Scientific Revolution, and the subjugation of women and nature across several short stories. Padilla's treatment of these themes reveals the ways in which science, knowledge, and commerce have been and continue to be harnessed to marginalize and control women and nonnormative subjects, seemingly rendering them analogous to mechanical androids or automatons. However, befitting Padilla's playful definition of himself as a "físico cuéntico" (physicist of the story), close readings of the stories reveal how this androcentric, mechanized order is subtly yet powerfully challenged through uncertain and unexpected acts of resistance and autonomy. Finally, I explain the ethical consequences of Padilla's depiction of reality that functions as an alternative to the mechanistic model of an inert natural world external to the humanist Cartesian subject.

Next, in "A Science of Good and Evil: Sabina Berman's Darwinian Ethical Turn," my analysis builds upon the aspects of ethics, humanism, and subjectivity that I explored in the previous chapter to analyze what I term Sabina Berman's Darwinian ethical turn. I demonstrate how, in response to what she sees as unbridled anthropocentric neoliberal capitalism, the playwright, author, journalist, and public intellectual puts forth the outlines of an ethical code largely inspired by Darwin's *On the Origin of Species* (1859) and *The Descent of Man* (1871). I determine that, when viewed collectively, Berman's four literary works of the 2010s—the novels *La mujer que buceó dentro del corazón del mundo* (*Me, Who Dove into the Heart of the World*, 2010) and *El dios de Darwin* (*Darwin's God*, 2014), the play *El narco negocia con Dios* (*The Narco Makes Deals with God*, 2012), and the short story compilation *Matemáticas para la felicidad y otras fábulas* (*Mathematics for Happiness and Other Fables*, 2017)—sustain a critique of Judeo-Christian morality, the Cartesian human-nature dualism, and neoliberalism as culpable in the degradation of both human society and the ecosystem. In particular, my analysis concentrates on the two novels that feature Karen Nieto as protagonist, in which the interplay of different levels of narration reveals an ethical system, a "Ciencia del Bien y del Mal" (Science of Good and Evil), as proposed by Berman's fictional Darwin. I then show that, unlike morality built upon theological or philosophical foundations, Berman looks to the more-than-human world as revealed through science, bringing together concepts of connectivity, cooperation, and mutual benefit, to construct an ethics, however utopic it may be, to confront the social and ecological crises of the present.

Continuing along similar lines of inquiry, "In Search of a New Language: Autopoiesis and the Anthropocene in Maricela Guerrero's *El sueño de toda* célula" engages poet Maricela Guerrero's *El sueño de toda célula* (*The Dream of Every Cell*, 2018) and its depiction of the relationships between scientific knowledge, language, and humanity's destructive impact on the ecosystem. In this chapter, I apply the concept of autopoiesis to Guerrero's portrayal of life, from its most basic units to its organization into larger systems, from networks of plants to the structure of human societies. By reading *El sueño de toda célula* through an autopoietic lens, I demonstrate how Guerrero repositions the human and the nonhuman within greater social and ecological systems to show how scientific knowledge can inspire alternatives to the extractivism and environmental degradation of the Anthropocene. Next, I analyze Guerrero's treatment of language—both human and more-than-human—and its potential for reordering humanity's relationship with other forms of life. I then conclude that Guerrero's call for a new language of commonality and trans-species kinship highlights the power of lyrical and literary discourse in ongoing political and environmental debates.

In the final chapter, "Dimensions of Embodied Experience: Space and Time in Elisa Díaz Castelo's *Principia*," I build upon the concept of autopoiesis and its impact on cognitive science and literature through my analysis of Elisa Díaz Castelo's poetry collection *Principia* (2018). First, I examine how Díaz Castelo combines technical and medical discourse with accessible verse to communicate an embodied human experience of and within both space and time, connecting the intimate with the more-than-human universe revealed through evolving scientific knowledge. Through an analysis of Díaz Castelo's treatment of the body and how it both experiences and produces spatiotemporal phenomena, I demonstrate how the fusion of sentimental themes such as memory, family, love, and death with analogous phenomena in the physical world not only functions as metaphor but also illustrates how embodied experience both emerges from and is integral to the more-than-human universe. Next, I expand upon how *Principia* presents a human subjectivity that emerges from the interplay of countless forces, bodies, and matter that unfold throughout space and time. In this way, this final chapter builds upon the analysis of the different aspects of ciencia-fusión from previous chapters and asserts the capacity for literature to express the entanglement of the material and the human.

In "Conclusions: Knowing and Belonging in an Entangled Universe" I synthesize how these authors utilize scientific knowledge, concepts, and discourse to reposition the human as emerging from and constitutive to nonhuman physical matter, forces, and phenomena. These texts, therefore, use science to provide readers with a deeper understanding not only of the universe itself, but also of innovative ways with which to confront the sociocultural and ecological issues of the present. The constant deluge of news about climate change, mass extinctions, violence, feminicide, and social injustice speaks to the urgency to rethink what it means to be human. Many of the concepts that feature in ciencia-fusión such as intra-action, autopoiesis, posthumanism, new materialism, necropolitics, and extractivism all emphasize relationality and entanglement among all living things and a material universe. Nonetheless, there also exist tensions between the concepts and what we are to make of matters of agency, the dignity of human and more-than-human life, as well as the ability of scientific concepts to destabilize literary discourse, identity, and human subjectivity. I argue that such destabilizations are the driving factor in the appearance of ciencia-fusión. The writers and texts I analyze in *Science Fusion* consistently depict interconnectivity and entanglements yet also harness the productive tensions that arise from heterogenous paradigms of what it means to be human and our relationship with each other and a more-than-human universe. Through its exploration of common themes regarding the human and the incorporation of scientific concepts in diverse literary texts, *Science Fusion* deepens our understanding of this current within contemporary Mexican literature and how these authors imagine new ways of being in and of the universe.

CHAPTER 1

Entangled Matter

THE SCIENCE POETRY OF ALBERTO BLANCO

Perhaps the best way to begin the first chapter of a book about science and the entanglement of the material and the human through literature is with a bit of biochemistry and one massive work of poetry. In particular, this chapter's journey is set in motion by the creative power of deoxyribonucleic acid, more commonly known by its acronym DNA, the famous molecule that carries genetic information for the development and functioning of all living things, including trained chemist and poet Alberto Blanco. It is also DNA that serves as the inspiration for Blanco's most audacious and hermetic work, *Antes de nacer* (*Before Being Born*, 1983), a book-length poem whose title's acronym spells out ADN, which of course is DNA in Spanish. Blanco tells of how inspiration for the work struck him in the middle of biochemistry class in 1972 when

> de pronto *vi* el poema. Yo me estaba volviendo loco en la clase, pues me sentía absolutamente incapaz de expresar o de transmitir o de platicar con nadie lo que yo estaba *viendo* en ese momento. Y sentía una pena terrible, desesperante, porque, paradójicamente, me sentía colmado por una felicidad extraordinaria. No podía compartirla ni expresarla.... ¿Qué podía decir? Una clase de bioquímica y lo que yo estaba viendo era *otra cosa*.[1]

> all of a sudden *I saw* the poem. I was going crazy in class, since I was feeling absolutely incapable of expressing or transmitting or conversing with anyone what I was *seeing* in that moment. I felt a terrible, desperate sadness because, paradoxically, I felt like I was overflowing with an extraordinary happiness. I could not share or express it.... What could I say? A biochemistry class and what I was seeing was a whole *other thing*.

This other thing, the thematic conceptualization expressed through the form of the poem that transposes the chemical carriers of genetic information to an

24   SCIENCE FUSION IN CONTEMPORARY MEXICAN LITERATURE

extended meditation on creation and awareness, is a poetic and visual representation of what Javier Galindo Ulloa describes as the image of silence through the paradox of what man has known since before the origin of his thought.[2]

As form and image are vital for Blanco, *Antes de nacer* is composed of dual tercets that are ingeniously spaced into two columns that, in addition to giving the impression of a two-dimensional rendering of the double-helix structure of DNA, allows multiple readings as the segmented verses representing acidic triads can be read vertically, horizontally, forward, or backward. Blanco, who originally wanted the poem printed in the form of a scroll or at least in a set of cards that could be removed and reordered by the reader,[3] in the end published it in bound-book form with 108 numbered pages through which the poem's 1,008 dual verses speak of the act of birth and creation that emerges from and returns to the chemical and material building blocks of life. The circularity of the poem is evident from the first verse, which begins in the lowercase, with the poetic voice stating "antes de nacer / reconocemos verdaderamente nuestra vida" (before being born / we truly recognize our life),[4] from which a plurality of readings spring forth depending on which way the reader arranges or, to extend Blanco's own analogy of genetics, encodes the different verses. The verses tell of how the human evokes and gives name to a world "de materia densa recién coronada" (of dense matter recently crowned),[5] highlighting the fusion of materiality and mysticism that infuses much of Blanco's poetry. In *Antes de nacer* we find the human as a spatiotemporal coming together that emerges from and melds back into flows of matter and energy in an endless cycle of beginnings and endings. Like in so much of Blanco's oeuvre, materiality is not just the stuff from which life is made but also the stuff that life makes in a process of perpetual motion and mutual constitution.

Likewise, this first chapter takes up how Blanco brings together science and art to portray the entanglement between matter and human experience. After examining how metaphor extends beyond its application in poetry to connect the human with the more-than-human world, I demonstrate how Blanco establishes an interconnectivity between science and art through several of his science poems and "Theories." By applying Niels Bohr's Principle of Complementarity as well as Karen Barad's articulation of reality as enactment through intra-action, I argue that Blanco's poetry conveys an ontology of process where reality emerges through the mutual constitution of entangled agencies. Human experience and metaphors of meaning find so many analogues in scientific discourse because both co-emerge from the same phenomena and mutually constitutive human-material agencies. In this chapter we will see how Blanco's poetics openly lays out theories, laws, and meditations on the relationship between science and literature that other works of ciencia-fusión likewise explore or incorporate in different ways. By examining how these themes and concepts are treated in various poems composed over the course of decades, I demonstrate how Blanco's poetry puts forth an image of reality that emerges from the continual intra-action of matter and forces in contrast to interactions between preexisting subjects and objects.

WE ARE NATURE'S METAPHORS: BETWEEN THE MATERIAL AND THE HUMAN

It is no small task to try to define or classify Alberto Blanco's prolific body of lyrical work. Chronologically, he falls into the Generación del Medio Siglo (Mid-Century Generation), which is also sometimes called the Generación del '68 (Generation of '68). Evodio Escalante groups Blanco with David Huerta, Gerardo Deniz, and Coral Bracho in what he terms the "vanguardia blanca" (white avant-garde) due to the influence that Octavio Paz and his innovative work *Blanco* (*White*) had on this group.[6] Juan Armando Rojas also links Blanco with Bracho as two poets born in the 1950s who renovated poetry due to their use of multiple forms as well as radical and innovative use of language.[7] Teresa Chapa lauds how "el gran dominio y respeto que tiene Blanco por las formas poéticas convencionales, combinado con su deseo constante de experimentar más allá de los parámetros de la tradición poética dan como resultado un corpus poético escrito con maestría e innovación" (the great command and respect that Blanco has for conventional poetic forms, combined with his constant desire to experimental beyond the parameters of poetic tradition result in a poetic body of work written with mastery and innovation).[8] Irma Chávez Robinson, in her study on Zen Buddhism and ecology in the poet's work, calls Blanco both a Zen poet and an ecopoet who invents a new language to express problems in Mexico and the world.[9] On the other hand, Christopher Domínguez Michael is not as generous in his estimation of how Blanco incorporates Eastern philosophy and religion into his poetry, which he says gives it a "timbre que remite a un mestizaje de los misticismos" (timbre that refers back to an intermixing of mysticisms),[10] which makes the poet a "bardo desdoblado en 'vidente consejero' que suelta *netas* de las cuales, no tan paradójicamente, brotan poemas a veces inspiradísimos" (a bard that doubles as "clairvoyant adviser" that drops truths from which, not so paradoxically, sprout poems that at times are quite brilliant).[11] In contrast, Ronald Friis explains how Blanco brings together science, mysticism, religion, and art to create what he terms "Blanco's poetics of empathy."[12] What is more, in his comprehensive study of the poet's extensive oeuvre Friis states that "the poetry of Alberto Blanco is a universe of verse—a large and complex body of meticulously structured and interrelated poems in a constant process of transformation."[13]

Transformation in Blanco's poetry is as multifaceted as his use of form and language as when it challenges anthropocentrism while expressing empathy and a deep engagement in affirming human dignity. In his poetry often what at first glance seems like contradictory opposition is ultimately revealed to be entirely consistent with complementarity in both Eastern philosophy and quantum mechanics, two of the many domains of knowledge that guide Blanco's work. Fritjof Capra, in his influential work *The Tao of Physics: An Exploration of the Parallels between Modern Physics and Eastern Mysticism*, observes how many concepts of modern physics, like complementarity, often show surprising commonalities to Asian religious and philosophical cosmogonies in that "the two basic themes of this conception are the unity and interrelation of all phenomena and the intrinsically dynamic nature of the universe."[14] As we will see in various examples, much of Blanco's work similarly fuses the scientific with the spiritual with the two functioning as complementary approaches to understanding the mysteries of the universe as both reveal a deeper interconnectivity among all things. If the impression is that Blanco's poetry is some sort of metaphysical or scientific mysticism, it is a badge that Blanco wears proudly, claiming, "Si por religiosa, o metafísica, o mística, entendemos una poesía y una conciencia que tienen que ver con saber que no estamos separados, que formamos parte de una inmensa red, entonces acepto la calificación gustosamente" (If by religious, or metaphysical, or mystic, we understand a poetry and an awareness that has to do with knowing that we are not separate, that we form part of an immense network, then I accept the description with pleasure).[15] For Blanco, the unity of all things is a metaphysical truth, with spirituality alongside science providing pathways of understanding. Blanco points to the origin of the word "religion," in the Latin verb *religare*, which means "to bind" or "to join together":

¿Qué persona que de verdad observa, así sea por un momento, no se da cuenta de que no estamos aislados, de que no estamos solos, de que formamos parte de algo muchísimo más grande, y de que estamos ligados, que estamos re-ligados en y con la inmensidad? Ese es el origen de la palabra "religión." Que no estamos separados. Sería imposible construir una metáfora si no tuviéramos esa posibilidad reunificadora de principio; sin aceptar esta convicción. Es imposible construir una metáfora—cualquier metáfora—sin aceptar la posibilidad de que las cosas están relacionadas, de que entre todos los seres existe una hermandad.[16]

What person that truly observes, even for a moment, does not realize that we are not isolated, that we are not alone, that we form part of something much, much bigger, and that we are joined together, that we are rejoined in and with the vastness? That is the origin of the word "religion." That we are not separate. It would be impossible to construct a metaphor if there were not that reunifying possibility of principle; without accepting this conviction. It is impossible to construct a metaphor—any metaphor—without accepting the possibility that things are related, that between all beings there exists a siblinghood.

ENTANGLED MATTER

For Blanco, metaphors not only reflect but are the direct consequence of a universe that features connectivity among everything. Given that research into cognitive linguistics has demonstrated that our conceptual system is fundamentally metaphoric in nature,[17] the movement between experiential domains that occurs is much more than its employment as linguistic or poetic device. For Blanco, poetry itself is an extended metaphor, a mediating and reunifying force that binds together science and the knowledge it produces with human experience and wisdom from the traditions of art, religion, philosophy, and, of course, poetry.

COMPLEMENTARITY, METAPHORS, AND BECOMING THROUGH INTRA-ACTIVITY

A central concept to understand how Blanco conceives poetry as something that binds, mediates, and reunifies is through the Principle of Complementarity. In the Eastern tradition it is often expressed through the interconnected forces of yin and yang that give rise to each other as they interrelate. Familiar to many through their graphic representation in the *Taijitu*, the dynamic interplay of yin and yang, "the essence of all natural phenomena,"[18] was particularly fascinating to physicist Niels Bohr, who saw the concept of complementarity as essential to understanding the universe.[19] Through his work and that of so many others including Louis de Broglie, Max Planck, Erwin Schrödinger, and Albert Einstein, to name but a few, discoveries in the nineteenth and early twentieth centuries showed that all quantum entities such as photons and electrons exhibit both wave and particle natures. These insights helped Bohr to reconceptualize the model of the atom and later his Principle of Complementarity that affirms that, while it is impossible to observe both wave and particle aspects simultaneously, a more complete description of the entity is possible only when taking both into consideration.[20] Similarly, often in Blanco's poetry what at first seems to be a paradox is ultimately revealed to be reciprocally affirming and complementarity aspects of a greater whole, offering a much more robust representation of an interconnective and mutually constitutive reality. Friis observes how complementarity functions in Blanco's poetry as his "work tends to reject hierarchical dualism (one element dominating the other) for the more Taoist concept of mediated and intertwined pairs of complements in what might be called a 'dialectical monism' in progress or under interrogation."[21] In *Antes de nacer* we see this dialectical monism that both encompasses and is constituted between the material and the human, both in the content of the verses and in the form of the poem itself, with its appearance of a double helix in constant movement through the predominance of the spaces between and among the verses, places where Evodio Escalante contends that the reader becomes the missing helix, actively participating in the act of creation.[22]

28 SCIENCE FUSION IN CONTEMPORARY MEXICAN LITERATURE

As we will see, Blanco often uses metaphors of complementarity as a sort of double articulation, with both concepts—metaphor and complementarity—respectively and mutually functioning through continual movement. It is telling, then, that in addition to being a trained chemist, poet, musician, and translator, among so many other callings, Blanco is an accomplished collage artist, reutilizing and reordering found materials to create works of art. Blanco sees collage as the basis of human creativity, given that "realmente no somos los creadores de nada" (really we are not creators of anything).[23] We can see the metaphor of collage already at play in the poem *Antes de nacer* where combinations and reconfigurations of already existing material form into the more familiar objects as well as the poetic subject. The word "materia" (matter) appears numerous times in the poem as being both content and form within an endless cycle of coalescence and formation. Declaring "cada cosa aparte / que se impone por su ser indescifrable" (each thing apart / that prevails through its indecipherable being), the poetic voice ponders subjectivity and its material foundations:

> tiene un peso que no guarda relación   con la materia densa
> con un valor absoluto en cada escala   el tiempo y su lugar
> es un cuadro nuevo para el hombre   cuando se le aparece
> la felicidad de estar   en esta materia que llega destinada
> a su lugar de siempre   en esta camisa de franela a cuadros
> para dar con la talla   forma definitiva a nuestro fuego
> hidrógeno genial   palmeras de vapor en el mar extendido
> molécula maestra   polaridad de las soluciones que pintan
> la tinta paralela   que corre con el consentimiento nuclear[24]

> has a weight that bears no relation   with the dense matter
> with an absolute value in each stopover   the time and its place
> is a new canvas for man   when it appears to him
> the happiness of being   in this matter that arrives destined
> to its lifelong place   in this plaid flannel shirt
> to find the right size   definitive form to our fire
> brilliant hydrogen   palm trees of vapor in the extended sea
> master molecule   polarity of the solutions that paint
> the parallel ink   that runs with nuclear consent

As matter coalesces in eternal flows, with iterations into objects mere layovers that occur within time and space, including that which is the ephemeral poetic "I," it is the fusion of the hydrogen of the Sun that releases energy and gives light and life to Earth. While the poet acknowledges the materiality of his existence, there remains something more to his being that has a weight independent of the mass of the dense matter that he is continually becoming. Although the verses render a multiplicity of readings, through various iterations the outcome often returns to the idea that happiness, the creation of art, and a sense of belonging in the universe are products of the same matter and energy that constitute everything. In Blanco's poetry, matter and human affects are not mutually exclusive domains or even objects to be found out there, but complementary phenomena that flow into and emerge from the poet, dissolving the idea that subjectivity is somehow distinct from the reality in contemplation.

In a similar manner, physicist-philosopher Karen Barad looks to Niels Bohr's insights into the relationship between materiality and discourse to formulate Barad's theory of agential realism, which conceives that the universe comprises phenomena that are "the ontological inseparability of intra-acting 'agencies.'"[25] Barad explains, "Remarkably, Bohr calls into question representationalism's taken-for-granted stance toward *both* words and things. That is, unlike (some of) the poststructuralist and science studies accounts, which fully explicate and emphasize *either* the discursive *or* material nature of practices, Bohr takes hold of both dimensions at once."[26] Barad builds upon Bohr's claim that knowledge-making practices are material enactments that contribute to and are part of the phenomena they describe to argue that "the primary ontological unit is not independent objects with independently determinate boundaries and properties but rather what Bohr terms 'phenomena.'"[27] Agential realism describes that "phenomena do not merely mark the epistemological inseparability of observer and observed, or the results of measurements; rather, *phenomena* are the *ontological* inseparability of agentially intra-acting components."[28] Reality is both material and discursive because "knowing is a material practice of engagement as part of the world in its differential becoming,"[29] a recognition likened in Blanco's poem as "la felicidad de estar / en esta materia que llega destinada" (the happiness of being / in this matter that arrives destined).

In *Antes de nacer* the (intra-)activity of becoming is a driving metaphoric force that is reflected in both the poem's language and its form. Blanco explains how the structure of this poem is like that of a zipper that opens and closes, with two long strings of verse that respectively open and close, speak and then remain quiet, all with the center space being the most important element of the poem because, "Lo que no es ni el lado izquierdo ni el lado derecho de la creación; ni la razón ni la intuición; ni el lado femenino ni el lado masculino; ni esto ni aquello. Allí es donde debe esperarse, o podría esperarse, el salto cuántico" (What is not the left side nor the right side of creation; neither reason nor intuition, neither the feminine side nor masculine; neither this nor that. That is where one should expect, or could expect, the quantum jump).[30] The quantum jump, the instantaneous transition of an electron, atom, or molecule from one discrete energy state to another introduced by Bohr in 1913, has itself become a metaphor in common parlance to represent any large and sudden paradigm change, often in English through the more widely known term "quantum leap."[31] In *Antes de nacer*, the space between words and verses as well as within and between matter itself is where the metaphorical quantum jump occurs, abruptly leading to a change or illumination in the reader. The form of the verses that is constantly changing, the possibility to affect a multiplicity of different arrangements and readings, and the overarching metaphor of life emerging in a constant flow of matter and energy all convey a sense of creation as perpetual movement. Teresa Chapa remarks how the textual configuration of *Antes de nacer* produces the sensation of an ever-continuing poem that "como el proceso vital mismo, se altera y sin embargo es interminable, y la circularidad del poema afirma el incesante movimiento de toda materia orgánica" (like the vital process itself, is altered yet is endless, and the circularity of the poem affirms the incessant movement of all organic matter).[32] The metaphor of DNA, as both molecule and movement, therefore, is central to the relationships between the human and the material that Blanco conveys throughout his poetry.

In this manner, *Antes de nacer* utilizes metaphor both in its traditional context as poetic device that establishes analogy or relations between different things as well as in a more expansive understanding of the concept as a central feature of communication. In *The Music of Life: Biology beyond Genes*, biologist Denis Noble argues that organisms are not simply deterministic products assembled and constructed by genes but rather emerge within and through a larger web of contexts, modularities, and processes.[33] From the interpretation of the code of DNA to the music that we make, life is communicative in nature. DNA in and of itself does not do anything; rather, according to Noble, it is "interpreted" by proteins within a system "that provides the semantic frame and gives the gene its functionality, its meaning."[34] With proteins that read off and interpret ACGT bases converted into seemingly semiotic combinations that accrue and change over millennia, "we can say that, as the genome has developed, nature has switched from one metaphor to another."[35] Of course, proteins do not interpret anything in the logocentric sense of the world. Rather, Noble's point is to argue against seeing the organism as the mere culmination of a reductionist chain. Instead, Noble establishes that metaphor, or the capacity for transference from one domain to another, is a feature of nature beyond human semiosis. Noble's meta-metaphorical approach to genetics leads Wendy Wheeler to remark, "We might say that we, the creatures who make metaphor in human minds and words, are ourselves first made in bodies which are swarms of nature's metaphors."[36] Reversing the direction of metaphorical transference in this way undermines the notion of the anthropocentric subject and highlights how all life, including humans and our capacity for metaphor, is in many ways the living and embodied output of biosemiotic communication.

Poetry, Science, and Theories of Everything

Although themes about the complementarity between science and poetry abound throughout Blanco's work, he most explicitly articulates their entanglement in

ENTANGLED MATTER 31

his series *Lecciones* (*Lessons*), *Teorías* (*Theories*), and *Mapas* (*Maps*), brought together in the collection *La raíz cuadrada del cielo* (*The Square Root of Heaven*), published collectively as part of the cycle *El corazón del instante* (*The Heart of the Instant*, 1998), later expanded and published as a stand-alone book for the first time in 2016. In grouping these series into one collection, Blanco postulates a collective meta-poetics that features many shared characteristics and themes that pervade later works of ciencia-fusión. Combining scientific language with metapoetic forms, Blanco expounds upon questions of complementarity, entangled human-material agencies, and interconnectivity between science and art, among the many themes that continue to be taken up time and time again by authors of ciencia-fusión. While one cannot say with certainty that later writers of ciencia-fusión explicitly draw upon Blanco's scientific poetry, it is evident that Blanco's work over the decades articulates in the most explicit manner the ways that scientific theories and discoveries have influenced and destabilized our understanding of reality. From matters of discourse and narrative to questions of human identity and life within a greater more-than-human world, careful readers will note striking congruencies between Blanco's poems and later works of ciencia-fusión as we will see in the following chapters.

Blanco opens *La raíz cuadrada del cielo* with the poem "Declaración de principios" (Declaration of Principles), which begins as a lecture or public reading with the poetic voice addressing his listeners/readers in a playful manner, reflecting the colloquial tone that runs throughout the collection:

Señoras, señores:

antes de comenzar esta lectura
quiero confesar aquí, del modo más natural,
un par de cosas de mucha o poca monta (según se vea)
y, muy probablemente, sin importancia alguna.[37]

Ladies and gentlemen:

before beginning this reading
I want to confess here, in the most natural way,
a couple of things of much or little significance (depending on how one sees
    them)
and, most probably, of no importance whatsoever.

The poet goes on to also "confess" that he is a chemist, couching this assertion by saying, "No quiero decir con esto que es todo lo que soy" (I do not mean to say that this is all that I am).[38] Instead, the poet's first confession suggests that his real transgression is that his scientific training causes him to agree with readers that $1+1 = 2$. He then lays out several corollarial equations that his interlocutors may or may not believe, including $1+1 = 3$, $1+1 = 3.1416\ldots$, or even

32   SCIENCE FUSION IN CONTEMPORARY MEXICAN LITERATURE

$1+1 = 0$, all propositions to which the poet agrees. These equations leave open to interpretation as to what values the figures could represent, generating a multiplicity of possibilities that intentionally could be anything and everything from logic puzzles to a transgressive invitation to overturn arithmetical reasoning. Presumably, these equations are among the titular ordering principles that the poet wishes to declare, establishing them as a counterpoint to well-known axiomatic mathematical and scientific laws built through experimental and logical methods. Blanco's equations acknowledge yet simultaneously contrast with foundational logic and methods such as those of *Principia Mathematica*, Alfred North Whitehead and Bertrand Russell's massive yet seminal work on symbolic logic, where the authors famously take over three hundred pages to prove axiomatically that indeed $1 + 1 = 2$.[39] The poet's second confession, "que siento una fuerte inclinación a creer que $1+1 = 1$" (I feel a strong inclination to believe that $1+1 = 1$),[40] further undermines both linear and logical coherency and establishes a parallelism between the equations in this confessional declaration and the prior. Carlos Zamora-Zapata sees the poet's phrasing of "sentir" (feeling) and "una fuerte inclinación" (a strong inclination) as expressing inertia instead of certainty, moving from one affirmation to another, contradicting the scientific method yet increasing the possibilities for different types of understanding.[41] This final equation, when considered along with Blanco's prolific body of work, points to the idea that everything in the universe is of the same monistic singularity. The question of complementarity remains central in the ordering principles that Blanco sets forth here, as the dual confessions—that of being a scientist yet also feeling an inclination to believe that $1 + 1 = 1$—are examples of Blanco's dialectical monism. In their complementarity, they express the potential for greater understanding that comes from the tension between objectivist and subjectivist approaches to understanding the universe.

We can connect Friis's observation that this last equation expresses how "everything is united through a plurality of theories,"[42] to Barad's assertion that all phenomena both arise from and constitute a singular universe. Conceivably, according to the principles Blanco lays out, one could add an infinite number of operators and terms to the equation and still come out with the same constant of one, a singular matter and energy that is the universe. A similar meditation involving the number one is explored in "Primera lección de geometría" (First Lesson of Geometry), where the poet describes a foundational ordering of the universe:

En el principio era el uno.
Más cerca del punto de la escritura maya
que de la raya vertical de nuestro sistema de notación.
El uno no era una cantidad;
era la pura calidad del Todo indivisible.
Y fue a partir del gran uno

que en un momento dado brotaron todos los números.
Primero nació el dos
y con él—de inmediato—el tres.
Luego, en vertiginosa sucesión,
surgieron todos los demás números.
Antes del uno no había más que el uno.
No el cero del vacío inexistente.
Ni el cero de la nada absurda.
El uno nada más.

In the beginning was the one.
Closer to the dot in Mayan writing
than to the vertical line in our system of notation.
The one was not a quantity;
it was the pure quality of the indivisible Whole.
And it was from the great one
that in a given moment sprouted all the numbers.
First born the two
and with it—immediately—the three.
Then, in dizzying succession,
arose the remaining numbers.
Before the one there was nothing but the one.
Not the zero of the inexistent vacuum.
Nor the zero of the absurd nothingness.
Just the one.

Although the poet begins with the words "In the beginning . . ." from the biblical account of creation found in Genesis 1:1, the unfolding of numbers quickly nullifies any understanding of creation as the making of something from nothing. Rather, all materiality comes from the one, echoing Borges's Aleph or Pacheco's drop of water where we find "todo el universo encerrado en un punto de agua" (all the universe contained in a point of water).[43] Furthermore, the one from which all materiality springs forth reflects monism in many Asian and Mesoamerican cosmovisions, as we can see in the Mayan system where the numeral one is denoted as a dot or point. Blanco's first geometry lesson incorporates the concept of one as point, which opens up the concept of unity in several ways.

Rojas Joo sees this mythical "one" as representing both beginning and end, an infinite element of eternity and simultaneity.[44] Geometrically, a point is the most fundamental representation of a position in space, yet in the terms of a four-dimensional universe that includes time, any two- or three-dimensional spatial mapping would not reflect diachronicity. In this way, the "one" as a point of origin in the poem aligns with what unfolded from time zero in Big Bang

34   SCIENCE FUSION IN CONTEMPORARY MEXICAN LITERATURE

cosmogony, where the universe expanded from an immensely hot and dense singularity. While it is hard to imagine, the universe did not expand into space but rather was the expansion of space itself, or as Katie Mack describes, "The Big Bang wasn't an explosion within the universe, it was an expansion *of* the universe. And it didn't happen at a single point, but at *every* point."[45] In a process explained through inflationary cosmology, which is remarkably similar to Blanco's "vertiginosa sucesión" (dizzying succession) in which "en un momento dado brotaron todos los números" (in a given moment sprouted all the numbers), gravity actually was repulsive for a mere 10^{-35} seconds, causing the universe to expand at speeds faster than light by a factor of 10^{30} according to the models of inflationary cosmology developed in the seventies and eighties.[46] The final stanza of the poem contrasts the mystical "one" with the conception of zero as nothingness or an integer representing an empty placeholder in place value systems. Here, Blanco's re-creation of the Big Bang through his first lesson in geometry suggests yet another similarity between Mayan numerals and a monistic universe. While the one is represented as a point, the zero in the Mayan numerical system is often represented with a seashell, possibly due to its roundness that, as Anthony Aveni explains, depicts the closed, cyclic nature of time because "unlike its Western counterpart, the Maya zero represented completeness rather than emptiness."[47] Furthermore, this conceptualization of zero is strikingly similar to the Buddhist idea of *sunyata*, the voidness from which reality emerges, defined not by emptiness but by undifferentiation. Like the Cosmological Principle, which essentially states that at large scales the distribution of matter in the observable universe is uniform and isotropic, this first lesson of geometry is a study in the properties of space and time that, when held together with the value of the mystical "one," sustains the poet's earlier assertion in the belief that, in spite of being a scientist, $1 + 1 = 1$ is a valid equation. By drawing together knowledge from science and religion in this way, the poet constructs a framework of complementary analogues to establish a principle of unity in the universe.

To speak of unity in the context of scientific principles will eventually lead to the question of a grand unified theory of everything, one of the great unsolved problems in physics. Currently the two major theoretical frameworks that we use to describe the universe are not wholly compatible. General relativity, for one, focuses on the force of gravity and accounts for larger scales and masses, while the other, quantum mechanics, focuses on the electromagnetic force as well as both the weak and strong nuclear forces to understand the small-scale world of atoms and subatomic particles. While various iterations of string theory hold promise to unifying the four forces under one framework, the confirmation of a "theory of everything" remains elusive. Similarly, in the poem "Teoría de Newton," the poet speaks of how Newton's framework of gravity and the movement of bodies was eventually replaced by general relativity and then challenged by quantum mechanics, illuminating phenomena that Newton's theory could not explain. Nonetheless, as with Newton's, these newer theories have yet to solve a greater question:

> Sin embargo,
> las nuevas teorías
> no han ido más lejos
> en un punto esencial:
> todo lo que existe
> —visible e invisible—
> se rige por las mismas leyes.
> Hay una sola norma
> en el universo que vale
> lo mismo para las estrellas
> que para las manzanas,
> las órbitas de los planetas,
> la forma de la luna
> y la velocidad del sol.
> Hay una sola ley
> que lo mismo gobierna
> la mente de un físico
> que los versos de este poema.[48]

> However,
> the new theories
> have not moved beyond
> one essential point:
> everything that exists
> —visible and invisible—
> is governed by the same laws.
> There is but one rule
> in the universe that is
> the same for the stars
> as for apples,
> the orbits of the planets
> the form of the moon
> and the speed of the sun.
> There is but one law
> that both governs
> the mind of a physicist
> and the verses of this poem.

Like Einstein, who spent the last decades of his career unfruitfully seeking to confirm his intuition that there must be a unified field theory, the poet affirms a unity that has not yet been articulated scientifically. In these final verses, the poet brings large bodies such as stars, planets, and even apples whose movement was unified in the Newtonian framework together with cognition, imagination, and poetry, phenomena that fall outside of the scope of physics. Similar to how electricity and magnetism were long thought to be different forces when in actuality they are one and the same, this novel theory would unify what in Western thought should pertain to separate domains.[49] From objectivism and subjectivism to the divide between materiality and discursivity, Blanco's dialectical monism proposes a theory built on complementarity that, not unlike the movement of metaphor or the interdependence of the yin and yang, presents a reality that is not a collection of things but rather a universe of process and continual intra-action.

Intra-actions: From Material Interconnectivity to the Meaning of Matter

We can see an example of how Blanco articulates this theory of reality as process in the poem "Teoría de la incertidumbre" (Theory of Uncertainty), which joins quantum mechanics through Heisenberg's Uncertainty Principle and the Observer Effect together with analogies of human behavior and, finally, the power of poetry. Though often conflated into one idea, the Uncertainty Principle and the Observer Effect are in fact related but distinct descriptions of the strange reality revealed by quantum mechanics. Alongside Bohr's Principle of Complementarity regarding the wave-particle duality, these form the underpinnings of the so-called Copenhagen Interpretation of quantum mechanics. In essence, the Uncertainty Principle reflects uncertainty as an inherent property of any quantum measurement. In its simplest terms, it states that at the small scales of quantum mechanics one cannot determine with perfect accuracy both the momentum and the position of an object at the same time.[50] Brian Greene explains that through this inherent uncertainty in measurement making, "Quantum theory thereby sets up its own duality: you can determine with precision certain physical features of the microscopic realm, but in so doing you eliminate the possibility of precisely determining certain other, complementary features."[51] While the Uncertainty Principle explains our limits of knowledge of the universe at microscopic scales, the Observer Effect explains how any experiment will necessarily disturb the very quantum system being observed as in the famous thought experiment known as Heisenberg's Microscope, described in the opening verses of Blanco's poem:

Heisenberg descubrió
que un investigador
asomado al microscopio
—se de cuenta o no—

ENTANGLED MATTER

es parte del experimento
que está llevando a cabo
porque la misma luz
que utiliza para observar
lo que está pasando
en su experimento
altera fundamentalmente
el orden de lo que observa.[52]

Heisenberg discovered
that a researcher
peeping into the microscope
—realizing it or not—
is part of the experiment
that is being carried out
because the same light
that they utilize to observe
what is happening
in their experiment
fundamentally alters
the order of what they are observing.

After concluding this first section of the poem by humorously establishing an analogy between the Observer Effect and the abrupt change in the behavior of children when an adult becomes present, the poet moves on to the second part of the poem where he zooms back into the atomic and subatomic realms, highlighting the strange world described by the likes of Heisenberg and Bohr. Stating that velocity changes the conditions of an object, the poet explains,

Si hablamos de las velocidades
cercanas a la de la luz
que rigen y dirigen
movimientos de los átomos
y las partículas subatómicas,
estamos hablando de una realidad aparte:
Un mundo impensable
donde no sólo se modifican
"los objetos"
—si cabe la expresión—
hasta dejar de serlo,
sino que las leyes mismas
que gobiernan la naturaleza son otras:
nada tienen que ver con "el sentido común."[53]

If we speak of velocities
nearing that of light
that govern and direct
movements of atoms
and subatomic particles,
we are speaking of a different reality:
An unthinkable world
where not only modified are
"objects"
—if the expression even fits—
to the point they cease to be that,
but also the laws themselves
that govern nature are others:
they have not a thing to do with "common sense."

Through the use of quotation marks for "los objetos" (objects) and "el sentido común" (common sense) the poet emphasizes the instability of these signifiers. In particular, the very idea of objects as determinant entities that can precisely be measured dissolves in the face of the new reality presented in the Copenhagen Interpretation.

Karen Barad observes how, for Bohr, scientific practices themselves must be understood as interactions between components of nature, emphasizing that according to Bohr's philosophy-physics one finds "the heart of the lesson of quantum physics: *we are a part of that nature that we seek to understand*" and that, as such, "our ability to understand the world hinges on our taking account of the fact that our knowledge making practices are social-material enactments that contribute to, and are a part of, the phenomena we describe."[54] We see this play out in "Teoría de incertidumbre" as the poet's treatment of the word "object" erases any pretension of a discrete subject-observer that from a detached distance contemplates objects found out there. Rather, the laws of nature themselves as well as the notion of subject and object of which the poet speak are modified in such a radical way that the experimenter is intrinsically entangled with the "objects" of the experiment. In this manner, the act of observing is less the "reflection of objects held at a distance," and more an activity of diffraction, which is "marking differences from within and as part of an entangled state."[55]

In "Teoría de incertidumbre" complementarity—here between the material and discursive nature of scientific practices—draws both together by establishing an analogous relationship between the uncertainty inherent in knowing the velocity and position of subatomic particles with the cultural and discursive practice of writing:

Lo mismo sucede con la literatura.
No es lo mismo una crítica inmóvil,

ENTANGLED MATTER

un ensayo erudito, una reseña estancada . . .
  que un poema
que se desplaza a gran velocidad.
Los poemas son rapidísimos . . .
No podemos conocer
—al mismo tiempo—
su forma y su contenido.
Y si conocemos la forma de un poema
nunca sabremos exactamente
de qué está hablando.[56]

The same thing occurs with literature.
Not being the same an immobile critique,
a scholarly essay, a stagnant review . . .
  as a poem
that moves around at great velocity.
Poems are so fast . . .
We cannot know
—at the same time—
their form and their content.
And if we know the form of a poem
we will never know exactly
what it is talking about.

In addition to highlighting the partial and, hopefully for those reading these words, not too slow-moving knowledge that works of literary criticism produce, the poet conveys that the power of poetry is its communicative capacity through complementary form and content enacted through reception. Like the wave-particle duality of the indeterministic quantum world, meaning in poetry is always an act of movement, repudiating any pretense to a fixed, nonchanging signified. Likewise, as we see the analogue with the Observer Effect, there is not a clean systemic break between the observer/reader/critic and the "object" of study, furthering the idea that the poem is enacted through material and discursive intervention to continually produce multiplicities of meanings.

Reality as intra-active enactment emphasizes that objects and phenomena do not precede their interaction but rather emerge through intra-actions emphasizing the relational nature of all matter and force in the universe. In Blanco's short poetic thought experiment "Teoría de conjuntos" (Set Theory), the poet ponders how objects emerge in such a universe:

En un cuarto a oscuras se enciende una vela.
Todo lo que en ese cuarto existe
se ve de pronto iluminado por un flanco

40 SCIENCE FUSION IN CONTEMPORARY MEXICAN LITERATURE

y proyecta sombra por el otro.
Todo lo que tiene luz tiene sombra.
La luz y la sombra van de la mano.
Pero, si la llama misma no tiene sombra,
¿De veras tiene luz la llama de la vela?[57]

In a dark room a candle is lit.
Everything which in that room exists
is suddenly seen illuminated on one side
and projecting shadow on the other.
Everything that has light has shadow.
Light and shadow go hand in hand.
But, if the flame itself has no shadow,
Does the flame of the candle truly have light?

Like in set theory in which mathematical objects are construed axiomatically through extension and abstraction, the poet here contemplates relations between objects through light and shadow.[58] The poet straddles between an almost atomistic conceptualization of light and the strange world of quantum mechanics. Friis notes how the poem employs the cryptic tone of the Buddhist sutras while at the same time alluding to key elements of Schrödinger's Cat and Heisenberg's Uncertainty Principle.[59] As the poem draws on the so-called measurement problem in quantum mechanics that both of these set forth, it also interrogates the ontological relation between the objects in the room. The setup of the poem itself indicates a linkage to complex concessive interconnectivities that transcend the boundaries of the verses such as the intervention of someone transferring heat to ignite the wick that consumes energy and puts out radiation that then collides with opaque surfaces creating the effect of umbra that is perceived by the human visual system, to give one example. While this framing supposes interaction among individual objects, when we view the process of lighting the candle as relational intra-action, we perceive how the phenomena that unfold in the room are the product of intra-acting components that emerge "in relation to their mutual entanglement."[60] At the risk of abusing the metaphor as turn of phrase, we can say that, in this light, the question posed in the poem is not about what light is as photon or electromagnetic radiation per se. Rather, it is to portray what light does as an optical phenomenon through seemingly countless intra-actions of entangled energy and matter.[61]

While the poems of *La raíz cuadrada del cielo* explicitly take up scientific themes, the same principles abound throughout Blanco's prolific body of work. In the collection *Relámpagos paralelos* (*Parallel Lightning Flashes*) we find the poem "Canto a no yo" (Song to Not Myself), a clear engagement with Walt Whitman's epic paean to humanity and the grand communion of the inclusive

ENTANGLED MATTER 41

"I," "Song of Myself." Whereas Whitman's song departs from a collective presence with "every atom belonging to me as good belongs to you,"[62] Blanco's begins with the concept of absence:

Celebro y canto la ausencia de yo.
Y si va implícito un yo en los verbos que utilizo
es porque no hay otra forma de hablar que pudiera resultarnos comprensible,
y lo que digo ahora de mí, lo digo de ti y de todos,
pues no hay un átomo en nuestro cuerpo
que no esté en continuo movimiento
transformándose incesantemente en otra cosa.[63]

I celebrate and sing the absence of me.
And if an I is implicit in the verbs I use
it is because there is no other way of speaking that would be understandable
and what I say now of myself, I say of you and of all,
since there is not an atom in our body
that is not in constant movement
transforming incessantly into something else.

Where the poet of "Song of Myself" affirms his birth and presence as emerging from a greater unity, declaring "My tongue, every atom of my blood, form'd from this soil, this air,"[64] Blanco's poet destabilizes the notion of presence as every fundamental atom is in a state of perpetual movement and change. We could say that while Whitman sings of being, Blanco sings of becoming.[65] Here the poet uses the collective first-person singular of "nuestro cuerpo" (our body) and questions "¿Cómo podría ser el yo?" (How could I be the I),[66] being continually formed of atoms and memories, gases and forms, with each cell carrying a code that carries the signature of a heritage that goes back beyond our unicellular past.

As the poet's focus moves backward in time and zooms smaller and smaller in scale, he concludes his initial question of how I could truly be the I:

si todo lo que nos constituye está cambiando constantemente,
se mueve, se forma y se transforma,
a una velocidad cercana a la de la luz?[67]

if all that constitutes us is constantly changing,
moving, forming and transforming,
at a speed near that of light?

The theme of movement that makes up the I is mirrored in the following stanzas of the poem where the poet zooms out to contemplate a cosmos that extends beyond what the "I" can see. First traversing to the edge of the observable universe that can be perceived only through radio telescopes and then beyond with "constelaciones escuchadas más que vistas, / y previstas más que escuchadas" (constellations heard more than seen / and predicted more than heard),[68] the poet connects the lyrical subject with unfathomable distances in space and time, only to come full circle to return to the theoretical dimensions of the universe conjured through human imagination beyond the limits of what can be "heard" but has never literally been seen by human eyes in the cosmic microwave background. Through perpetual flux, subjectivity is not a thing to be had but rather an ephemeral act of becoming, as can be perceived in the chiasmatic devices that proliferate in the fourth stanza:

> Vagamos de forma en forma,
> de cuerpo en cuerpo vagamos
> y nada de lo que somos es realmente nuestro.
> Y nada de lo que somos variada y sorprendentemente somos
> pues no somos una multitud a solas sino que somos uno.[69]

> We wander from form to form,
> from body to body we wander,
> and nothing of what we are is really ours.
> Nothing of what we are what we variedly and surprisingly are,
> because we are not a multitude by ourselves but rather we are one.

Whitman's famous phrase, "I contain multitudes," is turned on its head as Blanco's treatment of the concept is an impossibility as there is no subject, or I, to contain anything in and of itself. Instead, Blanco turns the concept of unity as communion into monistic subjectivity. In this way, Friis observes how Whitman's leaves of grass become Blanco's waves of a sea,[70] creating another doubly articulated metaphor of movement to express a singular universe of entangled, intra-acting matter and forces:

> Un mar donde la individualidad de cada ola
> no es sino el lujo de la forma en un instante
> hecho por su propia gracia y para ser
> consistente y solidario con el fondo del mar
> que en su continuo movimiento necesita de las olas
> pero que no es distinto de las olas.
> Un mar con olas que no es sino un lujo del lenguaje.[71]

> A sea where the individuality of each wave
> is nothing but the luxury of form in an instant
> made by its own grace in order to be
> consistent and in solidarity with the depths of the sea
> which in its continuous movement needs the waves
> but is not distinct from the waves.
> A sea with waves that is but a luxury of language.

Returning to discursive foundation of first-person subjectivity, the poet likens himself to a wave in an ocean, not as a separate object or subject, but as a movement of interconnected matter brought about by forces that give rise to his fleeting form. By equating his perceived subjectivity with incessant transformation, the poet frames himself as something that happens, arising from and returning to a continual flow of intra-actions. Like Barad's definition of agency as enactment, that is "'doing' and 'being' in its intra-activity,"[72] the poet transcends any notion of subjectivity and objectivity. Instead, the "I" of the poem is a discursive phenomenon, a luxury afforded through language made of its own grace. By contrasting this "Not Myself" with its true materiality, the poet shows himself to be both material and discursive, the paradoxical addresser and addressee of a song that is humbling and laudatory at the same time.

Another way that Blanco treats scientific themes is readdressing common metaphors or threads, establishing thematic and intertextual corollaries between works composed years apart as we can see in "El hombre" (Man), which intersects with "Teoría de conjuntos." Whereas in the "Teoría de conjuntos" the human is the implicit observer of and participant in the phenomena unfolding through the lighting of a candle, in "El hombre" the human is the product of intra-active and complementary phenomena. The poem is structured as a series of one-verse aphorisms about humankind, which, when viewed together with "Teoría de conjuntos," establishes elements of sets that fall under the signifier of "man." The first verse declares, "El hombre es un relámpago entre dos islas" (Man is a flash of lightning between two islands),[73] likening humanity to complementary movement between two polarities. Given that, for Blanco, lightning as both metaphor and allegory is "the essence of creation,"[74] the lightning strike from which man emerges establishes the creative intra-action of matter and energy. In another metaphor that places the lifespan of a human within space and time, vitality becomes a sense of movement and flow given that "El hombre es un reloj de arena: se va llenando de espacio, se va vaciando de tiempo" (Man is an hourglass, getting filled with space, getting emptied with time).[75] We see the clearest correspondence with "Teoría de conjuntos" in the final stanza of the poem—the only composed of more than one verse—where the poet again takes up the dialectic between light and shadow:

El hombre: mitad luz
    mitad sombra
mitad imaginación.[76]

Man: half light
    half shadow
half imagination.

Also recalling the equations from "Declaración de principios" where three halves can equal one whole, this final stanza alludes to both the materiality as well as the

44 SCIENCE FUSION IN CONTEMPORARY MEXICAN LITERATURE

ethical and creative capacity of humans. Recalling the earlier allegory of the flame, humans are subjects and objects, complementarily existing in the intra-activity of being and doing. Disregarding the logic of fractions, this final definition approximates man to an abstract machine that does not function to represent the real, but rather constructs a real yet to come.[77] Blanco's poetry, then, affirms the materiality of humans. Yet as in the equation of $1+1 = 1$ or the sum of three halves, for the poet there is something more to the formula of the human than a mere summation of matter and energy.

CHEMISTRY AND THE PROCESSES OF BECOMING

In the spring of 2022 Blanco published the series *Meditaciones* (*Meditations*) in the online cultural supplement for the *Milenio* newspaper. These meditations with one-word titles such as "Música" (Music), "Silencio" (Silence), and "Estrellas" (Stars) all depart from their named concept to ponder connections to greater cultural, political, and metaphysical questions. As this chapter begins with biochemistry, it also seems fitting to conclude it with a poem from *Meditaciones* about chemistry and genetics published nearly thirty years after *Antes de nacer*. In "Química" (Chemistry), the poet begins by stating that he knows of few cases where Nobel Prizes have been awarded to both a parent and a child, and in those rare cases both have been scientists with the most recent pair being Roger and Arthur Kornberg. In verse, the poet quotes the father, biochemist Arthur Kornberg, who postulated that "La vida es química: nada más / y nada menos—repite una y otra vez" (Life is chemistry: nothing more / and nothing less—he repeats time and again).[78] In his autobiography, whose title, *For the Love of Enzymes: The Odyssey of a Biochemist*, surely deserves a prize of its own, the elder Kornberg offers a reductionist model of cognition, where the brain is equated to a machine that outputs cognition as a result of biochemical processes under the guiding principle that "mind *is* matter and *only* matter."[79] Challenging the premise that life is solely a matter of chemistry, Blanco proposes the following thought experiment that composes the remainder of the poem:

Muy bien. Propongo el siguiente experimento
(y conste que yo también soy químico):
Hay que proveer a Kornberg y su equipo
de destacados investigadores en California,
una cantidad suficiente de carbono,
hidrógeno, oxígeno, nitrógeno, fósforo, etc.,
así como ingentes sumas de dinero
instalaciones y tiempo suficiente,
para que hagan su trabajo de laboratorio
y se compruebe el mysterium tremendum:

Todo es química.
Sentémonos a esperar entonces algo igual
—o mejor aún: superior—
a La adoración del Cordero Místico
de los hermanos Van Eyck,
o al Arte de la fuga de Bach.
O, para el caso, a un padre
y un hijo más agudos, talentosos e inteligentes
que Arthur y Roger Kornberg.[80]

Very well. I propose the following experiment
(and let it be known that I too am a chemist):
We need to provide Kornberg and his team
of distinguished researchers in California,
a sufficient amount of carbon,
hydrogen, oxygen, nitrogen, phosphorous, etc.
as well enormous amounts of money
facilities and enough time,
for them to do their laboratory work
and to verify the *mysterium tremendum*:
Everything is chemistry.
Let's sit and wait then for something equal
—or better yet: superior—
to the *Adoration of the Mystic Lamb*
by the Van Eyck brothers,
or the *Art of Fugue* by Bach.
Or, as is the case, to a father
and son more astute, talented, and intelligent
than Arthur and Roger Kornberg.

Blanco's bottom-up reconstruction experiment gets at the flaws of a purely reductionist view of complex life. No one would argue that this reductionist chain does not feature chemistry, but to equate life to nothing *but* chemistry is to ignore that life is not a thing, but an intra-active process that unfolds in space and time.

In *The Music of Life* Denis Noble carries out a similar thought experiment regarding the reconstruction of oneself, concluding that even if such an experiment were computationally possible, it would not provide the same human given that the indeterminacy inherent in the ever-increasingly complex systems involved could not be replicated as "structures and processes at a higher level simply are not visible at the molecular level."[81] Likewise, the poet's sense of awe before great works of art is an acknowledgment that they could never be replicated. While there is chemistry in the pigments of the paints on the *Ghent Altarpiece*, in the metal of an organ pipe through which air vibrates, or even in the neurons that fire as Blanco contemplates their beauty, none of these are simply a matter of chemistry. To try to replicate the diachronic processes and systems from which these works arose and achieve the same outcome would be a task impossible even for Borges's Pierre Menard. Moreover, we must remember that any such intervention would necessarily alter the system itself, irrevocably changing it as we have seen in the example of Heisenberg's Microscope. Instead, in "Química" and throughout Blanco's works, the *mysterium tremendum* of art or life is its very own process of unceasing irreproducibility. Life may be chemical, but it is never just chemistry.

As we have seen, Blanco's poetry over decades has continually affirmed a relation-oriented ontology in which the universe is constituted through ongoing diachronic processes, standing in contrast with any substantialist Cartesian or mechanistic understanding of matter. Such accounts of the universe as intra-action, intra-relation, or perpetual becoming abound in many of the works of ciencia-fusión that we will take up in the following chapters. What is more, one could argue that Blanco's poetry presents ciencia-fusión in its most explicit form given its propensity to overtly and knowingly wrestle with common conceptual themes and literary techniques embraced by other authors of ciencia-fusión. In particular, Blanco's use of metapoetry lays bare how ciencia-fusión utilizes the transposition of analogous scientific concepts to nonscientific contexts, the embrace of metaphor in scientific and literary discourse, as well as an open refutation of binary or dualistic imagery to reposition the human within an intra-active universe. In this manner, Blanco draws on the concepts of complementarity and perpetual movement to dissolve purported limits between subject and object, human and nonhuman, and even science and art.

With this in mind, Blanco does not shy away from affirming the materiality of human experience. From the subatomic composition of the self of "Canto a no yo" to the forms of dense matter in *Antes de nacer*, humans, like everything in the universe, are made up of matter and energy. Yet for Blanco, human and, indeed, all life is also more than the sum of its materiality. All movements, from subatomic particles to the stroke of a pen, are intra-actions of entangled matter and energy in a continual process of becoming. Drawing on the idea of complementarity both in science as well as in Eastern philosophies, Blanco puts forth that our understanding of this strange universe and our place in and of it is more fully known when we hold together seemingly distinct yet intra-related properties or phenomena. In Blanco's poetry we see that remote galaxies, the subatomic particles that make up humans, and even the metaphors of a poem or scientific concept are ephemeral entanglements of an intra-active and entangled universe. In his prolific and challenging body of work, Blanco takes us on a journey that encapsulates much of the work of ciencia-fusión, examining not only what matter is but, perhaps more importantly, what it is to matter.

CHAPTER 2

Quantum Mechanics, History, and the Question of Scale in Jorge Volpi's *En busca de Klingsor*

One would be hard-pressed to find a more striking, and horrifying, example of the power of scale than the atomic bomb that exploded over Hiroshima, Japan, on the morning of August 6, 1945. At the scale of the atom, a neutron was fired into the nucleus of an atom of uranium-235, causing it to split into two, emitting thermal energy, gamma rays, and two more neutrons to propel a chain of fission with surrounding nuclei, releasing incredible amounts of energy that would cause destruction and death on a scale that boggles the human mind to this day. The destruction of Hiroshima, and Nagasaki three days later, would bring a gruesome end to the race among rival powers of World War II to first harness the power of the atom as the ultimate weapon of war. Correlating the diminutive size yet immense destructive capacity that that initial fired neuron unleashed binds together the subatomic world with questions far beyond the domain of neutrons and atomic nuclei, as human concerns of ethics, politics, scientific knowledge, and morality all collided so many years ago. Upon hearing the news of the attack on Hiroshima, Werner Heisenberg, the German scientist whose collaboration or lack thereof in the Nazi atomic weapon program remains polemical to this day, expressed surprise at the scale of what the Americans had accomplished, famously retorting, "I don't believe a word of the whole thing."[1]

The magnitude of World War II in the Western imaginary has inspired countless literary works that probe its causes, the causality of events, as well as the outsized role that what we would term as chance played in the events that preceded its beginning through its final days that would usher in a new atomic age. Chance and Werner Heisenberg, it would seem, would also play a role in the creation of *En busca de Klingsor* (*In Search of Klingsor*, 1999), Jorge Volpi's

47

48   SCIENCE FUSION IN CONTEMPORARY MEXICAN LITERATURE

novel that re-creates events before, during, and after the Second World War. In the most well-known and critically celebrated work of ciencia-fusión, Volpi describes the novel's origins and its connection to Heisenberg in the epilogue to *Leer la mente* (*Reading the Mind*), his extended study on neuroscience and the art of fiction, where he interviews himself to humorous effect, describing how for a long time he had wanted to write a novel about scientists.[2] Volpi retells (to himself or is it us?) how his friend and fellow Crack writer Ignacio Padilla had invited him to spend the new year at an apartment that Padilla and his wife were renting in Florence, Italy, in December 1996. Given the apartment's lack of sufficient heating and its dilapidated state, Volpi tells of how he would wander the streets of Florence all hours of the day and night searching out the city's many ice cream shops and bookstores. In one bookstore that stayed open until midnight, Volpi tells how "por casualidad" (by chance) he stumbled upon David Cassidy's voluminous biography of Heisenberg, and how, as Volpi tells it,

> La devoré frente al hornillo de la cocina y *supe*, de inmediato, que había encontrado a mi protagonista—o antes lo supo mi cerebro. La idea, como queda demostrado, no me pertenecía: a un mero deseo inicial se antepuso, primero, mi ignorancia y, luego, una cadena de historias que, provista de una lógica propia, me conducía por sendas que nunca imaginé transitar.[3]

> I devoured it in front of the kitchen stove and *just knew*, immediately, that I had found my protagonist—or before that my brain just knew it. The idea, as has been shown, did not belong to me: a mere initial desire was preceded, first, by my ignorance and, then, by a chain of events that, provided with their own logic, led me along paths that I never imagined I would travel.

Describing the circumstances that led up to his discovery of the book and the inspiration it would have in creating *En busca de Klingsor*, Volpi purposefully diminishes his role as subservient to outside coincidences and "chains of events" that led him along unimagined paths set out before him. The self-referentiality of Volpi's retelling of the events that led up to him composing *Klingsor* is a wink to the novel's readers, who will undoubtedly recognize similar rhetorical positioning by *Klingsor*'s narrator, Gustav Links. That Volpi carries out the playful guise of an interview with himself to close a book titled *Leer la mente* through an epilogue subtitled "En la mente criminal del escritor (diálogo autorreferencial)" ("In the Criminal Mind of the Writer [Autoreferential Dialogue]"), suggests that Volpi is not quite done with Gustav Links and the paradoxes that his search for Klingsor elicits.

Published some three years later in 1999, *En busca de Klingsor* quickly achieved commercial success and critical acclaim due to its innovative treatment of its subject matter as well as its genre-bending format. The first novel in the Volpi's trilogy on twentieth-century history, which includes *El fin de la locura* (*The End of Madness,* 2003) and *No será la tierra* (*Season of Ash,* 2006), *En busca de Klingsor* is part crime novel, scientific history, historiographic metafiction, and postmodern polemic. Its plot revolves around the experiences of two main protagonists: Lieutenant Francis Bacon, a young American scientist pressed into military intelligence at the end of World War II, and German mathematician Gustav Links, who serves as Bacon's guide in his quest to reveal the identity of Klingsor, the code name for the rumored scientific adviser to Hitler in charge of directing all scientific projects of the Third Reich, the most notable of which, of course, is the quest for a functional atomic bomb. Throughout their search, the pair investigate the lives and work of scientists who, like Heisenberg, were working within the sphere of influence of the German academy and were responsible for so many of the great advances in physics and mathematics in the first half of the twentieth century. In addition to being Bacon's guide, Links enjoys the privileged role of narrator of the story that we are reading. Links narrates the novel's events while interred in 1989 in a mental institution in East Germany, where he is condemned to spend his days because decades earlier Bacon, under the influence of Soviet spy Irene, fingered Links as the true Klingsor. The central feature of the novel, that it is impossible for the reader—like Bacon—to know with absolute certainty the true identity of Klingsor, underscores how in *En busca de Klingsor* the groundbreaking discoveries in quantum mechanics serve as an analogue for the seemingly senseless history of the first half of the twentieth century. I argue that *En busca de Klingsor,* in addition to being an exploration of the repercussions of epistemological and ontological uncertainty, can be read as a meditation on the idea of scale in narrative, be that literary or historiographical. Through the transposition of discoveries about causality and chance in classical physics and quantum mechanics, Links, the narrator of the novel, seeks to find a greater meaning in history writ large by exploring the seemingly unpredictable actions, coincidences, and results of chance that undermine a deterministic view of history. Utilizing Hayden White's theories on strategies of explanation and narrativity in historical writing, it becomes evident that *En busca de Klingsor* demonstrates how the choice of historical scale between the micro and macro in a narrative brings to the foreground the notions of chance and causality, mirroring the fraught relationship between Newtonian and quantum mechanics explored by the historical and fictitious characters in the novel. In particular, through a narration that focuses microscopically on the seemingly random nature of humanity, the novel explores how intra-active agency brings a stochastic element to history that must be considered in order to better understand both the past and the present.

Most of the abundant literary criticism of *En busca de Klingsor* has focused on how the novel engages questions of epistemology as related to the influence of quantum mechanics on philosophy and the popular imagination.[4] For example, the Uncertainty Principle, introduced by Heisenberg in 1927, is one of the most

50 SCIENCE FUSION IN CONTEMPORARY MEXICAN LITERATURE

examined motifs in the novel. According to Heisenberg himself, the principle "can be expressed in its simplest form as follows: One can never know with perfect accuracy both of those two important factors which determine the movement of one of the smallest particles—its position and velocity. It is impossible to determine accurately *both* the position and the direction and speed of a particle *at the same instant*."[5] As we have seen, the crux of this groundbreaking discovery strikes at the long-held idea that science could provide humanity with certainty of knowledge in an increasingly uncertain world. That *En busca de Klingsor* is in many ways a meditation on the idea of certainty leads Robert Goebel to declare that "la novela de Volpi es la teoría de Heisenberg vuelta literatura" (Volpi's novel is Heisenberg's theory turned into literature).[6] Volpi affirms this approach to the text, stating that *En busca de Klingsor* "además de las historias que cuenta, pudiera ser un resumen de esa primera mitad del siglo XX, una historia de la incertidumbre en el siglo XX, o al menos en la primera mitad del siglo XX" (in addition to the stories it tells, it could be a summary of the first half of the twentieth century, a history of uncertainty in the twentieth century, or at least the first half of the twentieth century).[7]

That a Mexican novelist has written several books that take place in Europe with mostly European and North American characters has attracted much attention.[8] In addition to coining a new subgenre by classifying *Klingsor* as a work of ciencia-fusión, Guillermo Cabrera Infante famously asserts that *Klingsor* is "una novela alemana escrita en español" (a German novel written in Spanish).[9] Tomás Regalado López describes Cabrera Infante's characterization as

> un arma de doble filo. Inicia una querella entre localismo y cosmopolitismo que reedita antiguos debates desde la Independencia y el siglo XIX, y que ha tenido episodios claves en Hispanoamérica con el Modernismo, Contemporáneos, la Vanguardia, Borges, la Generación de Medio Siglo, incluso el Boom.[10]

> a double-edged sword. It initiates a dispute between localism and cosmopolitanism that rehashes old debates from Independence and the nineteenth century, and that has had key episodes in Spanish America with Modernismo, the Contemporáneos, the Avant-Garde, Borges, the Mid-Century Generation, even the Boom.

Volpi is one of the founding Crack authors, five friends who published in 1996 their "Crack Manifesto," in which they advocate a renovation in Hispanic literature based on a skepticism of the abuse of the exoticism of magical realism and the supposed decadence of post-Boom literature. Through their manifesto and subsequent works, all share a preoccupation with what they identify as universal subjects and narratives marked by cultural, structural, and formal complexity.[11] While the events in *Klingsor* occur outside of Mexico, the description of it

JORGE VOLPI'S *EN BUSCA DE KLINGSOR*

as a German novel written is Spanish seems particularly imprecise. Aníbal González argues convincingly that reading the novel "in the context of a Latin American tradition that has Jorge Luis Borges as its main literary model, and as a critical rewriting of the Boom's 'total novels,' allows us to appreciate this text as a profound reflection of the paradoxical links between science and magic, art and oppression, totalization and totalitarianism."[12] Moreover, Adriana López Labourdette contends that *Klingsor* disrupts dominant discourse through its innovative use of narrative and treatment of European history, observing that it should be positioned as a postcolonial novel given that "primero que todo, el hecho, quizá exclusivamente evidente como para insistir en él, de un novel autor mexicano que acomete el desafío de una periferia doble: la re-escritura, primero, de la historiografía desde la narrativa, y segundo, la del discurso del centro (Europa) desde los márgenes (Latinoamérica)" (first of all, the fact, perhaps overwhelmingly evident enough to insist on it, of a new Mexican author who undertakes the challenge from a double periphery: the rewriting, first, of historiography from narrative, and second, that of discourse of the center [Europe] from the margins [Latin America]).[13] That the novel was written from a double periphery in López Labourdette's terminology adds yet another element in approaching Volpi's text and its treatment of politics, power, science, and knowledge.

METAFICTIONAL PLOTTING: SCIENTIFIC/LITERARY ANALOGUES

Volpi describes how he came about utilizing the history of science in the twentieth century to describe something much more all-encompassing:

> Y sabía que quería hacer una novela sobre el mundo de la ciencia porque creía que tenía una gran cantidad de riqueza en imágenes, metáforas, símbolos, que permitirían no solamente explicar el mundo, que es lo que busca la ciencia, sino que servirían para volverse metáforas, símbolos e imágenes de las relaciones humanas y de la relación del hombre con su entorno.[14]

> And I knew that I wanted to write a novel about the world of science because I believed that it had a great amount of richness in images, metaphors, symbols, which would not only let one explain the world, which is what science seeks, but would also serve in becoming metaphors, symbols, and images of human relationships and the relationship between man and his surroundings.

While readers have correctly pointed out that in the novel there are instances of an oversimplification of scientific theories or errors in describing mathematical concepts, a careful reading of the text reveals various narrative winks from Volpi through the narrator Gustav Links about the distinction between physics

52 SCIENCE FUSION IN CONTEMPORARY MEXICAN LITERATURE

and the realm of the human experience.[15] At times, Links paradoxically seems to affirm the application of physical discoveries to the nonscientific realm. Speaking of Gödel's Incompleteness Theorem—roughly, that in any formal axiomatic system there will always be statements that while they may be true are unprovable within the system[16]—Links recognizes its implication to logic by saying, "Nadie estaba a salvo en un mundo que comenzaba a ser dominado por la incertidumbre. Gracias a Gödel, la verdad se tornó más huidiza y caprichosa que nunca" (No one was safe in a world that was beginning to be dominated by uncertainty. Thanks to Gödel, the truth became more elusive and capricious than ever).[17] At the same time, Links warns of the danger of applying a superficial understanding of physics to the realm of the moral and political. In the chapter playfully titled "El principio de incertidumbre" (The Uncertainty Principle), Links questions,

> ¿Quién dice la verdad? ¿y quién miente? . . . Al principio de incertidumbre le ha llegado a suceder la misma desgracia que a la relatividad de Einstein: miles de personas no entienden una palabra de física, provocadas por cientos de periodistas que saben aún menos, suponen que han comprendido el sentido profundo de la expresión por más que la sola unión de una incógnita y un número—¡ni por hablar de una maleducada letra griega!— . . . A Heisenberg no le fue mucho mejor. Su principio de incertidumbre sólo se refería, en realidad, al elusivo mundo subatómico, no a los amores ambiguos, a las promesas rotas o las traiciones venideras.[18]

> Who is telling the truth? and who is lying? . . . The same misfortune that happened to Einstein's relativity is beginning to happen with the Uncertainty Principle: thousands of people who do not understand a word of physics, provoked by hundreds of journalists who know even less, and assume that they have understood the profound meaning of the expression much less the mere union of a variable and a number—not to mention a pesky Greek letter!— . . . Heisenberg did not fare much better. His Uncertainty Principle only referred, in reality, to the elusive subatomic world, not to ambiguous loves, broken promises or future betrayals.

The contradictory message highlights a tension of which both Links and Volpi seem to be aware. While not mathematically and scientifically applicable to questions of morality, these earth-shattering discoveries occur, not coincidentally, at the same time as Europe descends into a turbulent period marked by two great wars and the disintegration of the moral and philosophical foundations of Christianity and the Enlightenment.[19] Volpi states that

> lo cierto es que no podemos negar que, ciertas o falsas, esas implicaciones sociales han sido muy importantes. Aunque la Relatividad de Einstein no hablara sobre la relatividad de todos los valores, en el momento que Einstein se

populariza, en los años veinte y treinta de nuestro siglo, la Relatividad de Einstein parece estar directamente conectada con la relatividad de valores que se está viviendo.[20]

the truth is we cannot deny that, true or false, these social implications have been very important. Although Einstein's Relativity did not speak about the relativity of all values, at the time that Einstein became popular, in the twenties and thirties of our century, Einstein's Relativity seems to be directly connected with the relativity of values that was being lived out.

In this manner, *En busca de Klingsor*, like much of ciencia-fusión, portrays through a metaliterary approach the impact of scientific discoveries and knowledge within the greater popular imaginary, demonstrating how science moves within our culture and, consequently, the writing and reception of literature. In the novel, the way in which these two realms are combined to great effect is through a narrative structure dependent upon a metaphorical transposition that is "construida sobre la base de una descripción minuciosa, tanto de la física cuántica como de los pensamientos de los personajes: funcionan como análogos, y no necesariamente como miembros de una implicación lógica" (built on the foundation of meticulous description, both of quantum physics and the characters' thoughts: they function as analogs, and not necessarily as members of a logical implication).[21]

The use of analogy in which scientific and mathematical discoveries become the lens through which history and the lives of the main characters are explored is made possible through the narrative structure of the novel, which, from the very preface on, directly connects history writ large to a personal, humanized perspective of one man condemned to die in obscurity, demonstrating how the narration eases from the macro- to the microscopic. In doing so, *Klingsor* features variations in scale in its narration of events, descriptions, and phenomena in order to show how seemingly unconnected or circumstantial facts are all interconnected. Joshua DiCaglio argues that, while often overlooked, an awareness of scale as "a tool for establishing a reference point for domains of experience and interaction," enlightens the exploration of relations both within and across disparate disciplines.[22] DiCaglio explains that "scale reworks our notions of process, relation, and organization. Scale presents not only new objects but a tangle of new relations in two senses: first scale reveals relationships that were previously not apparent simply because they were not discernible; and in turn, scale provides new possibilities for comprehending these aggregates and relations."[23] Approaching Links's narration with an awareness of how he utilizes scale to explain and exculpate his complicity in the events he is recounting allows us to view it in an entirely new light. As DiCaglio points out, "In short, scale changes everything because it changes what every thing means."[24]

The novel begins with a heterodiegetic description of Hitler hidden in his bunker as Berlin is falling, orgasmically delighting in the daily showing of a film of the

54   SCIENCE FUSION IN CONTEMPORARY MEXICAN LITERATURE

execution and torture of the conspirators from the failed assassination attempt on the führer's life on July 20, 1944. The narrator then moves to a telling of how chance and coincidence impeded the plot and allowed Hitler to escape, unleashing the cruel retribution of the führer on all suspected participants and accomplices. The narrator then abruptly becomes homodiegetic, telling how "cuando el 5 de septiembre vinieron por mí" (when on September 5 they came for me),[25] chance once again intervened when a bomb fell on the courthouse where he was to be sentenced to the same fate as the conspirators. The preface, signed by Gustav Links on November 10, 1989, sets up the frame of narration by stating "quizás porque otras coincidencias, no menos terribles, me han obligado a escribir estas páginas" (perhaps because other coincidences, no less terrible, have compelled me to write these pages).[26] Throughout Links's retelling, coincidence and chance play a fundamental role given that "a diferencia de otras épocas, la nuestra ha sido decidida con mayor fuerza que nunca por estos guiños, por estas muestras del ingobernable reino del caos. Me propongo a contar, pues, la trama del siglo. De *mi* siglo" (unlike other eras, ours has been decided more forcefully than ever by these winks, by these signs of the ungovernable rule of chaos. I am proposing to relate, then, the plot of the century. Of *my* century).[27] The preface of the novel, therefore, establishes a narrator whose motivation in narrating is both explicatory and exculpatory. By asserting personal possession of the century, the narrator creates a frame through which all the events will be observed on a personal level. Consequently, Links begins each of the three books in the novel with laws and postulates such as in the first book's "Leyes del movimiento narrativo" (Laws of narrative movement) that include "Todo narrador ofrece una verdad única" (Every narrator offers a unique truth) and "Todo narrador tiene un motivo para narrar" (Every narrator has a motive to narrate). Although Links reminds us that "nuestro gusto por las metáforas puede meternos en grandes aprietos" (our penchant for metaphors can get us in big trouble),[28] it is through these metaphors that Links will put his life on trial, inviting the reader to accompany him on the journey through uncertainty and chance with a task directed to the readers that "les corresponderá a ustedes, si aceptan el desafío—qué ampuloso; digámoslo mejor: el juego—, decirme si he tenido razón, o no" (it will be up to you, if you accept the challenge—how bombastic; let's rephrase that: the game—, to tell me if I was right, or not).[29]

As Volpi states in an interview, "[se hace] un paralelismo entre la investigación que lleva a cabo un científico y la de un policía, un detective. En ambos casos se plantea el mismo método inductivo, se trata de ir acumulando pruebas para probar teorías e irlas verificando o desmintiendo conforme van apareciendo nuevos elementos" (a parallel is drawn between an investigation carried out by a scientist and that of a police officer, a detective. In both cases, the same inductive method is proposed, it is about going around accumulating evidence to test theories and verifying or disproving them as new elements appear).[30] Nonetheless, the investigation is known only through the filter of the narrator, underscoring the epistemological complications in the reader's task. This signaling to the fact that the entire narration is dependent upon Links's experience and knowledge is evidence of Mikhail Bakhtin's observation that "when the novel becomes the dominant genre, epistemology becomes the dominant discipline."[31] The consequence, therefore, is that Links's history is discursive and textual by necessity. Although Links is a fictitious creation, his character stands in for the "trama del siglo" (plot of the century), and the text he presents the reader lays bare the idea of history as narrative. This linguistic turn in the philosophy of history can be found in the ideas of Hayden White, among others. By analyzing the structure of historical works, White delineates the ways in which historians make use of tropological strategies of prefiguration combined with various modes of explanation to show that historians do not simply find history but rather are narrators of stories.[32]

In her analysis of the postmodern novel, Linda Hutcheon takes up the idea that our accessibility to history in the present is "entirely conditioned by textuality."[33] This is to question not the existence of the past but rather how our knowledge of the past is conditioned by narrative. Hutcheon clarifies, "To say that the past is only *known* to us through textual traces is not, however, the same as saying that the past is only textual, as the semiotic idealism of some forms of post-structuralism seems to assert. This ontological reduction is not the point of postmodernism: past events existed empirically, but in epistemological terms we can only know them today through texts. Past events are given *meaning*, not *existence*, by their representations in history."[34]

The Role of Scale in Science, Literature, and Historiography

Links's story is in so many ways the story of the European twentieth century but told on a decidedly human scale. The idea of scale is fundamental in both historiographic narrative as well as fiction, which should be of no surprise given that DiCaglio argues that while "scale does not mediate our access to the world; it permits us to make sense of mediated, extended, and projected experience."[35] As an example, a macrohistorical study has as a focus a large topic or timeframe and seeks to identify patterns and common themes to explain historical processes and events. In contrast, a microhistory has a smaller, more defined focus to explore historical processes and events through a more detailed analysis of a reduced scale of investigation. The scale or scope of the narration, therefore, can be related to the different strategies of argument as proposed by White. In Volpi's novel, it can be said that Links's story is indeed a microhistory with the twist that the historian is also the historical subject. Through fusing both his story and that of renowned scientists and historical figures, the connection between the biographic and the historical is made manifest from within. As an example of how history is brought to the human scale, the narrator describes Bacon's thoughts while in the same bathroom of a Nuremberg hotel that Hitler once used. "Por todas aquellas superficies

56   SCIENCE FUSION IN CONTEMPORARY MEXICAN LITERATURE

se había deslizado, sin duda, la resinosa piel de Hitler; ahí había estado desnudo e indefenso, admirando la flaccidez de su sexo antes de sumergirse en el agua, y por ese mismo hueco habrían resbalado sus excrementos" (Across all these surfaces, no doubt, Hitler's resinous skin had slid; there he had been naked and defenseless, admiring the flaccidity of his genitals before immersing himself in the water, and through that same hole his excrement would have slid down).[36] While striking in vividly reproducing the frailty and humanity of a historical figure associated with cruel power on a grand scale, this style of narrative has been around for centuries, bringing to the reader's mind, for example, the description in Tolstoy's *War and Peace* of a fleshy and mortal Napoleon being dressed by his valet before the Battle of Borodino. Similarly, in *En busca de Klingsor* the scale of the historical object jumps between the macro and the micro, allowing a deeper examination of the themes of chance, coincidence, and causality.

While the biographies of scientists and explanations of the upheavals provoked by quantum mechanics serve as metaphors for the uncertainty in the search for Klingsor, these same analogies when applied to Bacon and Links's personal lives bring a greater understanding to the role that chance and causality play in making sense of history. Anderson notes the parallels between the investigation and Bacon and Links's relationships, remarking that "just as Bacon develops a view of behavior in the German scientific field, Links elaborates a relational understanding of identity, behavior, motivations, and betrayal among intimates. Following his training as a mathematician, Links articulates an arithmetic of the soul."[37] Volpi affirms this approach given that for the novel's protagonists personal sentimentality proves to be a superior motivator to other concerns such as reason, nation, patriotism, and logic:

> Para mí las historias importantes son las historias individuales de los personajes, las historias individuales que hacen que Bacon salga de Estados Unidos, las historias individuales de Links que están marcadas desde luego por su momento histórico, por la ciencia que practica, pero que son mucho más importantes que eso. Las decisiones que toman los personajes siempre tienen que ver con el amor; esa decisión trágica en medio de la incertidumbre siempre es apostar por el amor irracional.[38]

> For me, the important stories are the individual stories of the characters, the individual stories that make Bacon leave the United States, the individual stories of Links that are clearly marked by their historical moment, by the science that he practices, but that are much more important than that. The decisions that the characters make always have to do with love; that tragic decision in the middle of uncertainty is always betting on irrational love.

Reflecting both the sexism of the age as well as their primary function as narrative catalysts for the historically grand turns in the plot that center around male characters, Jorge Zamora points out that "las mujeres de *Klingsor* parecen operar en función de los personajes masculinos. Y todas sin excepción están de alguna manera reprimidas, explotadas o degradadas" (the women in *Klingsor* seem to operate in service of the male characters. And all without exception are in some way repressed, exploited, or degraded).[39] Both Links and Bacon's life trajectories, as well as those of various secondary characters, are abruptly altered by the mostly male response to love, betrayal, obsession, and infatuation of women. As a result, fate becomes obsolete and the present becomes the collapse of past possibilities to meld Heidegger's conceptualization to the language of quantum mechanics.

From the novel's preface to its final page possibility, fate, chance, and causality are explored, with Links pondering a type of alternate history. Links tells that during the assassination attempt on Hitler "un mínimo error de cálculo—una nimiedad: una de las bombas no pudo ser activada o acaso el maletín quedó demasiado lejos del lugar donde se sentaba Hitler—hizo que el plan se viniese abajo" (a minimal miscalculation—a tiny detail: one of the bombs could not be activated or the briefcase was left too far from the place where Hitler was sitting—made the plan fall apart).[40] Suggesting a chain of causation, Links declares that "un golpe de suerte salvó a Hitler. Si la segunda bomba hubiese sido puesta en funcionamiento por Stauffenberg, si el maletín hubiese quedado más cerca del Führer, si hubiese habido una reacción en cadena, si Stauffenberg se hubiese asegurado, desde el principio colocarse más cerca de él" (a stroke of luck saved Hitler. If the second bomb had been set off by Stauffenberg, if the briefcase had been closer to the Führer, if there had been a chain reaction, if Stauffenberg had made sure, from the beginning, to stand closer to him).[41] However, this chain of causation is unified by the idea of chance and luck, which becomes a recurring leitmotif throughout the novel. In the recorded dialogue that captures the German scientists held at Farm Hall debating why the Americans succeeded in creating the first atomic bomb, the idea of an alternate outcome is again raised when Karl Wirtz exclaims, "Planes, planes . . . si nos hubiésemos concentrado en una sola cosa desde el principio" (Plans, plans . . . if only we had concentrated on just one thing from the beginning).[42] Similarly, Links demands of his interlocutor in the mental hospital, "Analice mi relato: vea cómo fue una cadena de mínimos errores la que impidió su éxito . . . y, por un descuido, por un vaivén de lo que a falta de otro nombre conocemos como el azar, eso no pudo ocurrir" (Analyze my story: see how it was a chain of minimal mistakes that prevented its success . . . and, due to an oversight, due to a fluctuation of what for lack of a better word we know as chance, that could not happen).[43] Links's interpretation of history embraces causality within chains of events, yet it is also governed by the idea of chance and uncertainty, in short an indeterminate world. This is a radical departure from Links's

58　SCIENCE FUSION IN CONTEMPORARY MEXICAN LITERATURE

description of the nineteenth century, downright Hegelian in its determinacy, a time when

> mis padres, y los padres de mis padres, creían que la humanidad progresaba linealmente, desde el horror de la edad de cavernas, hasta la brillantez del futuro, como si la historia no fuese más que un cable tendido entre de postes de luz o, para utilizar la metáfora que mejor define al siglo XIX, como una vía férrea que une, al fin, dos poblados remotos.[44]

> my parents, and the parents of my parents, believed that humanity progressed linearly, from the horror of the cave age, to the brilliance of the future, as if history were nothing more than a wire strung between light poles or, to use the metaphor that best defines the nineteenth century, as a railway line that unites, finally, two remote villages.

In contrast, Links shares how the prewar period of instability led to the rise of Nazism and Hitler, observing that "el ambiente era propicio: el desorden sacudía a Alemania de un lado a otro. Revoluciones, asesinatos, saqueos. Todos queríamos un poco de paz y estabilidad, mientras que las posiciones de Einstein parecían representar la ruptura y el caos" (the atmosphere was propitious: disorder was shaking Germany from one side to the other. Revolutions, murders, looting. We all wanted a bit of peace and stability, all while Einstein's positions seemed to represent rupture and chaos).[45]

From this period of disorder and overwhelming chaos, Volpi found inspiration for the novel. "Me parecía una coincidencia fabulosa, que esta parte de la física que deja atrás la causalidad clásica y se adentra en la incertidumbre . . . ocurriese justamente en el período que va entre la Primera y la Segunda Guerra Mundial y que sus consecuencias fueran la creación de la bomba atómica" (It seemed to me to be a fabulous coincidence, that this part of physics that leaves behind classical causality and enters into uncertainty . . . would occur precisely in the period between the First and Second World Wars and that its consequences would be the creation of the atomic bomb).[46] In the novel, interestingly, it is Irene, in a debate with Links and Erwin Schrödinger, who best expresses how the idea of an extreme indeterminacy can suggest a total breakdown of the moral and ethical. "En un mundo indeterminado, donde no existe el bien ni el mal por sí mismos, los campos de concentración o la bomba atómica podían llegar a ser considerados normales" (In an indeterminate world, where there is no good or evil per se, concentration camps or the atomic bomb could come to be considered normal).[47] As Links (and Volpi through various interviews) sees it, the danger in an indeterminate world is that "en medio de la confusión permanente, nunca falta quien aprovecha la ceguera ajena para aliviar sus propios temores. Alguien se eleva por encima de los otros y . . . insiste en ser dueño de una verdad superior" (in the midst of permanent confusion, there is no shortage of people who take advantage of the blindness of others to alleviate their own fears. Someone positions themselves above others and . . . insists on owning a higher truth).[48] It is a well-worn proposition that a figure like Hitler often gains power by promising to bring order to chaos for a Faustian moral bargain. Although the novel highlights the element of chance and probability and how scientific discoveries upend our understanding of the world, when the question of an unmooring of morality is raised it is almost unfailingly refuted by scientists such as Schrödinger and Heisenberg. In the first section of the book, señor Bird takes up this question when recruiting Bacon. Referring to a popular interpretation of Einstein's theory of special relativity, "A mí no acaba de gustarme eso de la relatividad. Yo creo que hay cosas que no son relativas. Lo bueno y lo malo no es relativo" (I just can't get behind this relativity thing. I believe that there are things that are not relative. What's good and bad is not relative).[49] After pointing out that Einstein "sólo afirma que el movimiento es relativo para los observadores en movimiento" (only affirms that motion is relative to observers in motion), Bacon clarifies that Einstein "habla en términos físicos, no sociales. . . . Las cuestiones morales no tienen nada que ver con estos hechos, señor Bird" (is speaking in physical terms, not social. . . . Moral matters have nothing to do with these facts, Mr. Bird).[50] Nonetheless, this erroneous transposition of relativity in physics and ethics in the popular imaginary is facilitated by a world seemingly governed by indeterminacy and a lack of order. As in Links's narration that is the novel itself, many works of ciencia-fusión internally vacillate between an embrace of a direct transposition of scientific metaphor to the social and a more nuanced conceptual separation between the two realms. Like Links who repeatedly fluctuates between the respective poles represented in the previous passage by señor Bird and Bacon, works of ciencia-fusión utilize these conceptual entanglements in an often-complementary manner in a way not dissimilar to what we have seen in Alberto Blanco's concept of dialectical monism under constant interrogation.

NARRATING CHAOS, CAUSALITY, AND CHANCE

An example of the ways ciencia-fusión utilizes such conceptual movement can be seen in the treatment of the idea of chaos in Volpi's novel. In popular terminology, chaos is associated with an utter lack of order with its etymological origins in Greek as meaning *abyss* or *void*. However, in scientific and mathematical terms chaos put simply is a dynamic system whose complexity renders long-term predictions nearly impossible. That said, true chance does not enter the equation as chaotic systems are deterministic in that the smallest variances in initial conditions do determine the outcomes; they simply cannot be reliably predicted due to the complexity of the system itself. As Alberto Blanco expresses through his poem "Segunda teoría del caos" (Second Theory of Chaos), "El caos no es sino el orden / que no logramos comprender" (Chaos is but order / that we fail to understand).[51] One of the most revolutionary ideas of quantum mechanics is the strange idea that at the subatomic level every particle or quantic entity has characteristics of both waves and particles. At the microscopic, subatomic level, particles can be understood to behave like waves *and* particles in describing their behavior at the quantum scale. At this scale, matter seems to exist in a probabilistic milieu that can be described as a wave function that contains all the possible measurements for a system with the most likely being seen as a "crests" and the least as "dips" on a wave of probabilities.[52] While probabilistic, this does not mean that the universe is reigned by absolute chance. In response to Irene's idea of chance and radical indeterminacy, Schrödinger responds,

> Yo no soy bueno o perverso porque los hechos sucedan al azar: por el contrario, mis decisiones dependen de una gran variedad de motivaciones, desde las más mezquinas hasta las más sublimes, lo cual poco tiene que ver con decisiones tomadas en un marco aleatorio. Si bien es cierto que la mecánica cuántica considera que ciertos aspectos del universo permanecen indeterminados, al mismo tiempo realiza predicciones estadísticas que, en cualquier caso, no están basadas en el azar.[53]

> I am not good or wicked because events happen by chance: on the contrary, my decisions depend on a wide variety of motivations, from the pettiest to the most sublime, which has little to do with decisions made in a random framework. While it is true that quantum mechanics considers certain aspects of the universe to remain indeterminate, at the same time it makes statistical predictions, that, in any case, are not based on chance.

What seems like chance is actually characteristic of the indeterminacy in the system or as Links says when comparing the electron to a criminal, "la mecánica cuántica prefiere determinar estadísticamente, cuáles son las guaridas más probables en que el electrón decidirá esconderse una vez consumadas sus fechorías" (quantum mechanics prefers to determine statistically which are the most likely haunts in which the electron will decide to hide once its misdeeds have been accomplished).[54] This behavior seems counterintuitive to us because at the macroscopic level we do not observe this indeterminacy, thus the classical or Newtonian understanding of particles that occupy a definite place in space and time.

When describing the universe, the classical laws and formulas of Newtonian physics work efficiently to measure and predict on the macroscopic scale. It is only when scale is reduced and we enter the microscopic, quantic realm (or situations where temperatures are very cold) where we begin to see uncertainty and probabilistic systems in place of the world previously seen as orderly and entirely predictable. In *En busca de Klingsor* the personal and moral decisions that its protagonists Bacon and Links as well as the fictionalized historical personages make serve as a metaphor for how at a smaller, more human scale, the processes of the past can be seen as the outcome of seemingly coincidental but ultimately human choices. While Von Neumann condenses the aims and actions of the Axis and Allies into a simple diagram illustrating game theory to Bacon, the aims and actions of the human characters reveal a much more complex, probabilistic, even chaotic system. It is imperative to point out, however, that the two are not inseparable. The rules of quantum mechanics continue to exist at the macro scale, yet they are usually imperceivable. What is more, extrapolating quantum measurements at this scale causes calculations to become too complex when the rules of classical physics describe the same phenomena in a perfectly acceptable way. Von Neumann's simplified example of game theory is one we play, wittingly or not, when contemplating past chains of events. Regarding historiography, Reinhart Koselleck builds upon Heidegger's notion of possibility (*Möglikchkeit*) to emphasize that "chance is a pure category of the present."[55] Koselleck points out that from the perspective of the present looking to the past, chance "cannot be derived from a horizon of future expectation . . . neither is it possible to experience it as the outcome of past causes: for if this were possible then it would no longer be chance."[56] Therefore, chance "is more suited to depict the startling, the new, the unforeseen, and like experiences in history."[57] In *En busca de Klingsor* what we would term as chance plays a large role when the scale of the narrative focuses on small coincidences or when human sentimentality, love, and lust influence the characters' decision-making processes. In establishing the analogous relationship between science, history, and human behavior, the novel gives insight into how the question of scale impacts how we examine the past and the role human behavior and agency play in it.

In an analogous way, in historical studies the question of coincidence and causality is largely dependent upon the scope of the investigation. Olivier Hekster speaks to this phenomenon:

> Whether a historian interprets something as coincidental to, or a central focus of causality of, events depends somewhat on the historical scope of his or her analysis. The education of historical figures, for example, may explain their historical actions. Few biographers would formulate their protagonist's education as "mere coincidence," but for a historian who is interested in larger historical trajectories, the education that a single individual happened to have had, and which may explain specific actions that were part of a wider chain of events, has much less explanatory force. In such a reading the definition of historical coincidence becomes almost a matter of taste. To be more precise: the choice for the scale of a specific historical narrative decides whether certain events are coincidental to the history which is being described, or causal factors within that history.[58]

62   SCIENCE FUSION IN CONTEMPORARY MEXICAN LITERATURE

That is to say that the smaller the scale, or scope, of historical analysis the more events that seem coincidental to the action take upon causal characteristics.[59] What at first seems like coincidence becomes cause when the focus becomes smaller and smaller. In *En busca de Klingsor* the scope of the events occurs at both the micro and macro scales. On one extreme, Links describes in minute detail the ways in which small changes in timing or oversights change history. At first glance, these seem to be the product of pure chance. However, upon delving more deeply into the lives of just the two protagonists at hand, Bacon and Links, it becomes clear that what seemed to be chance is in truth the outcome of a probabilistic system. While Links's actions or lack thereof conceivably changed the course of history, on a scale of a lifetime Links declares that

> al contemplar mi vida desde la distancia que otorga el tiempo . . . me doy cuenta de que, desde mi nacimiento, mi destino ha estado ligado a la historia del siglo como una lamprea está unida fatalmente al cetáceo que le sirve de hogar y compañía. La mía es una existencia marcada por la turbulenta época que me tocó padecer y, sobre todo, por las personas que la fortuna puso en mi camino durante la primera mitad del siglo.[60]

> when contemplating my life from the distance that time grants . . . I realize that, since my birth, my destiny has been linked to the history of the century as a lamprey is fatally linked to the cetacean that serves as its home and company. Mine is an existence marked by the turbulent times that I had to endure and, above all, by the people that fortune put in my path during the first half of the century.

Links's almost deterministic view of his life and history appears to undermine his reasoning that "si me atrevo a unir hechos aparentemente inconexos, como la salvación de Hitler y mi propia salvación, es porque nunca antes la humanidad ha conocido tan de cerca las formas del desastre" (if I dare to link apparently unconnected incidents, such as the salvation of Hitler and my own salvation, it is because never before has humanity experience so up close the forms of disaster).[61] Through exploring these apparently unconnected events, Links shows how at the "microscopic" level what at first seems like coincidence and chance is actually nothing more than one more link in a causal relationship. As Hekster demonstrates, "The scale of the historical trajectory decides which events are too small (coincidental) or too big (background). In that sense, a historical coincidence is a cause (in the counterfactual sense) which is without explanatory force within the chosen narrative framework."[62] The primary example of how the idea of scale plays out in the novel can be found in the motivation and reasoning in Bacon's decision to finger Links to be Klingsor.

It is important to remember that, with the exception of the passages where there is what Mariela Insúa Cereceda identifies as a "traslado momentáneo de

JORGE VOLPI'S *EN BUSCA DE KLINGSOR*

la voz diegética pseudocientífica hacia instancias *poiéticas* que describen metafóricamente momentos epifánicos de descubrimiento" (momentary transfer of the pseudoscientific diegetic voice toward *poietic* instances that metaphorically describe epiphanic moments of discovery),[63] the entire novel is Links's diegetic explanation of his circumstances and defense of his innocence. His retelling of Bacon's turbulent relationships or his own complicated past with Marianne, Natalia, and Heinrich von Lütz functions as evidence to cast into doubt the events and reasons that Links is accused of being Klingsor. By taking the reader to the microscopic, quantic level where our ability to ascertain knowledge reaches its limits—with Heisenberg's Uncertainty Principle as its main analogy—and truths within axiomatic systems cannot be proven as such as posits Gödel's Incompleteness Theorem, Links creates a system where his own guilt, and innocence, cannot be completely proven. Bacon's search is destined to end in a deductive short circuit; as Giaconda Marún observes,

> Bacon en su ambición de encontrar la verdad termina al final de la novela donde empezó, arribó al punto de partida, probando así la teoría de la incompletitud de Godel, como también el concepto de infinitud, dado por la sucesión de interrogatorios que concluyen con la imposibilidad del conocimiento humano, incertidumbre que permea toda la novela.[64]

> Bacon in his ambition to find the truth ends up at the end of the novel where he began, arriving at the starting point and thus proving Gödel's theory of incompleteness, as well as the concept of infinity, due to the succession of questions that conclude with the impossibility of human knowledge; uncertainty that permeates the entire novel.

While protesting uncertainty, Links never proves nor disproves his own guilt in spite of feebly suggesting that Heisenberg was Klingsor. Instead, the analogous nature of his narrative reinforces the liminal space under the umbrage of uncertainty while he hopes to be exonerated in time. Telling Ulrich in the mental hospital, "lo único que puedo hacer entonces es conservar el consuelo de que no hay nada definitivo, de que mi papel en la historia nunca quedará definitivamente fijado, de que siempre existirá una posibilidad—antes se le llamaba esperanza—de que todo, absolutamente todo, no haya sido más que un error de cálculo" (the only thing I can do then is hang on to the consolation that there is nothing definitive, that my role in history will never be definitively fixed, that there will always be a possibility—before it was called hope—that everything, absolutely everything, will have been nothing more than a miscalculation).[65] As the investigation winds down and Inge/Irene's true identity is revealed, Bacon must make a decision. Links compares Bacon to a subatomic particle that exists in a probabalistic wave function: "Por primera vez en su vida, Bacon tenía que tomar una decisión. . . . Una y otra vez había sido como una partícula

64   SCIENCE FUSION IN CONTEMPORARY MEXICAN LITERATURE

subatómica, sometido a las imperiosas fuerzas de cuerpos mucho más podero-sos que él" (For the first time in his life, Bacon had to make a decision. . . . Time after time he had been like a subatomic particle, subjected to the overpowering forces of bodies far more powerful than himself).[66] Once Bacon accuses Links, the probability wave collapses and there is only one possible outcome to the system.[67] At this point quantic uncertainty dissolves as the more familiar causality of classical physics takes hold. Links connects Newton's Third Law with his own third *Ley de movimiento traidor* (Law of Traitorous Motion), titled *Todos los hombres son traidores* (All Men Are Traitors): "Cada vez que un ser humano toma una decisión, se esfuerza en sobrepasar sus límites o intenta doblegar la voluntad de otro, sea para enamorarlo, convencerlo o asesinarlo, cumple con las leyes de la mecánica clásica" (Every time a human being makes a decision, he strives to exceed his limits or tries to bend the will of another, be it to fall in love with the other, convince them or kill them, he complies with the laws of classical mechanics).[68] By connecting Newtonian laws of motion to his laws of the motion of traitors, Links is affirming a version of events in which Klingsor's identity can never be affirmed nor disaffirmed. Clemens Franken declares that "Volpi, al presentarnos al final no una solución del enigma, sino solamente dos versiones distintas y contradictorias, hace fracasar la búsqueda del criminal, es decir, de la verdad de los hechos" (Volpi, by presenting us in the end not with a solution to the enigma, but only with two different and contradictory versions, making the search for the criminal fail, or rather, the truth of the events).[69] Building on this idea, the narration moves beyond purely presenting an unsolvable mystery. By maintaining the focus of the narration on the human ele-ment of history, agency, and causality on a microscopic scale, Links highlights the stochastic nature of history writ small.

The unique position of Links as homodiegetic narrator, both detective and suspect, creates a double bind in the reader's quest for truth. To add another layer to the impossibility of absolute knowledge in the text, it is helpful to remember that Links positions his narrative as analogous to a scientific experiment. Links's observation and subsequent intervention in the sexual encounters between Marianne and Natalia in the chapter playfully titled "Los peligros de la obser-vación" (The Dangers of Observation) underscores the Observer Effect, which Links describes as "cuando un científico exploraba la realidad, ésta se modific-aba, de modo que era muy distinta *después* de haber sido medida. ¡Horror de horrores! El científico había dejado de ser inocente: su visión bastaba para alterar el orden del universo" (when a scientist explored reality, it was modified, so that it was very different *after* being measured. Horror of horrors! The scientist had ceased to be innocent: his vision was enough to alter the order of the universe).[70] In the novel, Links uses the Observer Effect to explain how he came to his present state and also to perhaps assuage some of his guilt over the tragic tra-jectories of the lives of the three members of the love triangle. In a similar manner, Links's entire narrative is contaminated by the Observer Effect given his intervention and participation in the extended metaphor of an experiment that is his own story.

What, then, can be made of the role of chance, human agency, and causality in both the novel and the exploration of the past both within the novel and outside of the pages narrated by Gustav Links? More than just a matter of literary criticism, Eduardo Santiago Ruiz argues that *Klingsor* literarily portrays a complex panorama of new ethical and philosophical problems brought about by advancements in science.[71] Ciencia-fusión's complementary approach that continually moves between direct and analogous transpositions between the scientific and the social, the human and the nonhuman, provides a novel way of approaching these problems. We are once again reminded of Karen Barad's formulation of agential realism and the implication that there is no privileged position from which one can simply observe reality in a neutral way, no matter the scale or the scope of study. Barad states, "Practices of knowing and being are not isolable; they are mutually implicated. We don't obtain knowledge by standing outside the world; we know because we are of the world. We are part of the world in its differential becoming."[72] The very apparatuses that we employ to examine the universe make what Barad calls agential cuts, which have ethical consequences, including and excluding certain aspects in material-discursive enactments. "Ethics is about being response-able to the way we make the world, and to consider the effects our knowledge-making processes have on the world."[73] The scale with which one approaches the object of study is in itself one of many ethical choices that are made, despite the appearance of exteriority, from within what is ultimately being examined. That is to say, the scale of the narrative itself, whether in historiography or fiction, determines what we see as coincidental, uncertain, or the product of chance. Hekster asserts that "for a systematic recognition of the role of coincidence in history, our analysis needs to be at the right scale. It needs to value *human agency*, and the *stochastic element* this brings into historical developments, whilst at the same time identifying the underlying processes which may be much more predictable."[74] In a similar way, the narration of *En busca de Klingsor* draws attention to the fact that, in spite of the scientific discoveries that upended our perception of the cosmos, it is the intra-active nature of agency that most renders the human experience of reality to be uncertain and probabilistic. Perhaps ciencia-fusión poet Gerardo Deniz expresses this idea in its most succinct form by asserting, "Sistemas y métodos presuntuosos, que se vayan al cuerno. En pequeña escala, en cambio, todo se vale" (Presumptuous systems and methods can all go to hell. On a small scale, by contrast, anything goes).[75]

By continually moving the lens of the narration between macro- and microscopic scales, Links's presentation and examination of history—perhaps unintentionally—shows that what at first glimpse is seen as mere chance or

66   SCIENCE FUSION IN CONTEMPORARY MEXICAN LITERATURE

uncertainty actually is the result of causal relationships. Although Links continually relays his sentiment and belief that chance governs the universe in order to make the case for his innocence, Links would know that while our knowledge is based upon probabilities and the limitations of observation, there is no chance in the truest sense of the word. When filtering the narrative on an analogously quantic level, Links's retelling reveals that while human behavior is inherently difficult to predict, it is causal even if the complexity of factors in the past renders them deterministically chaotic. It is this level that reveals a deeper narrative about history and reality itself. Much how classical physics and quantum mechanics accurately describe the same universe but on respectively different scales, there is a role for utilizing both macroscopic and microscopic scales in examining history whether through historiographic or fictional modes. In *En busca de Klingsor* scientific ideas serve as metaphors, images, and symbols of human relationship and the relationship between humans and their surroundings,[76] displaying and engaging through a metanarrative form how these entanglements are conveyed in works of ciencia-fusión. We can affirm that much how Alberto Blanco's lyrical subject proposes metapoetic laws and theories that unify science and art, Volpi's narrator through his corresponding narrative laws, theories, and corollaries, and most importantly through the intra-active act of narration itself, overtly depicts the formal and thematic mechanisms of works of ciencia-fusión that transpose the scientific to the literary. To visualize many aspects of quantum mechanics challenges and stretches our conception of how the world really is while introducing elements of probability in the place of certainty. Nonetheless, our understanding of the universe is much more complete as we learn more and more about reality at the quantic level. In a similar way, *En busca de Klingsor* invites the reader to enter the milieu of the twentieth century to understand the complex and ostensibly chaotic circumstances and, ultimately, very human causes behind many of the greatest and most impactful events in modern history.

CHAPTER 3

Automatons, Androids, and Androcentrism in Ignacio Padilla's *El androide y otras quimeras*

In his book-length essay on animism in contemporary times titled *La vida íntima de los encendedores* (*The Private Life of Lighters*, 2009), Ignacio Padilla recalls a popular legend that circulated in Europe in the seventeenth and eighteenth centuries in which none other than René Descartes had created the first artificial human, a mechanical automaton of a small girl he would come to call Francine, the same name as his daughter whose death from scarlet fever caused him unspeakable anguish years before. According to most versions of the legend, Descartes's fantastical progeny is discovered in his cabin during a voyage at sea by either the sailors or the captain of the ship who, horrified to find the automaton, cast it overboard.[1] While Descartes dabbled in constructing clockwork and lifelike automata, as was the rage in Europe at the time,[2] Padilla sees deeper logical roots to the apocryphal legend:

> No por nada fue él quien trazó las líneas que llevarían a la evolución de los estudios médicos que habrían reinstalado la tentación moderna de *ser como* los dioses para *ser* dioses. El vértigo de la ciencia, al que Descartes insufla un sistema en extremo energizante, nos habría animado a renegar nuestra corporeidad para sentarnos en el trono de la omnipotencia divina sobre lo animado y lo inanimado.[3]

> It is not by chance that it was he who drew the lines that would lead to the evolution of medical studies that would reinstate the modern temptation to *be like* the gods in order to *be* gods. The vertigo of science, into which Descartes breathes an extremely energizing system, would encourage us to deny our corporeity to sit on the throne of divine omnipotence over the animate and the inanimate.

67

68   SCIENCE FUSION IN CONTEMPORARY MEXICAN LITERATURE

As Padilla suggests, in addition to being the mythical father to mechanical life in popular folklore, Descartes's works give life to the philosophy of mechanism, establishing a radical dualism between *res extensa*, the substance of material things, and *res cogitans*, the nonphysical mental substance of the mind or soul. In the Cartesian mechanistic worldview, Nature, stripped of any divine or animate nature, is reduced to a lifeless measurable expanse external to the thinking mind.[4]

Although his reputed fondness for automata inspired his view that humans and animals are biological machines that in many ways function like clockwork,[5] for Descartes all nonhuman automata, be they mechanical or animal, are capable of performing only predetermined actions as they lack the immaterial soul of humans. As articulated in the celebrated phrase *I think, therefore I am*, it is only the thinking and rational human mind—unlike that of an automaton—that can prove its own existence.[6] Perhaps, then, it is fitting that one of the more entertaining challenges to Descartes's first principle comes from an automaton known as l'Ecrivain (the Writer), a mechanical boy that dips his functioning quill pen in an inkwell and shakes off excess ink with a flick of the wrist, while his eyes follow the text he composes with startling lifelike movement. Built by the Jaquet-Droz watchmakers more than a century after Descartes published his *Discourse on the Method*, the automaton is capable of drafting messages of forty characters or fewer, which are mechanically coded through a system of wheels and cams. Among the many messages that the Writer has purportedly been programmed to compose over the centuries, one statement in particular, "I do not think . . . do I therefore not exist?,"[7] tests Cartesian logic and captures best how automata have always had an uncanny ability to disrupt our notions of what separates the human from the nonhuman.

In his collection of short stories, *El androide y otras quimeras* (*The Android and Other Chimeras*), Padilla constructs various narratives involving mechanical automata and androids like the Writer as well as tales of subjugated humans that, like Descartes's classification of animal as automaton, portray characters who seemingly lack autonomy beyond predetermined actions. *El androide y otras quimeras* forms the second volume of Padilla's ambitious tetralogy, *Micropedia* (*Micropedia*), published in its totality posthumously in 2018. Much how friend and fellow Crack member Jorge Volpi utilizes scale to reveal new ways of seeing the familiar, Padilla's *El androide* reflects a dedication to exploring, through fiction, the primacy of the minute and the uncertain nature of historical events and characters. The stories of the collection, divided into two sections, titled "El androide en nueve tiempos" (The Android in Nine Times) and "Quimeras de tres orillas" (Chimeras from Three Shores), take place in disparate times and places but are all linked through a common tension between dualities: female and male, nature and commodity, as well as automation and autonomy. While almost all the stories feature male protagonists, the narrative is often driven by female or nonnormative individuals whose very autonomy is subjugated through various forms of patriarchal control. Androcentric desire is projected upon the female characters by inventors, paleontologists, authors, linguists, scientists, and even a magician, through the power of epistemic privilege, mechanization, and commodification. Through an exploration of the themes of automation and autonomy, the Scientific Revolution, and the subjugation of women and nature, *El androide y otras quimeras* reveals the ways in which science, knowledge, and commerce are harnessed to marginalize and control women and nonnormative subjects, seemingly rendering them analogous to mechanical androids or automatons.[8] However, evocative of *En busca de Klingsor*'s quantic stochasticity and befitting Padilla's definition of himself as a "físico cuéntico" (physicist of the story),[9] a closer reading of the stories reveals how this androcentric, mechanized order is subtly yet powerfully challenged through indeterminate and unexpected acts of resistance and autonomy.

In addition to creating critically recognized novels and essays, Padilla was a prolific writer of short fiction, having published close to a dozen collections of stories. Three such collections belong to the larger project of the Mexican writer titled *Micropedia*, defined by another friend and founder of the Crack, Pedro Ángel Palou, as "una enciclopedia, entonces, de lo pequeño, de lo mínimo, de lo nanoficcional, otra metáfora que le hubiese gustado" (an encyclopedia, then, of the small, of the minute, of the nanofictional, another metaphor that he would have liked).[10] Due to his untimely death in 2016, Padilla was not able to see his project come to complete fruition, as the final volume, *Lo volátil y las fauces* (*Flying Beings and Jaws*), was ultimately published in 2018 under the guidance of Jorge Volpi. The *Micropedia* project underscores the author's attention to the minute, in matters of both theme and form. Bruno Pardo Porto reminds us that Padilla "se definía a sí mismo como 'físico cuéntico,' una autodenominación que subraya esa precisión atómica con la que creó su gran proyecto" (defined himself as a "physicist of the story," a self-designation that underlines that atomic precision with which he created his grand project).[11] Each collection of stories reflects Padilla's penchant for baroque language and structure as well as an intense engagement with his literary predecessors, not to mention an uncanny attention to the minute as even the titles of the volumes themselves are all composed of dual complementary concepts totaling exactly eight syllables with subtitles that are likewise eight syllables each. Throughout *Micropedia* Padilla develops themes such as American bestiaries, exploration, or familial relationships, blurring the distinctions between fact and fiction, historical source and literary creation. In essence, "En su obra las dimensiones imaginarias irrumpen y trastocan constantemente la convención de lo real para adentrarse con perspicacia en las posibilidades paradójicas de lo real" (In his work imaginary dimensions barge in and constantly disrupt the convention of what is real in order to shrewdly penetrate the paradoxical possibilities of the real).[12]

70 SCIENCE FUSION IN CONTEMPORARY MEXICAN LITERATURE

This paradoxical nature of reality is what anchors *El androide y otras quimeras* in which Padilla utilizes the figures of the android and automaton to examine the processes and impacts of female and nonnormative marginalization through the past four centuries. The subsection of the volume titled "El androide en nueve tiempos" comprises nine stories, of which only two deal directly with what could be defined as "androids" in common parlance. Brian Stableford explains the evolution of the term, in usage long before George Lucas's impact on the popular imaginary, as having "originated in alchemical literature—rendered 'androides' in its first traceable appearance in English in 1727—with reference to rumoured attempts to create 'homonculi' by such alleged practitioners as Albertus Magnus and Paracelsus. The notion is sometimes traced back by historians to Jewish legends of golems."[13] The more contemporary meaning of the term replaces alchemy with technology, as it first appears in Auguste Villiers de L'Isle-Adam's 1886 novel *L'Eve future* (*Tomorrow's Eve*), and "in the context of modern science fiction, the term is usually employed in such a way as to differentiate it from robot, reserving it for artificial humanoids made from synthetic flesh rather than inorganic components."[14] Further complicating the various definitions of the term, in the eighteenth century the term "androide" was also used to refer to mechanical automata that uncannily played music, wrote missives, digested food, or even played chess, to the delight of crowds in exhibition halls and parlors throughout Europe and Asia. In *Living Dolls*, Gaby Wood traces the pursuit to create evermore complex and lifelike androids or mechanical automata over the past three centuries, declaring that "each of the projects blurred the line between man and machine, between the animate and the inanimate. The madness left over from darker times was all the more disturbing for being hidden beneath the mask of enlightenment."[15]

In the acknowledgments section of *El androide y otras quimeras*, Padilla recognizes that, among his inspirations, "debo poner a la cabeza de ellos *Living Dolls*, obra excepcional de Gaby Wood" (I should put at the top of them *Living Dolls*, an exceptional work by Gaby Wood),[16] as a number of his stories are born of the bizarre and moving history of the quest to become the next modern Prometheus. While historical creations such as Edison's talking dolls or Kempelen's "Turk" automaton provide the catalysts for a number of the stories, in reality the androids in Padilla's stories "son de carne y hueso y sin embargo se las arreglan para confundirnos y hacernos creer que vienen de un lugar carente de volumen y sustancia. Se muestran ante nosotros como si no hubiera otros lugares más trascendentes que el crepúsculo y el ensueño" (are of flesh and blood and yet they manage to confuse us into believing that they come from a place lacking in volume and substance. They appear before us as if there were no other places more transcendent than twilight and fantasy).[17] By reducing the human subject to an inert presence without volume and substance, many of Padilla's characters, at first glance, present themselves as lifeless, mechanized shadows of people, while at the same time it is often the machines, simulacra, photographs, and even a magician's props that seem to possess a life of their own. Siridia Fuertes Trigal signals that

> esta pérdida, confusión o mezcla de las fronteras entre el sistema humano y el sistema mecánico, puede ocurrir en dos sentidos distintos: o el humano tiende a la máquina o la máquina tiende al humano, idea que Padilla explota de una manera sutil en cada cuento, pero incidiendo en el género femenino.[18]

> this loss, confusion, or mix of the limits between the human system and the mechanical system can occur in two distinct senses: or the human approaches the machine or the machine approaches the human, an idea that Padilla subtly exploits in each story, but focusing in on the female gender.

MECHANISM, SCIENCE, AND THE HUMAN/NATURE DUALITY

It is not by chance that Padilla's stories of these android-like humans all take place during the past few centuries, when the concepts of mechanism and domination over nature become ordering principles. Jessica Riskin describes this shifting view of nature and life: "From the early to mid-seventeenth century, at the hands of mechanist philosophers, matter and its mechanical combinations would be divested first of soul and then of life."[19] Similarly, in her groundbreaking work of ecocriticism, Carolyn Merchant examines how many of the ideas of the Enlightenment and the Scientific Revolution radically changed the relationship between humanity and the natural world: "Two new ideas, those of mechanism and the domination and mastery of nature, became core concepts of the modern world. An organically oriented mentality in which female principles played an important role was undermined and replaced by a mechanically oriented mentality that either eliminated or used female principles in an exploitative manner. As Western culture became increasingly mechanized in the 1600s, the female earth and virgin earth spirit were subdued by the machine."[20] As a result, mechanism becomes associated with rational thought, order, and mankind's dominion over nature. Both implicitly and explicitly, nature, largely associated with the female in Western thought since antiquity, becomes an object to be controlled, harnessed, and exploited. In essence, "Mechanism rendered nature effectively dead, inert, and manipulable from without."[21] Gisela Heffes emphasizes that while anthropocentrism confers a superiority of mankind over nature, androcentrism professes the superiority of the male subject over the female, as the two elide given that "comparten una 'lógica de dominación' similar (que la mujer ha sido asociado con la naturaleza, lo material, lo emocional y lo particular mientras que el hombre ha sido asociado con la cultura, lo no material, lo racional y lo abstracto)" (they share a similar "logic of domination" [that woman has been associated with nature, the material, the emotional and the particular

72   SCIENCE FUSION IN CONTEMPORARY MEXICAN LITERATURE

while man has been associated with culture, the nonmaterial, the rational and the abstract]).[22] This dominion over nature, and consequently over women, is effectuated in Padilla's short stories through the protagonist of the scientist-inventor, epistemic privilege, and commercial capitalism, all of which frequently have been harnessed to marginalize female and nonnormative individuals.

The blurring of distinctions between human and machine as well as the anxiety of a growing sense of dehumanization have been featured in various works of literature from the industrial period to today. In her groundbreaking and influential *Cyborg Manifesto*, Donna Haraway looks at the subversive and chimeral potential that human-machine fusions provide and that wipe away essentialist notions such as nature, machine, and culture. Recognizing that thinkers from Herbert Marcuse to Carolyn Merchant have insisted on resistance centered on an imagined organic body, Haraway posits that "a slightly perverse shift of perspective might better enable us to contest for meanings, as well as for other forms of power and pleasure in technologically mediated societies."[23] Defining the cyborg as "a cybernetic organism, a hybrid of machine and organism, a creature of social reality as well as a creature of fiction,"[24] Haraway argues that the concept of the cyborg offers new possibilities to reconfigure feminism in that "cyborg imagery can suggest a way out of the maze of dualisms in which we have explained our bodies and our tools to ourselves. This is a dream not of a common language, but of a powerful infidel heteroglossia."[25] In Latin American literature in particular, J. Andrew Brown observes that for much of the nineteenth and twentieth centuries, artificial humans "have gathered at the periphery of Latin American cultural production," as "only recently has a consideration of corporeal identity at the encounter of the mechanical and the organic occupied a central space in Latin American culture."[26] Elizabeth M. Ginway examines the employment of cyborgs in Mexican and Brazilian speculative fiction as reflective of social and economic conditions throughout the twentieth century as "all of these entities—doll-like automatons, industrial robots, and posthuman cyborgs—capture the dilemmas of gendered labor and social inequities while simultaneously serving as a voice for those who have been silenced in the national collective memory."[27] Alicia Rivero traces how various Spanish American writers, from the *vanguardista* collaboration between Vicente Huidobro and Hans Arp to Mexican authors Juan José Arreola and Rosario Castellanos, have used gendered cybernetic organisms to explore questions of technology, communication, and autonomy. Highlighting the myriad uses of the cyborg in works from different periods with disparate themes, she observes that "mientras Huidobro y Arp problematizan el aspecto comunicativo de la cibernética, Arreola y Castellanos se centran en las implicaciones nefarias del control, sobre todo en lo tocante a la mujer" (while Huidobro and Arp problematize the communicative aspect of cybernetics, Arreola and Castellanos focus on the nefarious implications of control, especially in regard to women).[28] In his work on race and technology in post-Revolutionary Mexico, David Dalton incorporates a more expansive definition of the cyborg to show how "officialist cultural production invoked technological hybridity as a means for modernizing the indigenous body and assimilating it to the state."[29] While its depictions and deployments may vary, the cyborg in Latin America functions as a bodily site where discourse, technology, gender, race, and identity intersect. Moreover, Brown argues that in Latin American literature the question of the cyborg and the posthuman functions outside of the traditional confines of speculative literature and fiction, as typically the cyborg figure is not explicitly coded as would be typical in science fiction.[30]

As we can see in *El androide y otras quimeras* as well as other works of cienciafusión such as Rosa Beltrán's *El cuerpo expuesto* and Maricela Guerrero's *El sueño de toda célula*, intersections between the technological and the organic, concepts of cyborgs or material-technological amalgams are typically situated within decidedly historical or contemporaneous nonspeculative frameworks. Chela Sandoval argues that the material-semiotic cyborg is a particularly powerful figure of resistance of control and coloniality in Latin America given that "the colonized peoples of the Americas have already developed the cyborg skills required for survival under techno-human conditions."[31] Sara Potter identifies depictions of female bodies fused with technology in Mexican literature that have emerged in response to disruptive social and political events and engage with ongoing currents and conversations revolving around national identity and history.[32] Potter argues that these female human-technological fusions are "*technified* muses, each of whom incorporates these discourses into her very being, creating a hybrid, cyborgian and/or virtual being and establishing a powerful connection between memory and technology."[33] The muses' fusion with technology, then, empowers subversive and critical narratives that run counter to prevailing social and political discourse. Padilla similarly taps into this long tradition of Latin American and Mexican authors to imagine gendered androids and chimeras, whether fully mechanical, cybernetic, or organic, in order to bring together technology, humanity, and gender to challenge concepts of control and gender and reveal new perspectives on automation, autonomy, and resistance.

As is typical in many of Padilla's works of short fiction, most of the tales of *El androide y otras quimeras* are inspired by historical stories, often beginning with a somewhat well-known set of circumstances before slowly blurring the distinction between the real and fictional. Fuertes Trigal compares this technique with that of Borges, given that Padilla starts from "una serie de datos históricos y contrastados, para finalmente acabar fabulando sobre aquello que sus fuentes históricas no cuentan, que no se puede demostrar y que es imposible de rastrear" (a series of historical and confirmed facts, to finally end up fabulating about what his historical sources do not tell, that which cannot be proven and that is impossible to trace).[34] The source material for "Las furias de Menlo Park" (The Furies of Menlo Park), the opening story of the section "El androide en nueve tiempos," revolves

74 SCIENCE FUSION IN CONTEMPORARY MEXICAN LITERATURE

around what seems to be an amalgam of the Descartes automaton fable and Thomas Edison's well-known foray into the creation and production of talking dolls that, by 1890, turned out to be one of his few commercial flops. Embedded into the shell of a doll's body manufactured in Germany, a recorded voice resonated from a miniaturized tin and wax phonograph complete with a crank, producing an eerie recording of a nursery rhyme that one NPR commentator recently referred to as "the soundtrack to your nightmares."[35] Years later, even Edison himself would refer to them as his "little monsters."[36] While a far cry from the "paradoxical" android created by a fictitious Thomas Edison in Villiers de L'Isle-Adam's *L'Eve future*, the historical Edison's talking dolls undoubtedly represent an attempt to create and monetize a mechanized simulation with lifelike attributes. Given his recognition of the influence of Edison's toy while he composed these stories, it is fitting that the focus of Padilla's work mirrors Gaby Wood's historical observation that "nowhere was the mechanization of human beings more ironically in force than in the production, piece by piece and thousand by thousand, of Edison's talking doll."[37] It would be easy to assume that in Padilla's short story the central android figure is Edison's uncanny doll. However, in Padilla's hands, the dolls are only a means through which a flesh-and-bone character becomes this story's figurative automaton.

"Las furias de Menlo Park" is bookended by the destruction of two different sets of dolls, with the narrator opening the story by describing Edison's first order of European dolls that was lost in the Atlantic Ocean, where "seiscientas niñas de cerámica se ahogaron a escasas millas de Rotterdam sin que hubiera dios ni ayuda para impedir esa zozobra de encajes, piernas, brazos y ojos de vidrio que miraron sin mirar a los peces que no podrían devorarlas" (six hundred ceramic girls drowned just a few miles from Rotterdam where neither god nor help could prevent that sinking of lace, legs, arms, and glass eyes that looked out without looking at the fish that could never devour them).[38] In addition to tapping into the fable of Descartes's mechanical daughter cast into the sea, these opening images foretell later deaths, drownings, and destruction to unfold in the story. Upon learning of the loss of the first shipment, Edison then sends his associate, Charles Nervez, to procure a new order, which the latter accompanies from the European factory to Edison's workshops at Menlo Park, New Jersey. There, Nervez sees and hears the voice of Claudette Rouault, one of the women who, under the inventor's orders, toils past the point of exhaustion, as she mimics a child's voice to make recording after recording of a nursery rhyme to be uniquely implanted into each individual talking doll. While pitying the working conditions of the women, Nervez does not dare cross the Wizard of Menlo Park in his fanatical quest to produce his newest creation. Only later does Nervez seemingly learn of Claudette's suicide from drowning after she was summarily fired for having stolen one of the dolls from the factory. The narrator closes the story by describing Edison's parallel quest to reacquire and destroy another, lesser-known set of talking dolls that voiced a cryptic and menacing recording about a wizard, a curse, and a dead princess.

Like many of the stories in *El androide y otras quimeras*, a heterodiegetic narrator focalizes internally on a male character, in this instance Charles Nervez, yet the plot itself is driven by marginalized characters, almost entirely female or nonnormative, a process that in many ways reflects the androcentric protagonism of the male inventor or scientist. While in a fictitious setting, the glaring lack of voice and focus of nonmale characters aligns closely with the ways in which the history of scientific progress and technology has been written from a male perspective. Ruth Oldenziel describes how even the term "technology" itself is charged with significance: "Rather than a neutral term, *technology* is itself part of a narrative production or plot of modernism, in which men are the protagonists and women have been denied their part."[39] In "Las furias de Menlo Park," when being interviewed by reporters years later, Nervez expresses his unease with Edison's use of technology from the very beginning by using clearly gendered terms all while he "invocaría también, como quien narra sin desearlo un mal sueño, su entrada en el recinto amurallado de West Orange . . . donde máquinas dentadas y fonógrafos minúsculos aguardaban como larvas hambrientas la llegada de sus novias alemanas" (would also invoke, like someone unwittingly recounting a bad dream, his entry into the walled compound in West Orange . . . where machines with teeth and miniscule phonographs awaited like hungry larvae the arrival of their German brides).[40] The seemingly sinister references to the mechanized larvae that will reach maturity through mating with the shell of the doll bring to the reader's mind other modern promethean figures, both real and literary, and the cost to be paid for their hubris. Unlike life being created through selective breeding, strange chemicals, electrical sparks, or even alchemical methods, it can be argued that in "Las furias de Menlo Park" the true life source of the "little monsters" is the women whose voices are captured on the wax phonographic drums that will be placed in the torso of the dolls.

When entering Edison's factory, Nervez catches a glimpse of the women who are sequestered in a cell-like string of cabins where they "entonaban sin tregua la primera estrofa de *Jack and Jill* ante boquillas doradas que enseguida le hicieron pensar en una serpiente enhiesta e insaciable" (relentlessly intoned the first verse of *Jack and Jill* before golden mouthpieces that immediately made him think of an erect and insatiable snake).[41] The metaphor of the machine as a beast, with sexualized undertones to boot, devouring the life force of the female workers is likewise expressed through Nervez's first impression of Claudette, the object of his instantaneous infatuation, whose condition surprises him in that "una mujer tan joven pareciera no obstante tan agraviada por los años, tan maternalmente triste" (a woman so young seemed nevertheless so aggrieved by the years, so maternally sad).[42] Nervez's passion and its physical manifestation of a fevered state for over two days is inspired not by interaction with this woman

76   SCIENCE FUSION IN CONTEMPORARY MEXICAN LITERATURE

but through quickly glimpsing her and hearing her voice, or rather her imitation of a child's voice, as she works tirelessly to meet the demands of Edison's factory. It is no coincidence that the accumulating layers of simulacra—childlike dolls whose mechanical voices are recorded by women imitating children, who are in turn not treated as human beings—are driven primarily by male desire: Edison in his quest for creating mechanical life and Nervez in his obsession for a woman upon whom he projects his own fevered yearnings.

Nervez does not advocate forcefully to Edison on the workers' behalf, in spite of his genuine concern about the well-being of the women. In contrast to his predecessor, who was worried only that their ill treatment would negatively affect the sweetness of their voices in their recordings, Nervez at least internally expresses a modicum of empathy. While Nervez is perhaps the closest thing to an ally that the women have, his sympathy and later remorse do not supersede his financial and professional interest in working with Edison. In this way, Nervez through his inaction and Edison through his relentless action both project their desire onto the women. In the case of the famous inventor, the narrator describes how, "aunque estaba claro que a Edison le inquietaba poco el bienestar de las muchachas, era también evidente que estas provocaban en él una mezcla de despecho y fascinación rayana en la monomanía" (although it was clear that Edison was little concerned for the welfare of the girls, it was also clear that they provoked in him a mixture of spite and fascination bordering on monomania).[43] Regarding the historical figure, although he publicly championed some pro-women causes, Wood asserts that "there is evidence that Edison privately thought of women as perfectible creatures, machines or products."[44] While the drive for the perfectible product that ultimately fails in the market is an embarrassment for Edison, the deeper danger seemingly lies in the tension between automation and autonomy, as portrayed in the events leading up to and following the tragic death of Claudette.

After Claudette is fired for stealing a doll, the women attempt to convince Nervez to advocate on her behalf, intimating Edison's profound involvement as well as the maternal relationship between the woman and the doll as they plead, "dígaselo a Edison, señor Nervez, pregúntele cómo espera que esa niña pase el invierno, él sabe mejor que nadie que la muñeca que cogió le pertenece como si fuera su propia hija" (tell it to Edison, Mr. Nervez, ask him how he expects that girl to spend the winter, he knows better than anyone that the doll she took belongs to her as if it were her own daughter).[45] In contrast to Edison's perfectible product, Claudette's maternal relationship with the doll underscores the vital, personal imprint not unlike a Benjaminian aura that the recorded voice gives each creation.[46] With Claudette punished for expressing a maternal claim over her creation, the questions of artisanship and ownership stand in stark opposition to the commodification and mechanized production of the talking dolls. In his original, fevered state of infatuation, Nervez foretells the unavoidable and tragic end to this

IGNACIO PADILLA'S *EL ANDROIDE Y OTRAS QUIMERAS*   77

tension between autonomy and automation as he "soñó con los labios de la muchacha repitiendo su canción cien, doscientas, mil veces al día. Y acaso fue también
entonces cuando intuyó que el proyecto de Thomas Edison estaba irremisible-
mente condenado al fracaso" (he dreamed of the girl's lips repeating her song one
hundred, two hundred, a thousand times a day. And perhaps it was also then that
he sensed that Thomas Edison's project was irrevocably doomed to failure).[47] In
La vida íntima de los encendedores Padilla likewise emphasizes the abject failure
of Edison in his attempt to make lifelike dolls: "El fracaso automático del Prome-
teo de la Edad Moderna evoca un castigo divino, el mismo que en el imaginario
occidental habrían recibido el rabino creador del Golem, el mítico Gregorio
Magno y el propio Victor Frankenstein" (The automatic failure of the Prometheus
of the Modern Age evokes a divine punishment, the same that in the Western
imaginary the rabbi who created the Golem, the mythical Saint Gregory the
Great, and Victor Frankenstein himself would have received).[48]

In the story, the price for Edison's desire to create life is paid for by the death
of Claudette, but the punishment outlasts the death of the worker. As Nervez
contemplates her obituary and how he will speak of these events when he
approaches his own death in the future, more is revealed about both Claudette's
death and the collective action of her fellow workers:

> Casi pudo ver sus manos de viejo sobre la mesa, su cuerpo ansiando una muerte
> apacible y su boca desdentada hablando sin convicción de una ahogada encinta
> en un río o del escándalo, oportunamente silenciado, de una segunda serie de
> muñecas parlantes que extrañamente terminaban su versión de *Jack and Jill* con
> cierta estrofa inesperada y macabra. Algo cantaban esas voces de rencor, algo
> sugerían aquellos versos sobre un mago, un embrujo y una princesa muerta.[49]

> He could almost see his old man's hands on the table, his body yearning for a
> peaceful death and his toothless mouth speaking without conviction of a preg-
> nant woman drowned in a river or from scandal, opportunely silenced, of a
> second series of talking dolls that strangely ended their version of *Jack and
> Jill* with a certain unexpected and macabre stanza. They sang something, those
> voices of rancor, and hinted at something, those verses, about a wizard, a spell,
> and a dead princess.

By revealing Claudette's pregnancy and the idea of a scandal being silenced, the
reliability of a narration focalized through Nervez reminds us of Volpi's Gustav
Links, equally rendering relativistic instability to the text, as the two male protagonists share culpability, as told through a stylized fairytale about the death
of the princess. Nervez silences Claudette's voice by omitting the truth about her
being pregnant, at the same time as Edison seeks to acquire and destroy the dolls
whose altered recordings are an act of female autonomy and rebellion against
the patriarchal order. As a result, in "Las furias de Menlo Park" the mise en

78   SCIENCE FUSION IN CONTEMPORARY MEXICAN LITERATURE

abyme structure of embedded series of voices within voices, creations within creations, all narrated within the frame of two tales of destruction of dolls, lends a mythic quality to the events that transpire. While never mentioned in the story, the furies of the title recall the Erinyes, the goddesses of vengeance sometimes associated with fertility. In Hesiod's telling, they are born from the drops of blood from Uranus's severed genitalia that fall on the Earth.[50] Like the gendered manifestation of revenge, the voices of the final set of dolls stand in direct contrast to their lifeless sisters under the sea. They are products of an act of rebellion of the women who warn of the consequences of the inventor's relentless quest to create and control artificial life through the automaton, whereas, in reality, Edison has only morphed the autonomous into the automated.

The theme of commodification in the name of scientific advancement is explored in a different way in "Romanza de la niña y el pterodáctilo" (Ballad of the Girl and the Pterodactyl), inspired by the true story of Mary Anning, who seemed to have a preternatural knack for discovering dinosaur fossils along the southern English coast during the early 1800s. In spite of her numerous, impactful findings and well-documented and illustrated volumes, Anning, as a woman, was never fully recognized by nor accepted among the paleontological and scientific communities of her time.[51] Padilla's story departs from Anning's biography in numerous ways to offer a meditation on the themes of innocence, scientific commodification, and the relationship between humankind and the surrounding natural world. The fictional Mary Anning is portrayed through the narrated recollections of a male fossil collector who, against his financial self-interest, tells her impoverished parents of the true financial value of the fossils that their daughter finds. Instead of bringing financial bliss to the family, the parents' thirst for income, combined with the insatiable demands of the international market in dinosaur fossils, cause Mary to withdraw emotionally and physically from her family. Mary attempts, but ultimately fails, to keep a fossilized dinosaur, as well as her own innocence, safe and hidden from a world that sees them both as commodities to be exploited.

The stark contrast between how Mary and the male paleontologists view and interact with the natural world casts in relief the Cartesian distancing between the thinking subject and the external world. Stephen Shapin summarizes this philosophical shift as underpinning the first two fundamental characteristics of the Scientific Revolution: "First, the mechanization of nature: the increasing use of mechanical metaphors to construe natural knowledge processes and phenomena; second, the depersonalization of natural knowledge; the growing separation between human subjects and the natural objects of their knowledge."[52] In Padilla's story, the impulse to literally separate the human subject in Mary from the objects that she discovers and sees as companions is compounded by the financial interest of those with infinitely more capital and influence. This idea aligns with Merchant's observation that "as a conceptual framework, the mechanical order had associated with it a framework of values based on power, fully compatible with the direction taken by commercial capitalism."[53] The result is a self-perpetuating order, which serves to strengthen the position of power of male collectors and scientists over alternative worldviews that, as we see in Padilla's story, are finally rendered to be either premodern or childlike.

While one reading of the story would suggest that "Romanza" is simply a coming-of-age parable about the end of a child's innocence, the conflict between Mary and the paleontologists offers a glimpse into the structures that enable the exploitation and commodification of the natural world. When first meeting the family, the narrator takes pity on them and confesses to them the true worth in the international market of the "curios" they have been selling for mere pounds. The narrator describes sardonically how word was circulating among European paleontologists that "en las costas galesas una niña desenterraba fósiles del cretácico con el olfato y la aptitud del más notado paleontólogo. Por fortuna, concluyó Lebercor con su eterna sonrisa de hipogrifo, el talento de Mary Anning no incluía los asuntos pecuniarios" (on the Welsh coast a girl was unearthing fossils from the Cretaceous period with the nose and aptitude of the most noted paleontologists. Fortunately, Lebercor concluded with his always present hippogriff smile, Mary Anning's talents did not include financial matters).[54] All the while, Mary gives the dinosaurs names such as "Rapunzel" and seems to interact and even play with the fossils for whom "su pasión estaba sólo en descubrirlos, desenterrarlos y dibujarlos luego, con lujo de detalle, en un cuaderno que habría hecho palidecer a Darwin" (her passion was solely in discovering them, unearthing them, and then drawing them, in great detail, in a notebook that would have left Darwin pale).[55] The insatiable demands placed on Mary cause her to secretly curate and protect the most impressive specimen of all by hiding it from the outside world. In her analysis of the story, Socorro Venegas explains, "Este último acto de resistencia es quizás el anuncio del final de la infancia de Mary" (This final act of resistance is perhaps the signal of the end of Mary's childhood).[56] The narrator describes the fossil as a dragon that "estaba allí para cuidarla hasta el final de los tiempos o hasta que un príncipe del mar viniese a rescatarla" (was there to take care of her until the end of time or until a prince from the sea came to rescue her).[57] Mary's words reflect a child's imagination, yet her actions indicate that she has the maturity to understand and resist the demands of those who view the fossils only as inert, commodified objects to be acquired, sold, and studied. Like the most beautiful birdcage in the world in Gabriel García Márquez's "La prodigiosa tarde de Baltazar" (Balthazar's Marvelous Afternoon), the reader is told how Mary's pterodactyl is the most perfect specimen ever found, so complete and immaculately restored that its future owner gains immense fame but is forced to constantly defend its authenticity. Mary's painstaking recuperation of the pterodactyl can be seen as the ultimate act of love, as she sees herself as functioning in communion with the fossils and the greater natural world.

Mary's act of rebellion eventually comes to an end after her father's death, when she runs away with a young man to Ireland and tells her mother to sell the fossil at the best price she can get. The narrator notes that Mary never told anyone the name that she had given her most precious monster, the dragon. The narrator then tells how Mary was tragically abandoned by the young man, presumably a paleontologist himself, who "arrancó a Mary de las garras del monstruo" (snatched Mary from the monster's claws),[58] and left her destitute on the streets of Dublin. Mary's multiple betrayals whenever she participates in the adult and scientific worlds demonstrate how these make her an automaton of sorts, powerless to the whims and demands of the patriarchal order.[59] In "La romanza de la niña y el pterodáctilo," the innocent bliss of a world in which the subject is integral to the order of nature that surrounds her is incompatible with a more powerful worldview of nature as an external object to be exploited and commodified through technology and capital. It is significant that Mary finds a measure of stability only when, finally, "quiso al parecer su suerte que de allí la rescatase un viudo, con quien vive todavía sin niños en una casa pequeña que ella se encarga de mantener inmaculada" (it seemed it was her fate that the one to rescue her from there would be a widower, with whom she still lives without children in a small house that she takes care to keep immaculate).[60] Far from the happy ending to her fairy tale that the dragon's presence would protect, her life is the demonstration that, in addition to her relationship with the natural world, even Mary herself is incompatible with and must be domesticated by the prevailing androcentric order.

Autonomy and Resistance in an Androcentric World

The autonomy of another woman is similarly explored through the case of a famous android from a century earlier than Edison's dolls in the story "Las entrañas del Turco" (The Bowels of the Turk). The Turk, also known as "Wolfgang von Kempelen's Chess Playing Automaton," was a touring sensation in the late eighteenth and early nineteenth centuries that featured a cabinet structure topped by an exotically fashioned, pipe-smoking upper body of a "Turkish" mechanical man that seemed to play chess autonomously, besting rivals from chess masters to luminaries such as Benjamin Franklin and Napoleon Bonaparte. At the time many theories circulated on how the mechanism worked, only to be revealed years later that it was all an elaborate hoax. Padilla's short story does not take up whether the Turk was truly an automaton or not, considering it settled that it was indeed directed by a person inside the machinery. Rather, as Edmundo Paz Soldán points out, "Lo que le interesa al escritor mexicano es ver cómo cambia la subjetividad de los individuos cuando se los confronta con el autómata" (What interests the Mexican writer is seeing how the subjectivity of individuals changes when they are confronted with the automaton).[61] Padilla, however, is not the first to explore this terrain as writers such as Edgar Allan

IGNACIO PADILLA'S *EL ANDROIDE Y OTRAS QUIMERAS*   81

Poe, Ambrose Bierce, and even Walter Benjamin in the opening of the first of his "Theses on the Philosophy of History" take up the Turk as a metaphor for questions surrounding humankind, mechanization, technology, and authenticity.[62] Padilla's short story on Kempelen's creation is epistolary in form, as a male associate communicates the destruction of the Turk in a fire at the P. T. Barnum Museum to the last director of the automaton. While the Turk was destroyed in a museum fire, the fictional placement of the automaton in the namesake museum of the world's most famous showman and hoaxer underscores that, even fictitiously, the true nature of the machine is never in question. Instead, the narrator writes of encountering an elderly woman at the museum who tells him of when she directed the Turk and how the chess master, Italo Fabrizio, in his rivalry with the machine was driven to a madness that would ultimately lead him to take his own life. The woman is viewed as a harmless curiosity at the museum that she frequents to take care of the forgotten machine, and she disappears on the night of the fire that would once and for all destroy the Turk.

From the beginning of his missive, the narrator knows that the deceitful nature of the supposed android's inner workings does not prevent him from suggesting that the machine metaphorically and literally had characteristics of a living organism. Similar to the functioning machines in Edison's workshops, the Turk seems to have a parasitic relationship to humans, leading the narrator to confess, "No dejo de pensar que el Turco absorbió una buena parte de la vida de quienes alguna vez ocuparon sus entrañas para jugar al ajedrez por el ancho mundo" (I can't stop thinking that the Turk absorbed a good part of the life of those who once occupied his innards to play chess around the wide world).[63] Rehashing the many theories on how the machine operated, the narrator reminds his associate of the widely circulated drawing in which "la proporcionada pequeñez del jugador dibujado por Cumbert siempre me ha hecho pensar en una marioneta. Es como si el autómata dirigiese al hombre y no a la inversa" (the proportionate smallness of the player drawn by Cumbert has always made me think of a marionette. It is as if the automaton directed the man and not the other way around).[64] The story's Cumbert is likely inspired by the real engravings of Joseph Racknitz, who sought to reveal the hoax by conjecturing that a diminutive dwarf crouching in the cabinet works the controls yet is visually presided over by the much larger upper body and head of the Turk.[65] The narrator's observation of a machine directing a man stands in contrast to his shared knowledge that the Turk lacked any automation in the truest sense of the word. Nonetheless, the power between the "automaton" and the anonymous soul who directed it reveals a profound discomfort with the entire relationship between humankind and technology. Referring to how the Turk was portrayed in these engravings, Wood asserts, "It was not, evidently, just a machine, or just an illusion, but at times a kind of parasite. . . . Put this way, the tale of the Turk becomes monstrous, not a lifeless thing directed by a man (or a woman), but the puppeteer in service of the puppet."[66]

In *La vida íntima de los encendedores* Padilla argues that the attraction of the Turk was a shared suspension of credulity that spoke to deeper truths about humankind's place in reality.[67] In what may be an allusion to *Cien años de soledad* (One Hundred Years of Solitude) as well as "Un señor muy viejo con unas alas enormes" (A Very Old Man with Enormous Wings), where García Márquez explores the relationship between the real and illusion through the tale of the girl who was turned into a spider, Padilla states that "quienes se batieron contra el Turco no eran distintos de quienes iban a la carpa para conocer a la muchacha que fue convertida en araña por desobedecer a sus padres" (those who battled the Turk were no different from those who went to the tent to meet the girl who was turned into a spider for disobeying her parents).[68] By suspending their incredulity, they allow themselves to sense the unsettling reality that "cada director del Turco fue a su manera un títere en el interior de otro títere dirigido a su vez por un ser humano remiso a aceptar que también él, mal de su grado, era una precaria marioneta soñada por Dios" (each director of the Turk was in his own way a puppet inside another puppet, directed in turn by a human being reluctant to accept that he, too, against his will, was a precarious marionette dreamed up by God).[69] This Chinese box structure of infinite masters shares seemingly countless intertextual links with many of Padilla's literary predecessors such as the dreamers of Borges's "Las ruinas circulares" (The Circular Ruins) and the Red King that is actually dreaming Alice in Lewis Carroll's *Through the Looking-Glass*; or, in a similar fashion, a fictitious and dying Charles Dodgson who feverishly creates his definitive yet negative inversion of Alice in the companion story, "Las tres Alicias" (The Three Alices), found in the same section of *El androide y otras quimeras*.[70]

Like the other stories in the collection, the narrative focalization in "Las entrañas del Turco" is focused on the male figures, yet here the voice of the female protagonist is registered, albeit through the memory of the male narrator. When the elderly woman questions the narrator as to his plans for the Turk, she chides his supposed ignorance: "Usted no sabe cuánta vida encierra este muñeco" (You do not know how much life this puppet holds).[71] Having literally been enclosed in the space of the Turk's cabinet, the woman in many senses becomes the titular viscera, as she directed the machine's movements and reacted to her opponents' moves. Speaking of the various directors of Kempelen's automaton, Wood observes, "The life inside the box could only be a life of the mind, since the body had so little room to exist, and because the adverse effects were incremental."[72] In a twist typical of Padilla's fiction, the illusory automaton is what actually permits the woman to challenge the grand masters of her day, freeing her from being excluded because of her embodied identity. From within the Turk she is able to offer what David Dalton terms in other contexts "robo sacer resistance," a cyborg articulation of Agamben's homo sacer imbued with resistance qualities against the prevailing order.[73] The life of the mind and the appearance of a male, gendered machine liberate her, but also begin to change her in ways she could never have anticipated. Even though she is the heart of the illusion and knows it is an elaborate parlor trick, she confesses, "Allá dentro, señor mío, a una le entraban deseos de ganar la partida como si en ello se le fuese la existencia y a veces se te olvidaba que eras algo distinto del autómata" (Inside there, dear sir, you became taken with winning the game as if your existence went away and sometimes you forgot that you were something other than the automaton).[74] Seemingly one step removed from the cybernetic cohesion of Haraway's cyborg, the anonymity that frees her comes at the cost of relinquishing part of her own identity to become unanimous, of one spirit, with the mechanical Turk.

In a similar way, unexpected revelations of human encounters with autonomous technology, real or perceived, are what drive Italo Fabrizio to take his own life. The female director explains the paradoxical effect the machine had on those who operated and competed against it:

> Entonces podías ver íntegra el alma de tu contrincante, aunque no lo vieras, aunque sólo fuera por su talento o su torpeza para atacar o defenderse. Jugar desde el Turco te daba la facultad de ver lo que de otra manera no habría sido posible ver, ni siquiera columbrar. Cuando uno jugaba desde el autómata y contra el autómata todo se hacía plenamente humano y vulnerable.[75]

> Then you could see the whole soul of your opponent, even if you could not see him, even if it was only because of his skill or his clumsiness in attacking or defending himself. Playing from within the Turk gave you the ability to see what otherwise would not have been possible to see, or even glimpse. When one played from within the automaton and against the automaton, everything became fully human and vulnerable.

Therefore, the encounters between the Turk and Italo Fabrizio become a relationship between a human and a machine that uncannily strips interpersonal artifice under the appearance of automation. That a machine would seemingly possess a soul blurs the epistemological hierarchy between the thinking subject and the inanimate object. Adding to the disorientation is the fact that the opponent's soul is revealed in a paradoxically more human way through the Turk. The narrator emphasizes the relevance of a woman directing the automaton and then ponders, "Ahora lo sabemos, y no deja de resultar casi oprobioso pensar que la del siciliano no fue exactamente una historia de venganza, sino el producto de una pasión que a estas alturas no me atrevo a calificar" (Now we know, and nonetheless it is almost disgraceful to think that the Sicilian's story wasn't exactly one of revenge, but the product of a passion that, at this point, I do not dare describe).[76] These multiple epistemological shifts inevitably lead to the impossibility that Fabrizio confronts: if the machine is autonomous from man and yet is his equal or possibly superior, what does that mean for his place in the universe? For Fabrizio, the ramifications of such a question lead him to a final, desperate act of autonomy in his suicide. For the female director of the Turk, this same impossibility leads to endless remorse and the need to destroy the paradoxical machine that both liberated and assimilated her.

In all the stories of *El androide y otras quimeras*, it is the human characters, particularly female and nonnormative, that at first glance have no autonomy over their place in the world. They appear to be subordinate automatons to forces, epistemologies, and actors that control, constrict, and predetermine their actions and agency. However, it bears repeating that the narration of the stories mirrors the epistemic privilege inherent in both scientific and post-Enlightenment discourse, as the narrative focalization clearly rests on male protagonists, excluding female and nonnormative knowledge. By grounding the narration in gendered, situated knowledge, the male protagonists and narrators in *El androide y otras quimeras* give the impression of a state of helplessness in the portrayal of female and nonnormative characters. However, a deeper look at the "nanofictional" level of the stories, where glimpses of alternatively situated knowledge can be perceived, unveils a world where the appearance of a mechanized order is undermined by myriad acts of resistance and autonomy. The contradictory and paradoxical nature of this reality is analogous to the strange nature of the cosmos as postulated through quantum mechanics, which undermines the orderly and mechanized model of Newtonian physics. Much as Volpi uses measurements at the scale of electrons to illustrate questions of ethics in an indeterminate world or Blanco speaks of bodies, matter, and poetry that move at speeds approaching that of light, Padilla, the self-described *físico cuéntico*, offers a new, more inclusive perspective of reality through the *Micropedia* project.

As in Padilla's short stories, ciencia-fusión challenges long-held Enlightenment metaphors of reality as mechanistic clockwork as well as Cartesian dualistic accounts of matter and phenomena that compose our universe. As we will see in the following chapters, authors of ciencia-fusión likewise identify such Enlightenment epistemologies as underpinning social subjugations as well as the extractivism and environmental degradation that define the Anthropocene. In the next chapter I explore how authors of ciencia-fusión like Sabina Berman similarly challenge the pernicious nature of a Cartesian worldview that propels divisions between humankind and the more-than-human world. Through baroque style and plotting, in *El androide y otras quimeras* Padilla denaturalizes and portrays how these epistemologies have evolved over the previous centuries as questions of autonomy and automation, as well as of nature and commodity at first point to the subjugation of female and nonnormative characters through a mechanized, androcentric order. However, by focusing on the minute, microscopic, and quantic, Padilla reads and writes a much fuller narration of reality, depicting acts of resistance and autonomy that, much like the discoveries of quantum mechanics, reveal a reality that had gone unseen but was, ultimately, there all along.

CHAPTER 4

A Science of Good and Evil

SABINA BERMAN'S DARWINIAN ETHICAL TURN

Over the years, playwright, author, screenwriter, director, journalist, and public intellectual Sabina Berman has expressed what Jacqueline Bixler calls "a *causi* obsessive interest in Charles Darwin."[1] Known for readdressing, reworking, and adapting many of the same concepts, memes, and even entire works over and again, Berman, in the second decade of the 2000s, began to take up Charles Darwin and the complex legacy of Darwinism to engage questions of morality and ethics in a time of bloodshed, narcoviolence, political corruption, and ecological crisis. While Berman's work has always sought to destabilize and denaturalize, intentionally posing more questions than it answers, in her more recent literary pieces, interviews, and media appearances, Berman has put forward outlines of an ethical code inspired by Darwin's *On the Origin of Species* (1859) and *The Descent of Man* (1871). In response to what she sees as an unbridled anthropocentric neoliberal capitalism, it is perhaps logical that Berman would find inspiration in Darwin, given how his works disrupted paradigms, removed an active God as the mover of Nature, and—much how Copernicus reoriented our place in the Universe—helped to decenter humankind from its privileged place in the story of the Earth. I argue that Berman's four literary works of the 2010s—the novels *La mujer que buceó dentro del corazón del mundo* (*Me, Who Dove into the Heart of the World*, 2010) and *El dios de Darwin* (*Darwin's God*, 2014), the play *El narco negocia con Dios* (*The Narco Makes Deals with God*, 2012), along with the short story compilation *Matemáticas para la felicidad y otras fábulas* (*Mathematics for Happiness and Other Fables*, 2017)— when viewed collectively sustain a critique of Judeo-Christian morality, the Cartesian man/nature dualism, and neoliberalism as culpable in the degradation of both human society and the greater more-than-human ecosystem. Berman's emergent ethical system is most clearly articulated in the two novels that feature Karen Nieto as protagonist (*La mujer* and *Darwin*), in which the

85

86   SCIENCE FUSION IN CONTEMPORARY MEXICAN LITERATURE

interplay of intra- and metadiegetic levels reveal a "Ciencia del Bien y del Mal" (Science of Good and Evil), as proposed by Berman's fictional Darwin. Unlike morality built upon theological or philosophical foundations, Berman looks to the natural world, uniting concepts of connectivity, cooperation, and mutual benefit, not just between human actors, but among all living things on the planet.[2]

Throughout her career, Berman has shown no temerity in taking on polemical topics with a sense of irony and dark humor. Her dramatic works have challenged and subverted the status quo vis-à-vis questions of power, gender, sexuality, language, and history. After a particularly prolific run of critically and commercially successful plays during the 1990s and early 2000s including *Entre Villa y una mujer desnuda* (*Between Villa and a Naked Woman*, 1993), *Molière* (2000), and *Feliz nuevo siglo doktor Freud* (*Happy New Century Doktor Freud*, 2002), Berman's creative interests looked away from the stage to television journalism and film. Returning to fiction with the publication of *La mujer que buceó dentro del corazón del mundo* in 2010, Berman drew upon two themes that would run throughout her literary production in the subsequent decade: Darwinism and morality. The emphasis on reformulation, rewriting, and reimagining across Berman's works has been characterized by Stuart Day as "intersextualidad," combining the idea of intertextuality with an ever-destabilizing reformulation of sexuality.[3] Likewise, Bixler advises that "a dramatist as prolific and perfectionistic as Sabina Berman is best understood not through the reading or viewing of an isolated play, but rather by following the adaptation of that same dramatic meme over time."[4] In that same manner, in her literary works from the 2010s Berman continually revisits and evolves the overarching themes of Darwinism and morality while returning to several minor and major motifs and memes in what I contend be a markedly distinct cycle in Berman's oeuvre. These inter- and intratextual images, memes, and connections suggest a vaster network of meaning, an interconnectivity that is more readily discerned when viewed collectively.

The more obvious examples of Berman's intertextuality in this cycle, such as Darwin's *On the Origin of Species* and the recurring protagonist Karen Nieto, stand alongside more subtle, repeating intertextual links and motifs such as a flamingo that stands with its legs bent in a figure four, ants that crawl on a beach, or a story where an author literally shrinks with every word they write of their magnum opus. The repetitions, returns, and evolutions can be seen as visible manifestations of Berman's rhizomic project on Darwinian ethics, with interconnectivity being not only a narrative feature but also constitutive to its goals. Working to untangle and denaturalize the existing neoliberal order and the natural destruction that she considers a feature of capitalism, Berman's goal is to reverse "varios siglos de humanismo donde colocamos la autoridad en el ser humano, como el centro del planeta y de las decisiones" (several centuries of humanism where we place authority in the human being, as the center of the

A SCIENCE OF GOOD AND EVIL

planet and of decisions).[5] Berman's words echo Valerie Plumwood, who argues that global capitalism and late humanism go hand in hand as "Neo-Cartesian moral dualism is strongly entrenched, as an ethical expression of a corresponding form of life that is entrenched under global capitalism, the dualistic division between persons and property."[6] Over the course of her four literary works from the 2010s, Berman fictionalizes the ecological crisis wrought by extractivist capitalism and the dark side of humanism. Like Berman, Plumwood asserts that the current ecological and social crises of the present are in large part caused by the economic rationality of capitalism that supports strategies that minimize ethical recognition of the other-than-human world.[7] Berman argues that "el capitalismo ha saqueado a la naturaleza para traer a la burbuja humana todos sus tesoros, y en ese saqueo desmedido de la naturaleza ha desequilibrado todo y efecto de ello es lo que estamos viviendo" (capitalism has looted nature to bring all its treasures to the human bubble, and in this excessive looting of nature everything has been knocked off balance and the effect of this is what we are currently experiencing).[8] In the face of such a dire situation, Berman's recurring motif of the dream of an albino boy in a cave who draws a circle in the sand that takes form, rises, and rolls through the world for all to see represents her own attempts to call for systemic change through both her recent literary works as well as her appearances in the mass media.[9] As Berman states in the prologue to *Matemáticas para la felicidad*,

> Solo el soñador comprende su sueño. Yo comprendí el mío. El niño albino es la pura imaginación. El círculo que traza en la arena, una historia que, de cerrarse, perfecta, o casi, puede alzarse y salir rodando a la realidad, apta de ser vista por los Otros. Si pudiera, con el material de la realidad social coyuntural, contar historias imaginarias, que se levantasen de lo anecdótico y dijeran algo más pensé. ¿Qué más? Que transmitieran una moraleja, pensé. Una moraleja: una enseñanza sobre el Bien y el Mal.[10]

> Only the dreamer understands their dream. I understood mine. The albino child is pure imagination. The circle that he traces in the sand, a story that, if closed, perfectly, or almost, can rise up and roll out into reality, ready to be seen by Others. If I could, with material from the present social reality, tell imaginary stories, that would rise from the anecdotal and say something else, I thought. What else? That they should convey a moral, I thought. A moral: a lesson about Good and Evil.

In line with her long-established contrarian impulses, this ethical turn in Berman in many ways defines itself in opposition to the status quo. While featuring a markedly anticapitalistic and antihumanist stance, it also puts forth precepts and claims that, when considered holistically, construct an ethical system, however utopic it may be, that Berman believes crucial to confront the crises of the present.

Survival of the Fittest: Exhaustion in Times of Moral Morass

After a nearly decadelong period without producing a new work of theater, Berman returned to the stage in 2012 with the play *El narco negocia con Dios*, which explores questions of morality, narcotrafficking, violence, and corruption at both the interpersonal and national levels. Although a hallmark of Berman has always been to question and destabilize, *El narco*, in contrast, is marked by a sense of exhaustion before the moral morass of Mexico's *Guerra contra el narcotráfico* (War on Narcotrafficking) portrayed onstage, however humorously. Though the play does not overtly bring up Darwinism, the concept of survival of the fittest, or at least as it is often popularized in the popular imaginary, is applied to the current state of violence and narcoculture in Mexico.[11] Furthermore, Darwinism as methodology pervades Berman's work, given that the playwright's "interest in Darwin extends well beyond the titles and thematic concerns of her literary creations to the way she guides and adapts her texts from page to stage and from one performance to the next."[12] We see this textual and performative adaptation in the storyline of *El narco negocia con Dios*, itself an adaptation of a plot that Berman used in the earlier iterations *El gordo, la pájara y el narco* (*The Fat Guy, the Thieving Woman, and the Narco*) and *Krisis*, written in 1994 and 1996, respectively. In essence, the basic storyline of *El narco* and the earlier plays revolves around the lack of a coherent moral system within all institutions and sectors of society. Essentially, in *El narco* the action unfolds through verbal and physical violence among its characters, including Alberto, an impotent, drug-addled leftist public intellectual; his sister Gabriela, a sanctimonious and hypocritical religious prude; Patricia, Alberto's wife and polyamorous neoliberal who is having an affair with Ramón, the titular narco who makes deals with God to remit for his sins. As I have argued elsewhere, *El narco negocia con Dios* portrays how enmeshed relationships between Mexican civil society, government, and criminal cartels have undermined the coherency of long-held moral principles.[13] In Berman's play, the characters are able to assert sovereignty only through necropower and the subjugation of the life of others. When viewed through the lens of Slavoj Žižek's tripartite classification of violence, we see that *El narco* puts forth the argument that "the only way to end the more recognizable subjective violence is to combat systemic violence rooted within the current economic and political order."[14] While the farcically pulpy nature of the play allows the audience to laugh at the absurdity of it all, *El narco* dramatizes debates about topics with very real life-and-death consequences beyond the stage. At the same time that Berman emphasizes the impossibility of adhering to long-standing moral systems, she opens the door to a series of ethical propositions capable of cutting through the systemic violence inherent in the current neoliberal order.

A SCIENCE OF GOOD AND EVIL   89

We can perceive this shift in the play when Ramón, the narco, points out the hypocrisy related to corruption: "¿Qué culpa tengo que mis negocios sean grandes y los tuyos cositas? Tú sobornas policías de tránsito, yo a jueces estatales. A la hormiguita que se va a meter a tu postre tú la aplastas; yo al buey que me chinga un bisnes" (Why is it my fault that my deals are big and yours are tiny little things? You bribe traffic cops; for me, it's state judges. You squish that little ant that gets on your dessert; me, the fool that screws with my business).[15] In *El narco* defining what is moral is an unsolvable enigma given that all the characters participate in an inherently immoral configuration of religion, neoliberal economics, and a corrupt political state. Alberto's statement that "el único error de la gente buena: ser débiles" (the only mistake of good people: being weak)[16] suggests that survival is dependent on wielding necropower over others, a contemporary permutation on Octavio Paz's often cited maxim that "para el mexicano la vida es una posibilidad de chingar o ser chingado" (for the Mexican, life is a possibility of screwing someone over or being screwed).[17] Although one reading of *El narco* would suggest yet another misapplication of the Darwinian concept of survival of the fittest to sociology and politics, when viewed within the greater cycle of Berman's Darwinian ethical turn, *El narco*, instead, is clearly a critique of a misguided social Darwinism that distorts the true nature of the naturalist's works, replacing their empirical logic with capitalist economic and sociopolitical discourse.

In contrast to the narco's propensity to carry ethical propositions to their logical extremes, throughout the play his verbal rival Alberto argues that there is indeed an ethical red line that is crossed when one harms another human, as he explains in the following example: "El policía que muerde es el que muerde, ¿estás de acuerdo?; el que es mordido es el dañado. El juez que muerde es el que muerde; el que es extorsionado por el juez es la víctima. No somos iguales los villanos que las víctimas" (The cop that does harm for a bribe is the one doing the harm. Right? The one getting injured is the one being harmed. The judge that harms for a bribe is the one doing the harming; the person being extorted by the judge is the victim. We victims are not the same as the villains).[18] The gist of Alberto's argument—that individuals and society mutually benefit when respecting each other's sovereignty and the values of communality and cooperation—stands in direct contrast to the actions of the characters that function as types to represent neoliberalism, religion, and narcoculture. Alberto's words reflect the beginning contours of the ethical system, even though it is never expressed in an explicit manner in the play, that Berman will develop throughout her dramatic and fictional works in the 2010s that is inspired by Darwin's observations of social species in the natural world.

Berman says that in many respects *El narco negocia con Dios*, more than a critique of hypocrisy, is "una carcajada al sistema de valores religiosos, pero también al sistema de valores liberales" (a fit of laughter at the system of religious values, but also at the system of liberal values).[19] Irmgard Emmelhainz maintains that neoliberalism has brought change far beyond the liberalization of markets, to the point that its normative rationality has altered the ways in which Mexicans exist and behave and even how they relate with others and themselves.[20] This is apparent on both personal and planetary scales, as the rationality of neoliberalism "opera en nombre del desarrollo y la mejora (individuales). Nuestra era ecológica es la sexta extinción masiva y su causa principal es la transformación de la tierra por el hombre bajo la racionalidad del capitalismo industrial y global, que ha inaugurado un proceso de (auto)destrucción" (operates in the name of [individual] development and improvement. Our ecological era is the sixth mass extinction, and its main cause is the transformation of the Earth by man under the rationality of industrial and global capitalism which has opened up a process of [self-]destruction).[21] For Berman, the key to escaping the many crises of the present is to tear at the threads of anthropocentric liberalism, denaturalizing religion and neoliberal capitalism, and, most importantly, resituating the human within the more-than-human world: "Mi postura . . . es que tenemos que cambiar nuestro punto de vista. Colocar en el centro la naturaleza y nosotros como parte de la naturaleza. Y eso lo cambia todo" (My position . . . is that we have to change our point of view. Place nature at the center and ourselves as part of nature. And that changes everything).[22] For Berman, the alternative is a continuation of the systemic violence, corruption, and hedonistic consumption that harms individuals, but also causes the destruction of life on a planetary scale.

"I Am Therefore I Think": Descartes, Darwin, and the Anthropocene

In describing the inspiration for the novel *La mujer que buceó dentro del corazón del mundo* and Berman's growing interest in the relationship between humans and the natural world, the author recalls a fishing trip she took off the Pacific coast of Mexico:

> Fui a una pesca de atunes a la altura de Mazatlán. México tiene las atuneras más grandes del planeta y vi la pesca del atún. Y cuando termina la pesca del atún, el océano se vuelve 360 grados de sangre, de mar pintado de sangre. Esa imagen, empecé a soñar a con ella. Empecé a reflexionar con ella. Caramba . . . los humanos. . . . Entre los humanos y los animales y el resto de los seres vivos del planeta, hay un oceáno de sangre, más un océano de matanza.[23]

> I went to where they were fishing for tuna off the coast of Mazatlán. Mexico has the largest tuna fishing boats on the planet, and I saw them catching tuna. And when the catch ends, the ocean turns to blood for 360 degrees, a sea painted with blood. That image, I started dreaming about it. I began to reflect on it. Wow . . . humans. . . . In between humans and animals and the rest of the living beings on the planet, there is an ocean of blood, an ocean of slaughter.

A SCIENCE OF GOOD AND EVIL

Pondering the image of a sea of blood as far as the eye can see, Berman states that she realized that "la naturaleza se te vuelve un paisaje de tus acciones humanas. Así vivimos" (nature turns into the landscape of your own human actions. That's what we're living).[24] Born of the images of how humanity projects itself upon the environment, the novel is narrated as the autobiography of its protagonist, Karen Nieto, who goes from a speechless, neglected, and abused child to a world-famous zoologist. Over the course of years, Karen revolutionizes aquaculture practices and eventually severs all ties with the profit-making impulses of capitalism and creates a natural reserve, a "paradise for tuna," a place where the more-than-human returns to occupy the metaphorical center of the world. A large part of Karen's triumph is due to being on the autism spectrum, which differentiates her from what she calls "los humanos standard" (standard humans) and "mamíferos habladores" (talking mammals) and allows her to escape the pitfalls of logo- and anthropocentrism that confer humans an ontologically privileged position. Karen's autobiography touches on her personal, academic, and professional challenges and triumphs: her battles with faculty while studying animal science at Berkeley, the various innovations and more humane practices she installs as head of Atunes Consuelo, the uneasy but mutually beneficial partnership with Scottish mogul Ian Gould, her relationships with her aunt and others in her life, and finally her evolution from owner of a company that profits off the killing and mass consumption of tuna to an expert and innovator in how to sustain and support more-than-human life.

Karen Nieto's high-functioning autism conditions her worldview as her narrative denaturalizes the anthropocentric division between mankind and nature. This crucial advantage not only gives the protagonist-narrator the ability to see to the world differently but also gives her the tools to begin the work of ameliorating the ecological destruction that is characteristic of the Anthropocene. Karen's aunt compares her ability to focus obsessively with that of great geniuses such as Einstein, Beethoven, and Darwin, all autistic according to her aunt, declaring, "Son las personas con capacidades diferentes las que aportan cosas diferentes a la humanidad" (It's the people with different abilities that contribute different things to humanity).[25] In the character, Berman has attempted to create a bridge between the human and the more-than-human world, as when Karen's aunt declares to her that "tú eres la mediadora entre los animales que hablan y los que no. Tú eres la mutación de la especie para lograr otro pacto con la realidad" (you are the intermediary between animals that speak and those that don't. You are the mutation of the species to forge a new pact with reality).[26] The narrative effect of Karen's autism works both as a catalyst for the events in the novel and as a platform through which Berman communicates her critique of the current cultural, political, and economic order. María Bortolotto and May Farnsworth see particular value in Karen's lack of empathy not as an affective isolation but rather as "una posición estratégica que le permite ser, a la vez

92   SCIENCE FUSION IN CONTEMPORARY MEXICAN LITERATURE

que menos permeable a las 'caras' de los humanos, mucho más permeable a lo que ocurre en el mundo natural de los otros seres con los que convivimos" (a strategic position that allows her to be less permeable to the "faces" of humans while much more permeable to what happens in the natural world of the other beings with whom we live).[27] Similarly, Etna Verónica Ávalos Molina states that Karen's condition functions like a device that allows her to put in doubt long-standing gender and sexual paradigms in addition to capitalism and related neoliberal politics.[28] Alana Gómez Gray sees Karen's cold rationality as a counterpoint to the logic of capitalism that provides a meditation on the reason/emotion dichotomy that causes the reader to consider their own animal nature.[29] In a more critical evaluation, Eduardo Huchín Sosa states that in spite of its satirical advantages, Karen's autism blurs the individuality of other characters and reduces them to shadows.[30] Seeing Berman's employment of an autistic character indicative of what she identifies as literary hubris, Ana Ugarte describes "un exceso de confianza en los poderes del medio literario para traducir, representar o entregar la alteridad específica del personaje de Berman" (an excess of confidence in the power of the literary medium to translate, represent, or deliver the specific alterity of Berman's character).[31] I agree on the need for recognizing the limitations of the narrativization of the autistic condition by a neurotypical author in a novel written for mostly neurotypical readers. By doing so, I would argue that the narration itself can be read as an extended metafictive meditation on the danger of normative language to faithfully mediate an already-present material reality.

Tellingly, in the penultimate chapter as Karen is typing the book that becomes the novel we are reading, she brainstorms possible titles such as *Yo y el atún* (*Me and Tuna*), *Yo que buceé dentro del centro del mundo* (*Me, Who Dove in the Center of the World*), and *La fascinante coincidencia de ser yo* (*The Fascinating Coincidence in Being Me*).[32] One proposed title, *Existo, luego (y con dificultad) pienso* (I Exist, Therefore [and with Difficulty] I Think), an inversion of the Spanish translation "pienso, luego existo" of René Descartes's *cogito ergo sum* as declared in *Discourse on Method* is but one permutation of how Karen inverts Cartesian logic, which she sees as an existential danger to the planet. We can see this when Karen recalls her dismay at the phrase that she says puts distance between she and humans, recalling how "la oración me dejó la boca abierta, porque es, evidentemente increíble. Basta tener 2 ojos en la cara para ver que todo lo que existe, primero existe y luego hace otras cosas" (the sentence left me with my mouth open, because it's tangibly incredible. All you need are two eyes to see that everything that exists, first exists, and then does other things).[33] Karen's understanding of Descartes's statement—which is identical to what Berman has put forward publicly on numerous occasions—hinges upon a dubious application of the Spanish adverb "luego" (then/therefore), which can be either temporal or consecutive. Descartes's original statement translated from French,

A SCIENCE OF GOOD AND EVIL

"Je pense, donc je suis," supposes a causal or consecutive, not temporal, relationship between the act of thinking and the confirmation of being.[34] Although Karen's critique of Descartes often focuses on a misinterpretation of the philosopher's causal links between thought and proof of existence, the novel's greater engagement with the impacts of Cartesian dualism, particularly as it impacts humanity's relationship with nature, reflects this central feature of much ciencia-fusión and taps into the ecofeminist tradition of questioning what Freya Mathews calls "the distorting lens of dualism."[35]

In addition to identifying the culture/nature dualism as an ordering principle of Enlightenment thought as well as the Scientific Revolution, Plumwood argues that such dualisms create an ontological divide between man and everything else, providing the "logic of colonization" over nations, peoples, as well as the natural world.[36] In contrast to the thinking human subject, nature and the nonhuman are matter onto which human activity is projected, conceptually echoed in Berman's imagery of "paisaje" (landscape) and Karen's concept of the bubble in which standard humans live, which she describes as "una burbuja donde nada sino lo humano es oído o visto realmente, donde nada más que lo humano importa y lo demás es paisaje, mercancía o comida" (a bubble where nothing but the human is really heard or seen, where nothing but what is human matters and the rest is landscape, goods, or food).[37] In this conceptualization, humankind is the sole protagonist, projecting actions upon a soulless nature, emptied of its vitality and agential power.[38] It is telling, then, that what jars the memory of Karen's first encounter with Descartes is when she retells the day when the fishermen and managers gleefully hoist a dying swordfish onto the company's dock, torturing the animal in the most inhumane way without regard for any sensation or suffering the animal may experience.[39] Karen is able to silently observe the fish's suffering precisely because she is incapable of entering the human bubble conditioned by language and predicated on being distinct from nature. Instead, she questions how humans can believe that "thinking" is the ordering principle of all matter, pondering how in their bubble "todo aquello que no piensa no existe del todo. Los árboles, el mar, los peces dentro del mar, el sol, la luna, un cerro o una enorme cordillera: no, no existen del todo, existen con un segundo nivel de existencia, una existencia menor" (all that does not think does not exist completely. Trees, the sea, the fish in the sea, the sun, the moon, a hill or a huge mountain range: no, they do not exist completely, they exist on a second level of existence, a lesser existence).[40] Throughout the novel, then, humans are the sole specimens of Descartes's res cogitans, the thinking beings defined by free will, asserting their sovereignty and dominion over the exploitable res extensa, grouping together all that is nonhuman.

Mathews affirms that the assumption built upon Cartesian logic that humans alone possess cognitive attributes to confer intrinsic value on things denotes that "without mental attributes of some description, an entity cannot matter to itself

94 SCIENCE FUSION IN CONTEMPORARY MEXICAN LITERATURE

or in itself, since it cannot have meaning, value, interests or ends of its own."[41] Human actions upon the more-than-human, therefore, remain beyond the realm of moral and ethical consideration when one takes to the extreme Descartes's claim that his "practical philosophy" will "render us masters and possessors of nature."[42] Karen characterizes Descartes as "el loco" (the madman) and "el desquiciado" (the unhinged man), for establishing a firm line dividing human and animal.[43] Karen's contempt for the human/animal dualism runs throughout, as can be observed while as a student in the university course on Human Intelligence—itself essentially a compendium of the various theories on why humans differ from animals—she responds with the childish taunt "estúpido" (stupid) to each proposal, while naming animals that indeed have those very attributes, empirically undermining the logic that justifies seeing animals as simple material goods.[44] Instead, Karen insists that the only thing that separates humans from the more-than-human, including herself, is not thinking as a neurological process, per se, but rather the propensity to "estar siempre incomódos ahí donde están; y creo que esa incomodidad es lo que los hace estar siempre pensando en otras cosas en lugar de lo que tienen ante los ojos" (always being uncomfortable where they are; and I think that that discomfort is what makes them always think about other things instead of what is right in front of their eyes).[45] The protagonist's difficulty in comprehending the meaning of common metaphors—some, such as her riff on the tuna brand Chicken of the Sea, are quite humorous for the neurotypical reader—goes hand in hand with her inability to visualize nonliteral representations, such as when she draws blueprints to actual scale. We can argue that Karen's propensity to describe the world through literal and tautological propositions, combined with her ability to ascertain and concentrate on minute details gives her a unique ability to denaturalize existing suppositions about the natural world and, as the novel progresses, allows her to create innovative solutions to the damage humanity has inflicted on the ecosystem.

The character of Karen was surely based in part on Temple Grandin, the American scientist and animal behavioralist who, like her fictional counterpart, is on the autism spectrum. Grandin, an advocate for the humane treatment of livestock, affirms that animals and people with autism think in images and not abstractions.[46] Accordingly, the autobiographical text of the novel is accompanied by several drawings that Karen uses to replicate and convey to the reader the world as she perceives it. Navigating language as used by neurotypical humans is a constant struggle for her. In the opening pages of the novel, Karen's aunt encounters her in the abandoned family mansion as a neglected and abused child, "una cosa salvaje" (a savage thing),[47] endeavoring to "convertirla en un ser humano" (turn her into a human being), working tirelessly to teach the creature who will become Karen through the pronoun "yo" (I).[48] The protagonist's inability to grasp the representationalism of pronouns as well as her perception of her self-identity, the "yo," stands in contrast to what she terms as everything else, "el no yo" (the not I). While reminiscent of Ralph Waldo Emerson's idea of nature as the "NOT ME," Karen's subjectivity, unlike that of the transcendentalist, is not predicated on the immortal soul that operates outside of nature. Instead, Karen views her subjectivity as an intrinsic element of a larger interconnectivity within an ecosystem. For Berman's protagonist, the separation between human and more-than-human is not ontological but instead relational. The question of what separates humanity from nature, for Karen, is not the former's ability to think but conversely how it projects that thinking onto nature and the impacts that it creates. In recounting the parakeet, Max, whom Karen observes thinking and speaking, she further melds this distinction between humans and the more-than-human, even declaring that the natural world and Max are superior because "un humano standard vive separado por su pensamiento de las cosas naturales, incluso de su propio cuerpo, y como nada puede ser feliz si no es en su cuerpo real, el ser humano no es feliz" (the standard human lives separated by his thoughts about natural things, including his own body, and since nothing can be happy if it is not in its real body, the human being is not happy).[49] In this valorization, Cartesian duality, while not being wholly idealistic, removes humanity from its own materiality, creating a lacking that propels an endless cycle of consumption. Tables, chairs, buildings, books, universities all form an endless stream of fabricated "cosas humanas que durante siglos han ido llenando el espacio alrededor del ser humano: que han ido acumulándose para formar un mundo exclusivamente humano que tapa la vista del mundo no humano" (human things that for centuries have been filling the space around human beings: that have been accumulating to form an exclusively human world that obscures the view of the nonhuman world).[50] In Karen's estimation, therefore, it is the human ability to invent mentally and then project that invention onto the materiality of the world that both justifies and sustains the destructive anthropocentric order.

Karen recognizes that what she terms "the madness" begins not with Descartes but millennia before when the books of the Bible were being written, a theme that becomes central to the plot of Berman's next novel.[51] In interviews and commentary, Berman frequently uses the term "schizophrenia" to describe positions or belief systems that contain what she estimates as internal contradictions, such as Christians who believe in both evolution and God as "una inteligencia que nos está observando, cuidando y que hay un plan en la vida, que hay bien y mal" (an intelligence that is observing us, taking care of things, and that there is a plan in life, that there is good and evil).[52] Karen's outrage that the biblical God gives humans dominion over all living things with more-than-human life functioning as food, clothing, transportation, sacrifice, or, at worst, a metaphor

96   SCIENCE FUSION IN CONTEMPORARY MEXICAN LITERATURE

for something human or divine stands in direct contrast to the ants on the beach that devour a forgotten Bible and literally carry away, letter by letter, the remains of the sacred text.[53] In spite of Karen's supposed incomprehensibility of metaphors, the message is clear: the moral foundations that justify anthropocentrism and the destruction of the environment are immaterial products of language and rationalism, lacking direct relation to the true material nature of reality.[54]

In this conflict between the "human bubble" and material reality, Berman sees that only one narrative can win out, opting for the side of Darwinian empiricism. Although readers may question what would have been of Darwin without the foundations of Enlightenment thought, Karen sets up a dichotomous relationship between Descartes and Darwin, contrasting not only their works but also their philosophical/scientific processes. An example is when she mocks Descartes's rationalist impulses, wrapping himself in a cape and hiding away from the world, imagining him saying, "Voy a pensar, luego vuelvo al mundo" (I am going to think, and then return to world), emerging from his cape to declare that there is a line between humans and animals,[55] criticizing rationalism as a purely inward-facing activity. In contrast, Karen's Darwin looks to the external world, observing empirically that "todas las especies vivimos en el mismo planeta Tierra, interactuando y cambiándonos entre sí" (we species all live on the same planet Earth, interacting and changing among ourselves).[56] In contextualizing Berman's novel within her larger push toward a new ecological Darwinian ethics, it is important to note that Karen's attempts to work within the academic and scientific system all ultimately fail as when her article on zootechnics is published in the prestigious journal *Nature* only after the editors expurgate her footnote in which she wishes that at some point in the past they had gathered all of Descartes's books and burned them because "si hubiera sucedido, estas formas nuevas de relación con los animales se hubieran inventado en el siglo 19 y no hasta el siglo 21, cuando peligra la fauna del planeta" (if that had happened, these new ways of relating to animals would have been invented in the nineteenth century and not until the twenty-first, when the planet's fauna is in danger).[57] Although Karen's imperative to burn the books, along with her rallying cry, "¡Queménoslos!" (Let's burn them all!), perhaps unwittingly reinforce the duality between ideas and materiality, they clearly stand in for Berman's critique of the errant philosophical underpinnings of the Anthropocene. In addressing the difficulty in dislodging dualistic thinking, Mathews argues that "we cannot escape dualism by theorizing as theorizing itself perpetuates a dualism; rather it is through practice that liberates us from the 'unavoidable legacy of domination.'"[58] This bears out in the novel through Karen's inability to effect real change until she puts her unique sensibilities into action through her ownership of her family's tuna business.

A SCIENCE OF GOOD AND EVIL

TRANSMUTATIONS AND CONNECTIVITIES: CHANGE IN THE HEART OF THE WORLD

Karen's unique way of relating with the material world allows her to begin to make change to the system from within, slowly evolving and adapting her family's tuna company, Atunes Consuelo, from a traditional small-scale business being blocked out of the international market to an organization that practices more humane aquaculture.[59] It is only when she able to turn greed and overconsumption on their head and utilize other humans' propensity to employ figurative language that she is able to destroy the system of commercial tuna fishing itself, creating a new paradigm to ameliorate the human impact on the ecosystem. Although the infusion of capital investment as well as marketing acumen from international mogul Ian Gould allow Karen to implement changes to improve the conditions in which tuna live and keep them from extinction by overfishing and loss of habitat, the end result is that tuna is still a commodity to be bought, traded, and eventually consumed, in spite of Karen's good intentions. What is more, although the company's new iteration as True Blue Tuna is the public manifestation of the investment package, it is Karen's wildly successful invention of a better flytrap from years before that is the primary source of Gould's return on investment, emphasizing the impossibility of truly changing the paradigm of a system that is driven by the death of animals to satisfy ever-increasing demands of consumption. Karen understands that her uncomfortable partnership with Gould is transactional, stating, "La belleza de mi idea es que el asesinato humanitario de atunes conserva a la especie del atún" (the beauty of my idea is that humane murder of tunas conserves the species of tuna).[60] In the novel, the alternative to collaboration with the capitalist fishing industry offers even less satisfactory choices. The "pandillas ecológicas de gringos" (the ecological gangs of gringos),[61] the Animal Liberation Front, and the militant Animal Rights Militia all come across as ineffectual zealots, incapable of effecting lasting change in the world. This is no small part due to the intractability of the consumption of animals as part of a greater cultural ethos, embedded within humanity's relationship with the more-than-human world. Here Berman's positioning of capitalism is an example of new materialist criticisms in which "the capitalist system is not understood in any narrowly economistic way but rather is treated as a detotalized totality that includes a multitude of interconnected phenomena and processes that sustain its unpredictable proliferation and unexpected crises, as well as its productivity and reproduction."[62] The example in the novel of the international tuna industry, with countless connections to personal, economic, political, cultural, and ecological interests, demonstrates that it is not a self-contained phenomenon. These connections can be parallelly illustrated with Karen's electric flytrap, which is installed in restaurants, food processing plants, and hotels around the world. Invented to improve hygiene on the processing floor at Atunes Consuelo, it eventually enriches Gould, who publishes his best-selling book *Profit (A Love Story)*, the sales of which enable him to buy a new jet that will spew even more carbon emissions into the atmosphere. In a humorous flourish typical of Berman, Karen's flytrap even becomes the inspiration for an avant-garde installation at London's Saatchi Gallery, "donde un artista ha colgado un matamoscas eléctrico dentro de una vitrina junto con una costilla podrida de res, que asegura un flujo perpetuo de mocas a los tubos de luz, donde con un zzzzzz se achicarran" (where an artist has hung an electric flytrap inside a glass case along with a rotten beef rib, which ensures a perpetual flow of flies to the light tubes, where with a zzzzzz they get zapped),[63] a pointed metacommentary on the endless cycle of greed, killing, the consumption of even art, and, most importantly, hedonistic capitalism in the Anthropocene.

In a way similar to the Zapotec painter who uses his portion of Aunt Isabelle's inheritance to create what Karen calls a "templo darwinista" (Darwinist temple), secularizing and transforming a former convent into a green paradise completely unplugged from the national power grid, Karen uses the earnings and infrastructure of True Blue Tuna to create "tuna paradises," achieving the long-sought ovulation and propagation of tuna in captivity. The repeated use of the name "paradise" for what commonly would be called a refuge or sanctuary draws attention to the utopic nature of Berman's protagonist's project. The transformative power of the tuna paradises is that they are auto-generative spaces where, after initial human intervention, the natural world is allowed to return to pre-anthropogenic equilibrium. In this way, Karen's ecological legacy echoes the early imagery in the novel of the mass fishing of tuna as an open wound that violently opens and eventually closes as the blood diffuses and the color of the sea returns to blue.[64] The imagery of the sea as body onto which wounds are exacted would be metaphoric to what the protagonist calls "standard" humans. In light of Karen's inability to use metaphors, then, the idea of the sea as a living entity that bleeds and can be wounded indicates a literal materiality that belies its status as an inert resource to be plundered by human actants.[65] In such a vibrant materialism, which calls to mind Jane Bennett's assemblages of affective bodies,[66] tuna, krill, minerals, and even molecules of water are members of a greater assemblage that has agential qualities beyond a mere summation of each materiality considered alone. This interconnectivity, modeled in the tuna paradises, extends beyond any one geographic zone, encompassing an endless web of connections between all matter on the planet. In the novel's final pages Karen describes her heart attack while scuba diving that would have been her death if not for the jellyfish that pushed her up from the depths and gave her a shock that jolted her heart back into rhythm. Careful to not ascribe anthropomorphic or metaphoric intentions to a marine animal that was most likely simply rushing to escape a perceived predator, Karen describes her awe before the world *as it is*, saying, "Lo extraño . . . es que alguien necesitara imaginar un ángel o

A SCIENCE OF GOOD AND EVIL

cualquier cosa sobrenatural, si la realidad lo llena todo" (The strange thing . . . is that someone would need to imagine an angel or any supernatural thing when reality fills it all).[67] As Karen's near-death experience illustrates, humanity does not enjoy a privileged position within what we call nature. Instead, Karen at last finds true stasis with nature, seeing herself as one actor within a greater assemblage that she calls "reality," stating, "desde mi pecho pienso por primera vez sin borrar la realidad y sin que la realidad me borre a Yo" (from my chest I am thinking for the first time without erasing reality and without reality erasing me).[68] In almost mystical terms, Karen describes how reality speaks through her chest, revealing the trick to exist "en el centro de todo lo demás" (in the center of everything else), stating, "Éste es el truco, pensó la realidad desde mi pecho en el centro de 360 grados de mar y sol: No matar" (This is the trick, thought reality from my chest in the middle of 360 degrees of sea and sun: Don't kill).[69] The similarity of reality's imperative to not kill to the fifth of the biblical Ten Commandments is not by coincidence as there are several intertextualities with the Bible in the novel, including the three days and nights that Karen sweats out the jellyfish's toxins and the six phases of the operation to create a new world for tuna, a probable allusion to the six days of creation in Genesis. Replacing the supernatural with the natural, the painter's Darwinist temple, the tuna paradises, and Karen's union with reality all affirm the vitality of the more-than-human and the material, imagining ontologies informed by the interconnectivity between all matter and members, human and more-than-human.

Clash of the Narratives and Darwin's Search for God

In her 2014 novel *El dios de Darwin*, Berman positions Darwin in another dialectical battle of narratives, this time replacing the loathsome Descartes with religion, in particular the monotheistic Abrahamic faiths, as impediments to a more progressive and just world. The novel, Berman's first attempt at writing an intrigue thriller, is narrated once again by Karen Nieto, who is pulled into a country-hopping imbroglio involving Charles Darwin's *Theological Autobiography*, an undiscovered text that would have profound implications on the naturalist's legacy and the place of religion in the modern world. The novel begins a few years after the conclusion of *La mujer*, with Karen being called away from another discovery of a marine species to help solve the disappearance of her former classmate Antonio Márquez, who, after being granted permanent leave from his teaching post for lecturing in miniskirts, was working for the United Nations Office of Human Rights in the United Arab Emirates. The reader soon discovers that Márquez was kidnapped, tortured, and murdered by Islamic fundamentalists, but moments before his death managed to send out fragments of Darwin's censored text from his phone to Karen Nieto and three other trustworthy Darwinists. The existence of "Darwin's secret" sets into motion a struggle with secret alliances of Islamic fundamentalists and the highest echelons of the Roman Catholic Church against academics, polemicists, and scientists, all seeking to ensure that their metanarrative of nature and the divine wins out. Interspersed among the contemporary plotline is the text of Darwin's autobiographical text, which traces the British naturalist's evolving views on God, religion, and the natural world. The text of the *Theological Autobiography* embedded in Berman's novel is an impressive fictional re-creation of the religious, scientific, and cultural milieu in which Darwin struggled to align conflicting ontologies and value systems. In contrast, the thriller plotline frequently taps into tropes of the historical conspiracy subgenre to uneven effect, landing somewhere between Dan Brown's *The Da Vinci Code* and Arturo Pérez-Reverte's *La tabla de Flandes*.[70] All told, the shifting alliances and polemics of morality, faith, and science connect the eighteenth and twenty-first centuries and become the canvas on which Berman portrays an existential conflict between the narratives of monotheistic religion and Darwinian empiricism.[71]

Although there is violence in many forms in the novel, the true battle is over the power of narrative in defining morality, with consequences in both the human and the more-than-human worlds. Eduardo Parrilla Sotomayor argues that the novel weaves together two primary themes, "el de la 'confusión moral' al que ha devenido la Humanidad y el de la vía ética que hay que seguir para la solución de esta" (that of "moral confusion" to which Humanity has progressed and that of the ethical path that must be followed to solve this).[72] Reinforcing the repeating motif of the "Relato" (Story/Narrative) as the ordering force for defining morality, the structure of the novel itself is composed of embedded layers of narrative. While chapters jump between Karen's experiences, the recollections of others as told to Karen, and the text of Darwin's recovered *Theological Autobiography*, a chronological retracing of how Darwin's secret text arrives in the reader's hands proves revealing. The autobiography, in part dictated and written down by his secretary, is then fought over by his disciples, family, and the British Crown, only to be hidden away in a file in Westminster Abbey, discovered and encrypted by a twenty-first-century zoologist who sends its fragments in emails that are read and transcribed by Karen Nieto, who interweaves it with her own experiences, narrated in first person, filling in the gaps of the story with third-person recollections as told by others.[73] The effect, at times, is purposefully disorienting to readers, adding to the intrigue surrounding the authenticity and intentions of Darwin's secret text. By narrativizing the twists and turns in her own discoveries into Darwin, through both the plot and the structure of the novel, Berman foregrounds the processes through which narrating the past is an ethical and always political exercise, as evidenced in our study of similar positioning in Volpi's *En busca de Klingsor*. In this light, Berman's fictional *Theological Autobiography* picks up and gives new life to what Hutcheon would call the "textualized remains" of the past,[74] extrapolating from various

A SCIENCE OF GOOD AND EVIL   101

intertexts including Darwin's *On the Origin of Species, The Descent of Man*, and his posthumously published *Autobiography*, including the sections originally removed by his children, restored in its 1958 edition. In Berman's retelling, Darwin's search for God in nature in the nineteenth century becomes the inflection point in a centuries-old clash of cultures between science and religion. Considered together, Karen's observations on empiricism along with the "positive laws" that the fictional Darwin posits in the recovered autobiography put forward an ethical code derived from the natural world that will prove incompatible with the a priori moral certitude of Western religion and capitalism.

It is significant that *El dios de Darwin*, which is an extended meditation on narrative and reality, is framed by opening and closing passages that speak directly to the relationship between language, representation, and reality. The first lines of the novel are Karen stating, "Fuera de las palabras hay un lugar interminable. Se llama Realidad" (Outside of words there is an endless place. It's called Reality),[75] which is bookended when the narration concludes 135 chapters later with a drawing, to exact scale, of a tuna larva that is preceded with the words, "Éste es su tamaño real y acá Yo termino mi relato" (This is its real size and here I end my story).[76] As in *La mujer que buceó*, Karen's privileged position exterior to the bubble of language allows her to occupy a space outside of the battle of narratives between religion and science, which only confuses her own "ordenado Relato darwinista" (tidy Darwinist Narrative), saying, "Por suerte Yo no tenía que elegir entre los 2 relatos de la Realidad, el de la Religión y el de la Ciencia, porque tenía una 3ra opción. La Realidad misma, ese lugar interminable. Sólido" (Luckily I didn't have to choose between the two stories about Reality, that of Religion and that of Science, because I had a third option. Reality itself, that endless place. Solid).[77] Through her words and actions, the narrator is sympathetic to the side of science but is careful to make a marked distinction between scientific empiricism and Science as metanarrative, which she writes with a capital S as, for her, the latter term stands in for greater social, political, and epistemic systems. Jean-François Lyotard's description of the postmodern as "incredulity towards metanarratives"[78] is echoed in Berman's longtime impulse to question everything. Although Karen's insistence on also capitalizing "Reality" suggests she is replacing one metanarrative for another, throughout the novel reality is portrayed as a materiality that exists outside of language, and therefore outside of any metanarrative. The danger, according to Berman, is in believing that any narrative intervention (including her own) is capable of representing the real:

> No es accidental que sea el momento en donde como cultura nos damos cuenta de que todas las historias son ficción, pero creo que estamos entrando a otra época, por lo menos personalmente yo sí estoy entrando a donde dices: OK, todo es ficción, pero vamos a elegir las ficciones que van a regir nuestras vidas.

Tengamos confianza en el lenguaje, como lo que es, no como nuestros abue-
los creían que era.[79]

It's not by chance that this is the moment when as a culture we realize that all
stories are fiction, but I think we are entering another era, at least personally
I am entering where you say: OK, everything is fiction, but we are going to
choose the fictions that will govern our lives. Let's have confidence in language,
for what it is, not as our grandparents believed it to be.

Berman's assertation on the constitutive nature of discourse, like Donna
Haraway's reminder that "it matters what stories make worlds, what worlds
make stories,"[80] affirms the power of storytelling and language, not as replica-
tors of reality but rather as strategic tools with which to approach and mediate
our place within the material world. In this way, Berman's recent work, like
much of ciencia-fusión, moves beyond postmodern awareness of the referential
instability of discourse to seek out both novel and subjugated ways of perceiv-
ing and communicating a material universe. Berman declares, "El lenguaje es
una cosa y la realidad otra" (Language is one thing, reality another),[81] a statement illustrated in the novel in various moments such as the public debates on
faith and science, which Karen describes as mere "palabras y más palabras. . . .
Y lo que importa es si Dios existe en la Realidad, no dentro de las palabras"
(words and more words. . . . What matters is if God exists in Reality, no inside
of words).[82] Like Karen's observation that unicorns exist in words,[83] the fictional Darwin asserts, "Un relato no es la realidad. Un relato está hecho de palabras, no de materia sólida. De palabras que se refieren a materia sólida pero no
lo son" (A narrative is not reality. A narrative is made of words, not solid matter.
Of words that refer to solid matter, but are not that themselves).[84]

A Science of Morality Inscribed in Life Itself

The novel's Darwin, recounting his conversation with Queen Victoria, explains
the process through which humans developed their narrative about the divine:
"Habían inventado una geografía imaginaria sobre la geografía real y la habían
poblado con seres imaginarios" (They had invented an imaginary geography over
the real geography and they populated it with imaginary beings).[85] In his search
for the divine, Berman's Darwin reverses this process, looking to reality to offer
insights into the nature of the metaphysical. The *Theological Autobiography* portrays Darwin's evolving view of God from an external force that acts upon a
mechanistic and inert nature to one where the divine is a non-supernatural vitality intrinsic to nature itself. The historical Darwin, while more agnostic than
his literary counterpart regarding a divine first cause, indeed attacked the idea
of an external design as contrary to all evidence: "There seems to be no more
design in the variability of organic beings and in the action of natural selection,

A SCIENCE OF GOOD AND EVIL   103

than in the course which the wind blows. Everything in nature is the result of
fixed laws."[86] In Berman's novel, Darwin's search for God is the search for
these fixed laws embedded within nature itself, which, taken together, would
represent an empirical counternarrative to Judeo-Christian morality, "una Ciencia del Bien y el Mal" (a Science of Good and Evil), as Darwin explains to Queen
Victoria.[87] However, a major stumbling block in Darwin's quest to any thetic
interpretation of natural selection is the question of biological altruism, the altru-
istic actions that occur frequently in social species that would harm the surviv-
ability of the individual and its offspring, seemingly contrary to the axiom of
survival of the fittest. We can affirm that the historical Darwin glosses over biological altruism in animals and obliquely addresses the question in humans,
describing examples of self-sacrificing "savages" who "were always ready to give
aid to each other and sacrifice themselves for the common good, would be victori-
ous over most other tribes; and this would be natural selection."[88] Darwin's example of altruism, derived from a colonial anthropological gaze on the "savage," a
human that straddles the space between animal and civilized man, actually reinforces an anthropocentric ordering as the traits that Darwin attributes for
within-group selection such as "tribes," "sacrifice," and "common good" are
human cultural constructs. This framework of within-group selection to explain
altruism was favored among neo-Darwinists for almost a century until challenged by the concept of kin selection proposed by William Hamilton in 1964.[89]
This gene-centered view of evolution, which explains altruism through the propagation of the shared gene rather than the individual organism, gained greater
cultural cachet with the publication of Richard Dawkins's best-selling *The Selfish Gene* in 1976. Berman's fictional Darwin, while obviously unaware of modern genetics, in a similar way looks for an explanation for altruism and morality
in nature itself, outside of traditional subjectivist and cultural constructs.

The fictional Darwin's observation that "las especies sociales son la respuesta
de la Naturaleza para suspender la lucha atroz por la existencia" (social species
are Nature's answer to suspend the atrocious struggle for existence) becomes a
turning point in his articulation of what he later terms the "leyes positivas" (positive laws) of Nature.[90] These laws, in comparison to the God-given Ten Commandments that provide the moral underpinning in Abrahamic monotheism, do
not seek to establish order upon nature from an exterior position.[91] Rather, these
laws, articulated by Darwin a posteriori, are inherent to matter itself, revealing an
agential and material vitality not dissimilar to Bennett's proposition that matter
in relation to other matter exercises an affective "force."[92] This "Moral Natural"
(Natural Morality), "más antigua que la Religión o el ser humano" (older than
Religion or human beings),[93] is articulated through a set of seventeen propositions embedded within the text of the *Theological Autobiography* that Darwin
later identifies by marking each with a roman numeral. In essence, they are an
amalgam of Darwin's known asseverations from *On the Origin of Species, The*

Descent of Man, and his *Autobiography* with a few creative interventions by Berman thrown in for good measure. Laws XVI and XVII summarize the general direction of this natural ethics, stating respectively, "Lo malo es lo que causa malestar general al grupo" (Bad is that which causes general discomfort to the group) and "Lo bueno es lo que causa bienestar general al grupo" (Good is that which causes general well-being to the group).[94] Many of the laws, like the preceding two, which intertextuality correspond with Alberto's explanation of morality in *El narco negocia con Dios* or the moral of several fables in *Matemáticas para la felicidad*, have clear implications when applied to human society. Law VIII, which mirrors Berman's pluralistic inclination, states, "Cuanta más variedad de anomalías, es decir de formas minoritarias, contenga una especie o grupo, más oportunidades hay para su sobrevivencia" (The more variety of anomalies, that is to say minority forms, that a species or group contains, the more opportunities there are for its survival).[95] Through these laws, Berman sketches how in natural selection a vital force emerges from matter acting upon matter, intra-relations that are neither bestowed by a supernatural being nor products of an anthropocentric rationalism.

To identify "God" as a vital force intrinsic to materiality itself, then, means that neither the Western theological narrative of religion nor the prevailing constructivist narrative of science can fully reconcile itself with reality. Berman provides what we could call Karen's/Darwin's "third way," a ciencia-fusión narrative that is self-reflexive by nature and seeks to reverse its gaze back to the materiality of nature itself. For the human to narrate that reality is always a provisional exercise as is illustrated throughout *La mujer que buceó* and *El dios de Darwin* and in Darwin's final positive law: "Así como la Tierra continuará rodando, así como las formas naturales continuarán variando, así el relato humano igual seguirá ajustándose y explayándose, y de cualquier forma, nunca será perfecto y nunca abarcará la vida entera" (Just as the Earth will continue to spin, just as natural forms will continue to vary, so the human story will continue to adjust and expand, and in any case, it will never be perfect and will never encompass all of life).[96] Far from a postmodern exploration of the futility of narratives, Berman's work to break the hold of anthropocentrism reveals ciencia-fusión's potential to provide glimpses into a post-Cartesian intra-relationality of all matter and, in the case of Darwin's positive laws, provides the contours of an ethical paradigm that promotes cooperation, dignity, and respect for life.

Un final natural para el capitalismo

In her ongoing series of columns for the newspaper *El Universal*, which began in 2016, Berman returns time and again to the ethical framework that her fictional Darwin articulated in *El dios de Darwin*. Through the frequent use of fables and tall tales, Berman mines the intersections of ethics, nature, and politics

A SCIENCE OF GOOD AND EVIL   105

to question and subvert the status quo, speaking truth to power regardless of political orientation.[97] In the collection *Matemáticas para la felicidad y otras fábulas* Berman brings together revised versions of many of her columns from 2016 and 2017, with the intention of sharing fables "sobre mi realidad y bajo el signo de la moral natural que he venido a abrazar en mi vida. Una moral que se depende del estudio de la Naturaleza" (about my reality and under the sign of the natural morality that I have come to embrace in my life. A morality that depends on the study of Nature).[98] These stories are where Berman's ethos, revealed in earlier works, engages with current events and personalities, critiquing neoliberal capitalism as the driver of economic injustice, political corruption, and ecological catastrophe. In many of the tales the natural world is held up as offering alternate ontologies to totalizing capitalism. In others Berman's focus on materiality denaturalizes the subjectivist dichotomy between person/property that sustains an insatiable extractivism and accumulation of property that is anathema to her new ethical framework. Through these short, witty fables Berman illustrates absurdities and challenges the totalizing logic of global capitalism that she contrasts with intraconnectivity in nature and the more-than-human world.

In addition to animals and fantastic creatures, many of Berman's fables feature fictionalized versions of characters ranging from Warren Buffett and Vladimir Putin to a hologram of the president of Mexico that fully takes on the duties of the office without anyone realizing it. John Nash, known to most through Russell Crowe's portrayal of him in the popular film *A Beautiful Mind*, features in several of the fables. In "Matemáticas para la felicidad" the narrator submits that Nash was awarded the Nobel Prize due to the rise of neoliberalism in the 1990s politics when economics had become a form of competitive game, for which the Nash Equilibrium was its central instrument.[99] Compared to his earlier neoliberal embrace of competitive game theory, after being diagnosed and treated for paranoid schizophrenia Nash reconsiders his theories as he is sustained by the selfless kindness of his wife and the university, which keeps him employed out of compassion. The competing models of compassion and competition in the story further develop and apply the ethical dictums stipulated earlier in *El dios de Darwin*. Comparing the social behavior among species, Nash speaks of how, in contrast to humanity's current Model of Scarcity, bees have developed over millennia a Model of Abundance in which the individual acts to add to the group's resources, with the respective outcomes being as such that "la escacez perpetúa la competencia, la abundancia perpetúa la felicidad" (scarcity perpetuates competition, abundance perpetuates happiness).[100] Nash's novel insights correspond to the fictional Darwin's positive law XV, where moral conduct works to halt competition, a clearly anticapitalistic precept given Mabel Moraña's observation that "la condición enemiga del capitalismo no es la de la escasez, sino la de la abundancia, ya que ésta hace tambalear la racionalidad del

106   SCIENCE FUSION IN CONTEMPORARY MEXICAN LITERATURE

mercado, siendo la carencia, real o artificial, la que mantiene en marcha la dinámica de productividad y consumo" (the enemy condition of capitalism is not that of scarcity, but that of abundance since it rattles the rationality of the market, as scarcity, either real or artificial, is what keeps the dynamics of productivity and consumption going).[101] In the story "El dinero desaparece" (Money Disappears), Nash strikes again, this time orchestrating a power outage that converts every numeral on electronic devices around the world to a zero. Nash's anarchistic act reduces the world's financial wealth to nothing, underscoring the immateriality of modern currency and markets, showing them to be another human construct projected onto a material real. It seems, then, that in many ways Berman's Nash embodies Deleuze and Guattari's nomadic schizophrenic, whose unique abilities allow him to resist oppressive power as his "is not the identity of capitalism, but on the contrary its difference, its divergence, and its death."[102]

The story "El fin del capitalismo" brings together several of Berman's memes related to Darwinian ethics, capitalism, the Anthropocene, and humanity's place in the world and marks a logical bookend to her decade's literary work. The humorously dystopic imagery of the final days of life on Earth as humanity knows it is juxtaposed with cheery language that conveys a future posthuman ethos where humanity has reoriented its place within the more-than-human world. Here, in the quest to secure more and more fossil fuels, a diver knocks an underwater ice column that leads to a domino effect of the world's seas rising fifteen meters in the span of days. While the cities flood and churches submerged under water fill with fish and dolphins (another repetition of the motif of "Darwinian temples"), the sixty-four richest people in the world board a transatlantic cruise ship that will become a Noah's Ark for the world's wealthiest until it sinks literally under the weight of the gold bars in its bowels. Berman's metaphor recalls countless examples throughout history and literature, but takes on a deeper meaning when viewed within her Darwinian ethical turn. Here again, the confluence of the material in the weight of the element gold and the immaterial value that humans project onto it conditions their perceived reality and threatens the survival of the species, from the fittest to the most unfit. The captain's log found years later in the depths of the sea reflects his astonishment at the idiocy of the passengers: "Siempre fue una ironía llamar a un planeta cubierto en tres cuartas partes de agua, La Tierra" (It always was an irony to call a planet covered in three-quarters with water, Earth).[103] Berman's critique is clear: humanity's failure to see reality as it truly is causes our remove from the more-than-human world and ultimately ensures the destruction of our species as well as much of the life on the planet. Moreover, the way that capitalism's metaphorical ship goes down brings yet another one of Berman's repeating memes to the foreground. As we have seen, *La mujer que buceó dentro del corazón del mundo* marks the literary beginning for Berman's Darwinian ethical turn by focusing on what her protagonist calls "la burbuja humana," a

A SCIENCE OF GOOD AND EVIL

place where logocentrism and Cartesian human detachment from nature are ordering principles. In this fable, the literal weight of capitalism creates one final bubble, as "el Independence no se fue a pique. Se hundió parejamente, de popa a proa, y del golpe, por el peso del oro, y formando en la superficie una burbuja de 300 metros de diámetro, que luego explotó con un ¡plop!" (the Independence didn't slowly go down to the bottom. She went down in one fell swoop, from stern to bow, and with the impact from the weight of the gold, formed a bubble three hundred meters in diameter on the surface, which then exploded with a plop!).[104] Sinking to the depths of the sea, capitalism and the Anthropocene end how they began, with an anthropocentrically produced bubble.

In her groundbreaking 1974 work *Feminism or Death* Françoise d'Eaubonne first introduced the term "ecofeminism." While I have not found evidence of Berman making reference to d'Eaubonne in any public forum, there are striking similarities between the French thinker's manifesto and Berman's ecological ethics. Citing the need for a thinking that transcends current ideologies, d'Eaubonne calls for a global "mutation of the totality."[105] Like her protagonist Karen who becomes the mutation of the species to forge a new pact with reality, Berman's Darwinian ethical turn proposes that for the survival of our species and, by extension, all life on the planet, humanity must move beyond existing narratives and reposition ourselves within the natural world. There we will find that we are not the center of the world but rather one element in an intraconnected reality. This idea of intraconnectivity and the act of writing from within a material existence allows works of ciencia-fusión, like Berman's, to articulate humanity's relationship with the world and the subsequent ethical implications in more robust ways. As Karen Barad argues, "Ethics cannot be about responding to the other as if the other is the radical outside to the self. Ethics is not a geometrical calculation; 'others' are not very far from 'us'; 'they' and 'we' are co-constituted and entangled through the very cuts 'we' help to enact."[106] For Berman, the crises of the Anthropocene are not solvable through a closer attention to or a more rigorous application of any morality that only reinforces the false dualism between humanity and nature. Instead, she pleads that we must reorient humanity's place in reality and emulate examples of cooperation, altruism, and commonality in the more-than-human world, themes that strikingly all feature in Maricela Guerrero's *El sueño de toda célula*, the topic of the next chapter. For Berman, the first step in a new environmental ethics is embracing, as does her fictional Darwin, that our species is but another mutation within an intraconnected reality.

CHAPTER 5

In Search of a New Language

AUTOPOIESIS AND THE ANTHROPOCENE
IN MARICELA GUERRERO'S *EL SUEÑO
DE TODA CÉLULA*

In June 2017 the taps in San Pedro y San Pablo Ayutla suddenly went dry, leaving the more than five thousand residents of the small town in Oaxaca without access to potable water. Unlike many places where overuse, poor resource management, and climate change have caused aquifers to become depleted, the freshwater spring that feeds the town, known as Jënanyëëj in Ayuujk Mixe, never stopped flowing. Instead, for months in the spring of 2017 tensions had been growing between Ayutla and the neighboring town of Tamazulápam del Espíritu Santo over access to the waters and finally erupted in violence when heavily armed residents of Tamazulápam raided and destroyed neighboring farms, fields, and infrastructure. When the aggrieved Ayutla farmers visited the contested area with state prosecutors, armed groups blocked the caravan's passage, first with rocks and machetes and then with high-caliber gunfire, severely injuring six and taking the life of thirty-five-year-old Luis Juan Guadalupe.[1] In the following months and years, the outreach and engagement of local activists, including the well-known linguist and advocate Yásnaya Aguilar, cast a spotlight on the plight of the people of Ayutla through the #AguaParaAyutlaYa campaign, which ultimately attracted the attention of prominent scholars, journalists, and cultural figures including Julieta Venegas and Juan Villoro. Aguilar argues that the crisis in Ayutla is the product not of a local dispute between indigenous peoples, as it is often framed by government officials, but of systemic racism and governmental complicity in violence that has an incredibly disproportionate impact on women.[2] In the face of governmental nonaction and violence by armed groups that use the kidnapping and rape of indigenous women among their tools of intimidation, the people of Ayutla would remain steadfast in their nonviolent reclamation of the dignity of life and the basic right for access to the water that springs from the earth. Aguilar affirms the determination of the community:

109

"A pesar de las múltiples voces que se han unido a la exigencia de agua, lo cierto es que a casi tres años de estas agresiones seguimos denunciando; nuestra voz, aunque con sed, no ha muerto" (Despite the many voices that have joined our demand for water, what's certain is that after almost three years of these aggressions we continue to denounce; our voice, even with thirst, has not died).[3] The people of Ayutla would have to wait almost four years to the day to reconnect to the waters of Jënanyëëj when a federal judge finally ruled that the town could regain access to the spring.

The natural wellspring in the town of Ayutla is one of many streams and flows that reach their confluence in Maricela Guerrero's *El sueño de toda célula* (*The Dream of Every Cell*) (2018), where fluxes of life, communication, and even packs of wolves offer alternatives to ongoing extractivism and ecological destruction. The forty-three poems that make up Guerrero's book vary in tone and form, from free verse to prose poetry, yet are all connected thematically, advancing threads of a cohesive story when read in their collectivity. Adding to these flows, the poetic voice frames the collection through the fond memories of her teacher, Maestra Olmedo (Ms. Olmedo), who taught her and her classmates about scientific knowledge and gave them a language and the tools with which to understand the natural world more deeply. Through the knowledge and wisdom that Maestra Olmedo imparted on her pupils, the poet contemplates society's relationship with the more-than-human world, exposing the destructive drives and devastation of what she terms "imperio" (empire) while illuminating a space for resistance and forward-looking dreams of care and communion to flourish. While several motifs like the mother wolf and the tree-sitting protestor tie the poems together, the concept of flow, through communication and perpetual becoming, is the thread that runs through the poems themselves and shows humans to be part of much more expansive and intraconnected networks of life. In my analysis, I contend that Ms. Olmedo's lesson and the book's recurrent phrase—that "El sueño de toda célula es devenir células" (The dream of every cell is to become cells)—can be read as a reflection on the concept of autopoiesis, essentially the capacity for life, from the cell up to complex living systems, to produce and maintain itself by creating its own parts or components. By applying the concept of autopoiesis to Guerrero's unique portrayal of life, I demonstrate how *El sueño de toda célula* places humans and the more-than-human world within greater social and ecological systems to contest the destruction of extractivism while offering alternative ways of becoming where all living things have space to breathe. In particular, Guerrero's reterritorialization of language—both human and more-than-human—offers a place to dream of commonality and trans-species kinship while providing a framework of resistance to an unsustainable system that is destroying all forms of life on earth.

Science, Language, and Lessons in Care

While Maricela Guerrero's poetry is diverse in its themes—ranging from the utterances of macaws to the extended metaphor of traveling by train in Africa—it is at its core a poetry that mediates the bonds between bodies and language. From the internal and external nebulae of *Se llaman nebulosas* (*They're Called Nebulae*, 2010) to the inexpressible dark matter that gives impulse to our bodies in *Peceras* (*Fishbowls*, 2013), Guerrero has frequently drawn on scientific concepts to explore language and the interconnectivity of human and more-than-human bodies. In this way *El sueño de toda célula*, her ninth published collection, is an extension of this ongoing work, as it takes up and redefines ideas of language to reconceptualize the human as part of internal and external networks of life. Intersectionality is central in *El sueño de toda célula*, which Elena Gómez del Valle describes as "un libro de poesía de protesta transversal" (a book of transversal protest poetry), in which the author critiques climate change, irresponsible consumption, and the systemic rejection of balance and harmony at both the cellular and ecosystemic levels.[4] Ignacio Ballester Pardo notes how this work gives the impression of being an essay or an encyclopedic treatise that engages expressions of colloquial speech in order to "desautomatizarlas y generar la narración de una historia en la que el sujeto poético va reproduciéndose en contacto con demás células, voces, visiones" (deautomatize them and generate the narration of a story in which the poetic subject reproduces herself in contact with other cells, voices, visions).[5] Similarly, Ignacio Ruiz-Pérez indicates how Guerrero utilizes language and discursive strategies to reveal greater interconnectivities, remarking that "lo que más llama la atención en la poesía de Maricela Guerrero es la mezcla y la disolución de fronteras textuales, y el descentramiento del discurso poético para construir un espacio propio de articulación cuya dicción rizomática y acéntrica desterritorializa lenguajes e ideologías" (what is most striking in Maricela Guerrero's poetry is the mixing and dissolution of textual borders, and the decentering of poetic discourse to build its own space of articulation whose rhizomatic and acentric diction deterritorializes languages and ideologies).[6] We can therefore affirm that, like the Deleuze-Guattarian rhizome, Guerrero's exploration of language opens into multiplicities demonstrating how "a language is never closed upon itself."[7] By resisting structures of domination inherent in unitary expression, Guerrero's poetry overturns the epistemological underpinnings of the language of "empire" and makes visible the false foundations of what Walter Mignolo and Catherine Walsh term the "colonial matrix of power."[8] In *El sueño de toda célula*, the language of cells, animals, and trees contrasts with the deterritorializing language of empire in order to denaturalize and transculturate its representational foundations, offering new ways of being that embrace the true interdependent nature of all materiality.

The epistemological and ontological challenges that *El sueño de toda célula* presents are representative of larger trends in Mexican and Latin American eco-literature within ciencia-fusión and beyond. Gisela Heffes argues that Latin American ecocriticism, while sharing similar goals and strategies with literature around the globe, necessarily must differ to provide novel ways of addressing the crises of the present with an autochthonous discourse tied to nature and its exploitation incorporating local exigencies and recuperating indigenous and other marginalized cosmogonies.[9] Laura Barbas-Rhoden observes the emergence in recent decades of works of Latin American literature that reconfigure natural space through a "discourse of nature" that is a literary response to neoliberalism and part of a broader critique of economic systems of subjugation.[10] Ecological devastation is systemically tied into greater racial, ethnic, and linguistic subjugation in Latin America, and for Macarena Gómez-Barris extractivism in this context references "the dramatic material change to social and ecological life that underpin this arrangement."[11] What is more, *El sueño de toda célula* taps into the longtime tradition in Latin American literature to utilize plants and vegetal life to address questions within human culture. Lesley Wylie describes how the "recourse to the language of plants in order to grapple with questions of cultural identity and expression is recurrent in Spanish American literature, where the pervasiveness of botanical imagery indicates the defining role of the natural world and enduring concern about the relationship between people and plants."[12]

Within the literary context of Mexico, we situate *El sueño de toda célula* within a growing number of works of ecological poetry that map alternative geographies or timescales that Carolyn Fornoff identifies as "planetary poetics," through which "Mexican poets broach matters of planetary concern in ways that reach beyond national borders and even the bounds of species. These spatial, temporary, and ontological jumps are a defining characteristic of contemporary Mexican poetry concerned with environmental themes."[13] While incorporating the tradition of ecological awareness and call for alarm in precursors such as José Emilio Pacheco and Homero Aridjis, the newer voces of planetary poetics like Isabel Zapata and Karen Villeda eschew the former's "melancholic, apocalyptic register" in part to avoid the perceived abrasiveness of and distrust toward environmentalism that has often counteracted its intended impact in Mexico.[14] Similarly, the tone of *El sueño de toda célula* balances a sharp critique of extractivism and its culture of death with an optimistic affirmation of life and the possibility for a more just future. Robin Myers observes that the poems in Guerrero's collection "open themselves with warmth and compassion" and shares that in writing the book Guerrero "wanted to make poems that would feel inviting to the people she sustains intimate conversations with in her everyday life: her parents, her children."[15] The entire collection is framed as a conversation of sorts, with several poems that address second-person interlocutors and others that speak from a first-person plural to recollect and reflect on the lessons of the poet's beloved childhood science teacher. Furthermore, many of the poems present themselves as lullabies and fables, bringing a childlike quality in both their verbiage and outlook on the world. Guerrero shares how, in composing *El sueño de toda célula*, "yo más bien lo que quise recuperar fue un lenguaje quizá un poco más esperanzado de reconectar con la forma en cómo uno conectaba con los árboles en la infancia" (really what I wanted to recuperate was a language, perhaps a little more hopeful, of reconnecting with the way in which one would connect with trees in childhood).[16] The book, which Guerrero explains was originally titled *Arbolitos* (Little Trees) after her experiences of getting in touch with trees as a child in Mexico City,[17] invites readers to see the world through the eyes of a child in order to defamiliarize the language and the framework with which we see our place in the world. Although much of *El sueño de toda célula* is ostensibly about trees, Guerrero's innovative treatment of the multiplicitous interconnectivities in both language and the more-than-human world dispels any notion of what Deleuze and Guattari would call arborescent thinking, as knowledge sprouts in a rhizomatic fashion within and among the poems of the collection.[18] In this way, *El sueño de toda célula* is also a work about opening a space to reimagine the world. Guerrero connects the physical space of the forest or even the empty lot next door to more figurative spaces where life can flourish, or as the poet states in the book's epigraph, "Célula quiere decir hueco: / como una hoja para ser escrita" (Cell means space: / like a leaf, a page to write on).[19]

The image of the leaf in the book's epigraph is representative of the overall movement in the collection as the blank leaf waiting to be written orients itself toward future possibilities but also allows the poet to move backward in time, recalling how she learned of the natural world. The titles of the book's four sections—"Maestra Olmedo" (Ms. Olmedo), "Reino *Plantae*" (Kingdom *Plantae*), "Lobos: Lecciones de cuidado" (Wolves: Lessons in Care), "Reino *Linguae*" (Kingdom *Linguae*)—underscore the complementarity and continual movement between the empirical study of life through scientific taxonomies and the nurturing care of life through the actions of maternal figures that unfold throughout the collection. The book's first poem, "De la voz" (On Voice), introduces many of the book's recurring images in a prose-like stream of consciousness that flows backward toward the idyllic time of nostalgia, as each action of remembering shoots toward other memories in a rhizomatic movement through topics and time:

> La recolección decía con una voz que subía y bajaba del grave al grave al agudo agudísimo: agudeza de botánica de bióloga, oropéndola de la recolección decíamos: anotar el nombre común y la forma de hojas recordar: yo recuerdo un patio de árboles centrales yo recuerdo un aire fresco: yo recuerdo, decía cuando esto eran milpas cuando se transitaba en trajineras: las hojas,

114   SCIENCE FUSION IN CONTEMPORARY MEXICAN LITERATURE

recuerden que no había sustracciones; y recuerdo idílicamente, aunque puede que me falle la memoria.[20]

The recollection spoke in a voice that rose and fell from low to low to the highest high: the heights of botany of biology, the golden oriole of memory we said: jotting down common names and the shapes of leaves, remember: I remember a yard with trees in the middle I remember a cool breeze: I remember said the voice when all of this was milpas when people moved about in wooden boats: the leaves, remember, there was no subtractions; and I remember blissfully, although my memory may fail me.

The themes introduced in this first poem—scientific knowledge, the considerate collection and study of specimens, and the subtraction of life—emerge from a rhizomic web of memories and recollections where the distinction between the "I" of the poet and the "I" of Maestra Olmedo blur into each other. Furthermore, the phrasing in this prose poem undermines the univocality of the themes themselves. When we compare Robin Myers's expert English-language translation with the original, Ruiz-Pérez's assertion that Guerrero decenters language becomes even clearer through her use of multivalent terms such as "sustracción," which is both a subtraction and a theft, and "recolección," which is both the act of collection as in scientific study as well as that of remembering. In this way, each phrase of prose unfolds without clear punctuation or contextualization, rendering multiple meanings to the language employed. The first phrase offers several possibilities for the grammatical subject including the "la recolección" as in Myers's translation or conceivably that of Maestra Olmedo as the poet recalls the first words of her teacher's lesson on scientific collection. This careful employment of polysemy is a feature of Guerrero's poetry and in *El sueño de toda célula* it conveys how scientific study, language, and even human coexistence with the more-than-human world offer contradictory possibilities: either that of nurturing and caring for life or that of distancing from and destruction of the world through subtraction.

As we will see, in *El sueño de toda célula* language expands beyond acts of semiotic communication. The first poems of the book trace the ways that Maestra Olmedo introduced her pupils to a new way of seeing and conceiving the world through strange terms that illuminated connections and new depths to reality, as in the poem "La Maestra Olmedo" (Ms. Olmedo), where the poet explains, "La maestra Olmedo enseñaba ciencias y nos dio las bases de la taxonomía y un método para recolectar, resguardar y clasificar especies vegetales. También nos dijo que un árbol no es individuo sino que forman una red" (Ms. Olmedo was the science teacher and she taught us the basics of taxonomy and a method to collect, protect, and classify plant species. She also told us that a tree isn't an individual, but part of a network).[21] Teaching the students words like Linnaeus, mitochondria, and dicotyledon, Maestra Olmedo employs the language of science in a spirit of reverence for the complexity of life, a space for rapprochement through the care and study of the natural world. Science allows the students to learn of other types of language such as the methods of communication among trees or ever-deepening webs of intra-activity at the molecular level of the earth as when the poet remembers how Maestra Olmedo "con su voz de subida y bajada nos llevó al lenguaje de humus de nitrógeno de nutrientes y de la canción de cuna bajo los lentes del microscopio" (led us with her rising and falling voice into the language of humus of nitrogen of nutrients and lullabies under the microscope lens).[22] The striking manner in which the poet juxtaposes images of the workings of the scientific method and technical terminology with lullabies under the lens of the microscope suggests, as is typical in ciencia-fusión, a metaphorical transposition of the otherwise empirical scientific language of the poem. Just as Maestra Olmedo is a nurturing maternal presence for the students as they grow to learn about the world through science, she teaches the students that the sole purpose of life is to create life. Using the human metaphor of dreaming to impart the lasting lesson that becomes the overarching theme of Guerrero's book, Maestra Olmedo illuminates the processes that bring forth life and the resulting interconnectivity between humans and all living things. The poet recalls, "Y un día nos dijo que el sueño de toda célula es devenir células, y millones de ellas participan de esta: nuestra respiración" (And one day she told us that the dream of every cell is to become more cells, and millions of them take part in this: our breath).[23] The becoming of cells into other cells produces the perpetual motion of breathing—in essence the activity of life—and highlights that in *El sueño de toda célula* life is less a thing that something *has* and more a something that living things *do* in a perpetual drive of becoming.

Autopoiesis: The Making of the Dream of Every Cell

Maestra Olmedo's lesson about cells becoming cells is remarkably similar to autopoiesis, the concept neurobiologists Humberto Maturana and Francisco Varela developed to describe how a living system produces and maintains itself through the creation of its own parts or components. It is through autopoietic processes that these systems continually self-realize at every living moment.[24] Central to Maturana and Varela's conceptualization is the idea of perpetual relationality among all living things—from single cells to complex organisms—and their environments. We can observe autopoietic processes throughout the poems of *El sueño de toda célula* as in the poem "Miedo" (Fear), which begins with "Células, siempre se trata de células: de respiración, intercambios, reproducción y diferenciación" (Cells, it's always about cells: about breath, exchange, reproduction, differentiation),[25] or when the poet explains the process of breathing as "ardor y combustión" (ardor and combustion) in the poem "Pulmones" (Lungs):

> que así en algunos modos se respira:
> y el dióxido de carbono
> es a la vez requerimiento para producir azúcares,

clorofila y verdor: metabolismos, transformaciones
de sustancias en sonoridades y azar.[26]

that this is in some sense how we breathe:
and carbon dioxide
is a simultaneous requirement for producing sugars, chlorophyll,
and green: metabolisms, transformations of substances into
sonorousness and chance.

Of note is the way that the poet again combines chemical and biological processes with metaphorical products through sonorousness and chance metonymically representing life as process. Moreover, by expressing the process of respiration and photosynthesis as an intrinsic link between animal and plant kingdoms, the poem binds the autopoiesis of all living beings in a collective intraaction of breathing that occurs on a planetary scale.

Like the entangled relations between plants, animals, chemicals, and biological processes, autopoiesis is dependent upon such interconnectivities, what Maturana and Varela term "structural coupling," that is, the "recurrent interactions leading to the structural congruence between two (or more) systems."[27] Like the process of photosynthesis described in "Pulmones," these structural couplings form a network of actions, which generate phenomena that no isolated organism could generate on its own.[28] As part of these networks of coordination of actions, autopoietic organisms, including individual cells, practice effective actions such as allowing only certain molecules to enter the cell, expanding the definition of cognition as "not the acquisition of knowledge by a 'knowing subject,' or an epiphenomenal by-product of neuronal activity in the brain, but rather the organizing activity of living systems (i.e., their autopoiesis). This activity manifests itself from the dynamics of the individual cell all the way up to the self-regulatory capacities of the planet."[29] Maturana and Varela argue, then, "*Living systems are cognitive systems, and living as a process is a process of cognition.* This statement is valid for all organisms, with and without a nervous system."[30] The coordinated conduct among organisms involved in structural coupling is the action of communication, and therefore, as Paul Bains explains, "communication exists in a social field in a flow of interactions, not 'in' an individual agent."[31] To view communication as a key component of autopoiesis allows us to consider communication as process, opening up the concept of language—both human and more-than-human—as also occurring outside of the domain of neural cognition.

In *El sueño de toda célula* flows of communicatory interactions between cells or even vegetal organisms disrupt what constitutes language as in "¿El abedul y el abeto?" (The Birch and the Fir), where the poet expounds in essay-like form

IN SEARCH OF A NEW LANGUAGE

on a scientist from Canada who asked herself exactly how birch and fir trees communicate among themselves:

> Planteó un problema y lo resolvió con un método y un orden de investigación. Resulta que el abedul y el abeto no sólo se hablaban en el idioma del carbono sino en nitrógeno y fósforo y agua y en signos defensivos, en alelos químicos y hormonas a través de redes de hongos diminutos y bacterias.
>
> Resulta que hay familias de árboles que debajo de las ramas en su lengua de átomos, moléculas y enlaces se convierten en formas novedosas de la vida: fósforo, nitrógeno, carbono; que se reparten los nutrientes, que se cuidan su crecimiento y se procuran; aunque a veces transmiten información equivocada, es el azar y la contingencia: son las células, lo que no sabemos; por eso hay que dejar ventanas abiertas.[32]

She posed a problem and solved it with a research method. As it turns out, the birch and the fir converse not only in the language of carbon, but also in nitrogen and phosphorous and water and defensive signs, in allelochemicals and hormones through networks of tiny mushrooms and bacteria.

It turns out there are families of trees who, beneath their branches, in their language of atoms, molecules, and bonds, become new forms of life: phosphorous, nitrogen, carbon; that they distribute nutrients to each other, that they take care of and tend to each other as they grow; although they can transmit mistaken information, that's chance and possibility; cells are what we don't know; that's why we should keep the windows open.

The language of the fir and the birch is not an abstract activity, nor does it involve representation. Instead, the network of communication takes place in the domain of material relations, what the poet terms their "lengua de átomos, moléculas y enlaces" (language of atoms, molecules and links), moving the act of languaging from the domain of the organism to that of atoms and molecules from which it emerges. In particular, the poet emphasizes the collective nature of these transformative actions that create life-utilizing anthropomorphic metaphors such as "familias de árboles" (families of trees) that "se cuidan" (take care and tend to each other).[33] Following the inspiration of Maestra Olmedo, who combined scientific discourse with poetic metaphor, the poet blends extrinsic language and metaphors of care to further illuminate the connectivity among fir and birch trees and their environments. These metaphors of collective nurturing describe the intrinsic language of plants, "the modes of communication and articulation used by vegetal species to negotiate ecologically with their biotic and abiotic environments,"[34] and reflect how ontogenetic processes of development and growth can occur only within larger organic-inorganic networks that produce life. Autopoietic cognition, the organizing activity of living systems, then upends the

118   SCIENCE FUSION IN CONTEMPORARY MEXICAN LITERATURE

paradigm of communication as interaction, as can be seen in the intra-active network of birch, fir, funguses, and individual molecules that produces transformation and brings forth new life. Reminiscent of Barad's argument that intra-action is always material-discursive, cognition and communication, in this light, are not the sole domain of humans or even complex organisms. Instead, effective actions and life itself emerge at microscopic levels, or, as the poet ruminates, "son las células, lo que no sabemos" (cells are what we don't know).[35]

LANGUAGE, EMPIRE, AND SUBTRACTION

In contrast to the communication and different languages in the more-than-human world, what the poet terms "la lengua del imperio" (the language of empire) works as an antagonistic and destructive force. In a possible allusion to the etymology of the cell as "a space," in the poem "Datos" (Data) the language of the empire is described as information that fills both physical and social spaces, encoding them according to its own logic:

> La lengua del imperio de nuestros días está cifrada en estadísticas, en ríos de datos fluyendo por redes de energía y siliconas, sales: que acumulan reglas y multas y cárcel a los que van en contra del imperio y a nuestra forma establ-ecemos formas de resistirnos a esa lengua: a veces nos sale, a veces no.
>
> El imperio habla en monedas y talentos que absorben y cercan ríos que destrozan territorios y extraen minerales y ríos y personas: que disuelven, trozan y acumulan.
>
> Intervienen procesos metabólicos: sustraen.
>
> Acumular es una lengua imperiosa.
>
> Competir es una tarea imperial.[36]

The imperial language of our present day is encoded in statistics, in rivers of data flowing through webs of energy and silicone and salt: amassing rules and fines and prison to those who oppose the empire and in our own ways we wage resistance against this language: sometimes it works, sometimes it doesn't.

The empire speaks in currencies and talents that absorb and fence in rivers that demolish land and strip-mine minerals and rivers and people: that dissolve, cut up, accumulate.

They intervene in metabolic processes: they subtract.

Accumulation is an imperious language.

Competition is an imperial task.

While the language of the more-than-human world is one of communication and networks of life, the language of empire is one of subtraction through individual accumulation, echoing the Darwinian-ethical propositions that Sabina Berman puts forth in her recent works. The language of empire in *El sueño de toda célula* also harkens to Michael Hardt and Antonio Negri's concept of "empire" as the emerging globalized economic and political configurations that function as a decentered and deterritorializing apparatus of rule.[37] In essence, Guerrero's language of empire is the logic of extractive capitalism, known in Spanish as *extractivismo*, which Gómez-Barris explains is "an economic system that engages in thefts, borrowings, and forced removals, violently reorganizing social life as well as the land by thieving resources from Indigenous and Afro-descendent territories."[38] The verbs that the poetic voice uses to describe the language of empire all refer to stops and disruptions to natural flows, as the logic of extraction cuts, removes, closes off, partitions, and subtracts in a never-ending drive to accumulate wealth.

In particular, it is the language of the empire that imposes new meaning and ceases effective flows of communication. In the following stanza, the poet describes the pain of extractivism that is grafted upon bodies:

> Imponer es la masmédula de esto que hasta ahora vislumbro como lengua imperial inserta y dolorosa: aguda, punzante: imponer es una forma de dolor que se introyecta y envenena.
> Hace pensar en sustracciones.[39]

> Imposition is the moremarrow of what I've glimpsed only now as a painful grafted imperial language: sharp and piercing: imposition is a kind of pain that pollutes and introjects.
> It makes me think of subtractions.

To describe the imposition of the language of the empire onto the world, the poet invokes the image of the "masmédula," a clear allusion to Oliverio Girondo's avant-garde *En la masmédula* (*In the Moremarrow*, 1954), where the Argentine poet overpowers and blurs both the mimetic and lexicographic limits between words and reality.[40] The unconscious and hidden ways that the language of empire introjects itself into everything, including both the metaphorical and physical body of the poetic voice, give its deterritorialization an air of naturality. However, as Susan Antebi argues, to view bodies marked by difference—what the poet here calls "inscriptions" and "subtractions"—we better perceive the "permeability between bodies and their environments, between human and nonhuman bodies, and between the material and the social."[41] Rebecca Janzen argues that marginal bodies, through "their illnesses, disabilities, or other unusual lived experiences suggest that they do not fit in to the Mexican state's vision of its national body," yet they conversely "allow us to imagine an alternative non-hegemonic collective body that might challenge this state."[42] Like the grafting and subtractions of the language of empire onto bodies both human and nonhuman, extractivism and dispossession depend upon the rhetoric of modernity that creates separate ontological entities such as Nature, which then becomes a resource to transform, manage, and exploit.[43] As we have seen in other works of ciencia-fusión including Berman's Karen novels and Ignacio Padilla's short fiction, these ontological shifts are often viewed as the paradigmatic dark side of the Scientific Revolution, highlighting these authors' often paradoxical stance that embraces much knowledge produced through scientific work while criticizing many of its philosophical underpinnings and disciplinary matrices. In *El sueño de toda célula* Guerrero employs scientific thought in a decolonial way, emphasizing the many ways the language of empire works upon bodies both physical and imagined, deterritorializing humans from greater networks and systems of living, essentially severing human and more-than-human organisms from each other.

In the poem "La lengua del imperio" (The Language of Empire), the poetic voice expounds upon how languaging in regard to nature has been a critical tool in colonialism, citing Charlemagne's eighth-century *Capitullari de villis* that stipulates the number and variety of fruit trees, herbs, and the like that must be planted in conquered territories through a language precisely adapted to the dispositions of the growing empire. In this way, "La lengua del imperio es la lengua de nombrar reinos, especies, subespecies y la forma de las hojas: patronímicos: la lengua del imperio exige lo imposible: los subordinados al imperio interiorizan las reglas y asumen que esa es la forma, aunque también alimentan angustia" (The language of empire is the language of naming kingdoms, species, subspecies, and leaf shapes: patronymics: the language of empire demands the impossible: imperial subjects internalize the rules and accept them as the proper shape, although they also feed distress).[44] In clear contrast with the warm way that the poet recalls Maestra Olmedo's lessons on scientific classification, within the frame of language of the empire, the action of differentiation through taxonomies and nomenclature becomes a tool of division and mastery, what Mary Louise Pratt would call "totalizing classificatory schemas."[45] Similar to what Aníbal Quijano conceives as relations of domination that come to be considered "natural" within the coloniality of power,[46] the codification of differences in the language of empire is a tool of domination instead of contemplation. These artificial cuts, to extend Barad's concept of the term, break the relations between humans and the more-the-human because "en la lengua del imperio se rompen vínculos entre redes de plantas y ciclos y personas" (in the language of empire, the bonds connecting plants and cycles and people are broken).[47] The poetic voice's use of polysyndeton underscores these chains of interconnectivity that conceivably extend themselves beyond even the concepts enumerated, drawing attention to the ways in which the language of empire disrupts autopoietic processes of life.

We see Guerrero's embrace of polysemy in the example of classification and differentiation. Within the language of empire, they are tools of subtraction to facilitate the mastery over nature in "una carrera por la incomunicación" (a race for incommunication).[48] Likewise, the poetic voice contrasts the allegory of competition with that of cooperation, observing that "en la lengua del imperio no se trata de reconocer que una célula proviene de otra célula sino de determinar qué célula llegó primero" (the language of empire doesn't care about recognizing that a cell comes from another cell; it only wants to know which cell came first).[49] In the framework of competition, the cell comes to a static finality at the end of a race, contrary to viewing the purpose of the cell's existence as one of dynamic becoming. Following Maestra Olmedo's example, scientific language and classification can also work as a tool for reterritorialization when applied in a spirit of care. Studying the cell as autopoiesis opens new ways to reaffirm the intraconnectivity of humans with the more-than-human world. The more expansive definition of cognition that the framework of autopoiesis provides "comes to assist decolonial thinking in its endeavor of reducing Western knowledge (scientific, philosophical, theological) to size and opening it up to pluriversal epistemic ontologies."[50] The poetic voice reminds us, "En la lengua del imperio un microorganismo no deviene microorganismo sino artefacto adosado a los objetivos del imperio" (In the language of empire, a microorganism doesn't become a microorganism; it becomes an artifact adhered to the empire's objectives).[51] The stark contrast between the perpetual autopoietic process of cells becoming cells and the cell as artifact or stable thing suggests that anthropocentric language itself can obscure the vitality of the world at the molecular level. By using the language of science to open up multiplicities that were paradoxically obscured in that same discourse, Maestra Olmedo puts into action Héctor Hoyos's assertion that "extractivism continues in language, and so in language it must be, at least partially, dispelled."[52]

Ballester Pardo argues that in *El sueño de toda célula* Guerrero uses colloquial expressions of language to deautomatize them as we can see when the poetic voice explores the last name "Olmedo" (which translates to "elm grove" in English). The poetic voice recalls the root word "olmo" (elm), and its usage in the popular turn of phrase "pedir peras al olmo," literally to "ask for pears from an elm tree," akin to the idiomatic expression in English "to get blood from a turnip/rock/stone." From this turn of phrase, the poet puts forth a meditation on language, history, and genealogy, noting that surnames with trees in them are ancient. After tracing linguistic genealogies that become rhizomatic networks of connectivity between people and their relationship with the earth, the poet states, "Rastrear apellidos es una forma útil de tender las redes que involucran a personas y otras personas" (Tracing the roots of names is a useful way to weave the web that connects people to other people).[53] This deeper understanding of the connectivity between people and agrarian words such as "olmedo" defamiliarizes the deterritorialization that the language of empire obscures. In this manner, the poet connects her teacher's last name with the ability to wish for the seemingly impossible within the logic of extractivism:

> La maestra de biología tenía un apellido de un conjunto de árboles que no dan peras:
>
> historias y formas de clasificación que entonces no sabíamos cuánto nos harían falta para recuperar y crear nuevas redes que nos protegieran de las sustracciones.[54]

> The biology teacher was named after a group of trees where pears will never grow:
>
> stories and forms of classification we didn't yet realize how urgently we'd need to recover and weave new webs to protect us from subtraction.

The language of science, in Maestra Olmedo's hands, is a means to move closer to the world in all its complexity and interconnectivity. By giving her students the ability to establish connections between organisms and to understand how life emerges through the dream of every cell, she lays a foundation for forms to not only recuperate networks but also imagine and create new human–more-than-human networks through a process of transculturation. Like proverbially getting pears from an elm tree, what seems impossible in the language of the empire is actually quite possible in the language of cells in their continual process of becoming.

In the language of cells, becoming is movement in a constant flow of life. In contrast, in the language of empire, movement is a race or a competition, a drive to extract and accumulate at any cost. The poem "Hidrocarburos" (Hydrocarbons) addresses the force of extractivism, opening with a first stanza that rings almost of a Futurist manifesto, with aggressive and violent imagery of machines in perpetual motion. The poet conflates units of force such as newtons, dynes, and volts with energy in calories and electromagnetic flow in amperes along with commodified minerals and hydrocarbons, joining in a rush of displacements of capital, data, and people. These metaphors of movement of subtraction are ultimately contrasted through both the poem's form and the starkly different tone of the couplet that closes it, as can best be appreciated by reproducing the poem in its entirety, including its spacing:

> Hidrocarburos
>
> En tanto que motores de cuatro tiempos con pistones: impulso: velocidad y fuerza: desplazamientos que empujan territorios e ideas de progreso que hoy son nodos de información y publicidad de magnitudes:
>
> Caballos de fuerza, calorías, dinas, newtons, amperes, voltios, toneladas equivalentes de petróleo en carbón: millones de dólares de euros monedas y magnitudes de energía, lingotes de oro: reservas internacionales de óxido de silicio y germano.

IN SEARCH OF A NEW LANGUAGE   123

Y amplias cantidades de información para que seamos una masa de datos engaños coloridos y ajenos que abren abismos de comunicación entre comunidades, que determinan atributos y arrojan personas, plantas y animales de su casa.

Industrias y quehaceres que atraen luchas por la respiración y bufan, chirrían, alarman, rugen, roen, rasgan: hidrocarburos para la alimentación de máquinas feroces y inabarcables.

A veces detenerse
  es otra forma de fluir.[55]

Hydrocarbons

As four-stroke motors with pistons: thrust: speed and force: displacements that shove territories and ideas of progress that are now nodes of information and advertising for magnitudes:

Workhorses, calories, dines, newtons, amps, volts, equivalent tons in petroleum in carbon: millions of dollars of euros currencies and magnitudes of energy, gold ingots: international reserves of oxide of silicon and germanium.

And vast quantities of information to make us a mass of data deceits colorful and external to us that open abysses of communication between communities, that determine attributes and expel people, plants, and animals from their homes.

Tasks and industries attracting struggles for breath and snort, screech, startle, roar, gnaw, scratch: hydrocarbons for the nourishment of fierce and unfathomable machines.

Sometimes to stop
  is another way to flow.

The first four stanzas convey acceleration with enumerations of nouns and verbs that fire off in quick succession with an almost breathless quality. The metonymic ferocious machines that displace and destroy take on animal-like qualities, roaring and scratching and displacing the beings that carry out

124   SCIENCE FUSION IN CONTEMPORARY MEXICAN LITERATURE

these actions as part of their living. Like the "luchas por la respiración," the spacing before the final stanza draws on the poet's prior pleas for a space to breathe. In contrast with the language of empire, the poetic voice reterritorializes what it means to stop and flow. While the unending and destructive drive for extraction through flows of energy and capital creates fissures and disrupts flows of life, the act of simply stopping to contemplate, imagine, and dream opens up a space to breathe, allowing the process of becoming within and among all living things.

Like the lesson that "the dream of every cell is to become cells," the phrase that "to stop is another way to flow" appears throughout the book, forming complementary principles in a new language of life. In "Preguntas" (Questions), the poet takes up these ideas and ponders the role of poetry in the struggle to foster a culture of life:

> ¿Escribimos poemas para preservar la especie?
> Escribimos poemas y trazamos rutas para
> transmitir una información que muestre cómo
> seguir la vocación de alegría:
> luciérnagas
> bacterias luminosas.
> Echarse al lomo de la loba bosque arriba.
> Detener es otra forma de fluir.[56]

> Do we write poems to save the species?
> We write poems and map routes
> to convey information that teaches us
> to follow joy as a vocation:
> fireflies
> luminous bacteria.
> To nestle against the she-wolf's back on the mountainside.
> To stop is another way to flow.

The poetic voice conceives of poetry as a space to breathe and to territorialize the world. Like Maestra Olmedo, poetry provides a language with which to appreciate and care for life, literally and figuratively finding illumination in the more-than-human world. In this way, the poetic voice proposes that poetry allows us to explore what Gómez-Barris calls "life otherwise," "the emergent and heterogenous forms of living that are not about destruction or mere survival within the extractive zone, but about the creation of emergent alternatives."[57] As much as *El sueño de toda célula* is a denunciation of extractivism, it is also a guidebook on alternative languages of commonality and cooperation, recuperating and imagining different ways of becoming.

IN SEARCH OF A NEW LANGUAGE

Reclaiming Language, Embracing Fear, and Nurturing Life

In the section "Lecciones" (Lessons) Guerrero acknowledges the real-life stories of care and generosity that she consulted when composing the poems of *El sueño de toda célula*. These stories inform the narrative threads that run throughout the book including the rerelease of wolves into Yellowstone National Park, the story of Julia Butterfly Hill who sat in a giant California sequoia to prevent it from being felled, and the Russian scientist Nikolai Vavilov who created the world's largest seed bank and his fellow botanists who died of hunger protecting its archive of life. Among these stories of activism and environmentalist triumph, Guerrero highlights the water crisis in San Pedro y San Pablo Ayutla. For many, the face of mobilization and resistance in the town has been Yásnaya Aguilar, who demanded justice in a speech before Mexico's congress in the Cámara de diputatos. Aguilar delivered her speech titled "Nëwemp, Ja nëëj jëts ja ää ayuujk" (Mexico: Water and Word) in Ayuujk Mixe to connect her language with the more-than-human world. Accusing the Mexican state of complicity in the cultural, political, and natural crises affecting her region, she declared,

> Son la tierra, el agua, los árboles los que nutren la existencia de nuestras lenguas. Bajo un ataque constante de nuestro territorio, ¿cómo se revitalizará nuestra lengua? Nuestras lenguas no mueren, las matan. El Estado mexicano las ha borrado. En pensamiento único, la cultura única, el Estado único, con el agua de su nombre, las borra.[58]

> It's the earth, water, trees that nurture the existence of our languages. With our territory under a constant attack, how will our language be revitalized? Our languages don't die, they are killed. The Mexican State has erased them. In singular thinking, singular culture, the singular State, with the water of its name, erases them.

The poetic voice in "Introducciones" (Introductions) similarly connects the languages of the people of Ayutla with the ecosystems in which they live, inviting readers to ponder the maps that document where the Jënanyëëj spring "deviene y augura paz" (becomes and augurs peace) and to then consider,

> Han pasado más de cuarenta días y el manantial sigue bajo resguardo de personas armadas y muchas células se plantean preguntas en lenguas inusitadas y minerales. En variadas lenguas vernáculas se plantean preguntas a los lagos y las montañas, en muchas lenguas, millones de células piden paz y devenir.[59]

> More than forty days have passed and people with guns still patrol the spring and many cells ask questions in unusual mineral languages. In varied vernacular languages they ask questions of the lakes and the mountains; in many languages, millions of cells seek peace and justice.

By using the cell in the literal sense and as synecdoche for the people of Ayutla, the concept of language expands to incorporate both marginalized human linguistic systems as well as communication as interactive flow between structurally coupled autopoietic systems. In the following stanza the poetic form changes as the prose poetry of the previous sections gives way to verse:

> Devenir lengua en agua que fluye:
> sílabas, sonidos, fonemas que en combinaciones
> inusitadas y variables
> resuenan
> como un conjunto de árboles:
> alamedas, pinales, plantaciones, bosques, selvas:
> el baldío de al lado:[60]

> Becoming words in flowing water:
> syllables, sounds, varied and unusual combinations
> of phonemes
> resounding
> like a group of trees:
> poplars, pine groves, crop fields, jungles, forests:
> the vacant lot next door:

The selection of the word "lengua" (language) as something that becomes only in water that flows brings to light the systemic totality in contrast to the term "lenguaje," which would refer to acts of language. Like a baptismal rebirth, a new system of communication emerges from marginalized languages both human and vegetal. The poetic voice affirms the potential for indigenous languages to recuperate lost knowledge and to imagine ways of being outside of the logic of the empire. In the rush of verses that follow, the poet recalls Maestra Olmedo's words, imploring her students to just imagine "expandir el corazón: brotan manantiales en difusas y / posibles lenguas en químicas orgánicas e inorgánicas" (your heart expanding: springs springing forth in hazy and possible / languages in organic and inorganic chemicals).[61] When we open up language to incorporate any effective system of interactive communication, as Maestra Olmedo proposes, it is no longer "the mechanical result of an individuated living subject (plant or otherwise) but as an ecology produced by organisms in an interdependent and multispecies interrelation."[62] Viewing language in this way reorients the relations between all living things within larger interdependent networks. Maturana and Varela affirm that through autopoiesis every act of human languaging is ethical given that "human linguistic behaviors are in fact behaviors in a domain of reciprocal ontogenic structural coupling which we human beings establish as a result of our collective ontogenies."[63] Similar to Karen Barad's assertion that reality is material-discursive in its intra-activity, Maturana and Varela affirm that "every act in language brings forth a world created with others in the act of coexistence."[64] As such, the human and more-than-human alternative languages that the poetic voice seeks out provide ways of living that are simply impossible within the language of the empire.

In order to communicate in alternative languages, the poet must confront the fears, intrinsic to the language of empire, that distance humans from the ecosystem as well as from each other. Using antimetabole to bring together both plants and human students under the same threat of extraction, the poet emphasizes the human cost of extractivism:

He escuchado el miedo.
Jóvenes de secundaria pública recolectando ejemplares en una ciudad con variedades mixtas. Jóvenes de secundaria mixta ejemplares de una variedad a resguardo, teniendo miedo de las extracciones.[65]

I've heard the fear.
Public middle school students collecting samples in a city with mixed varieties. Mixed middle school students, samples of protected variety, fearing extraction.

The threat of violence renders students as an endangered species, intimating the cruel reality of violence against young people and students such as the forty-three students from Ayotzinapa Rural Teachers' College who were kidnapped and massacred in 2014. Through the power of extraction, modern-day Mexico necropolitics ensures "a power of life not in spite of death, but through it."[66] The poet contrasts her almost quaint childhood fears of extraterrestrials or of being separated from her parents in public with the "niños que no ponían el abandono en términos de extraterrestres sino de militares y cercos: cierres de caminos" (children who didn't put abandonment in terms of aliens but of soldiers and siege).[67] In the poem "Miedo" (Fear) the poet deftly presents images and anecdotes of the fear of subtraction as she grew up, from childhood fears like the memory of her mother taking her little brother out of the theater because the film *E.T.* proved too frightening, to her fear of losing her parents, and finally to the subtraction of extractivism. Citing the power to destroy entire ecosystems, the poet speaks of fear as being "como en todos los lugares donde la minería a cielo abierto crea páramos desolados" (like every place where open-pit mining creates desolate wastelands).[68] Thus the fear of subtraction by abandonment surpasses what a child or even Hollywood can imagine, transforming the land itself as all life is extinguished.

In the poems placed sequentially earlier in the collection, the image of the wolf inspires a deep-seated fear in the poet given its power to hunt prey. As she

128   SCIENCE FUSION IN CONTEMPORARY MEXICAN LITERATURE

comes to observe carefully how the wolf functions in its habitat, she quickly realizes that there is another apex predator that truly imposes terror:

> En realidad cuando se trata de grandes depredadores, hay que tener mucho cuidado: concebir la cadena alimenticia, porque en realidad los grandes depredadores son más bien una concatenación de métodos de acumulación y extracciones de riquezas comunes y ajenas de inoculación de sueños que se perturban: insomnios: sustracción de las lenguas no imperiales e inoculación de la lengua de publicidad y banqueros: no son lobos: son personas con hambre de acumulación y garras para sustraerlo todo.[69]

> Actually, when it comes to large predators, it's important to be careful: to grasp the food chain, because in fact large predators are actually a concatenation of methods of accumulation and extractions of communal riches and separate from the inoculation of dreams unsettling each other: insomnia: subtraction of nonimperial languages and inoculation of the language of advertising and bankers: they aren't wolves: they're people hungry for accumulation with claws to abduct it all.

In contrast, the wolf reveals itself as a symbol of the flowing of life, as in the following stanza where the poetic voice equates wolves to "manifestations of love":

> De los lobos de su gracia y su dejarse correr y su habilidad de cazadores diremos hermosas manifestaciones del amor:
> aromas y otros fluidos que comunican: sudor, lágrimas, mocos, saliva, linfas que guían y cuidan: células que provienen de otras células:[70]

> As for wolves, we'll say of their grace and their running free and their aptitude as hunters: beautiful manifestations of love:
> aromas and other communicating fluids: sweat, tears, mucus, saliva, lymphs guiding and taking care: cells coming from other cells:

The poet dreams of wolves as maternal guides and protectors and imagines herself riding on the back of the she-wolf up a mountainside. In other moments, she describes fear as a wolf that nestles at her feet like a beloved pet. Having embraced fear, the poet sees that true danger comes not from the natural world but from the language of empire that justifies extraction and subtraction. Following the lesson of care of the mother wolf, the poet asks, "De qué manera una madre y sus cachorros comunican en líquidos y respiración: / Cargar cachorros en el lomo: devenires" (How do a mother and her pups communicate in liquids and breath: / carrying her pups on her back: becomings).[71] While at first glance it would seem that the poet's use of the word "love" to describe motivations and actions in nonhuman animals and plants screams of anthropomorphizing, in *El sueño de toda célula* to love moves beyond a human sentiment to denote the fostering of life through structural coupling between and within all living things

IN SEARCH OF A NEW LANGUAGE   129

and their environment. It is, in its essence, autopoietic activity. Maturana and
Varela caution that what we commonly term "love" is actually a biological
dynamic with deep roots that "defines in the organism a dynamic structural pat-
tern, a stepping stone to interactions that may lead to the operational coher-
ences of social life."[72] To love in Guerrero's poetry is to mutually and collectively
foster life within a perpetual process of autopoietic becoming that involves couplings, interdependence, and interconnectivity.

Life and the Flow of Autopoiesis

As with the etymology of the surname "Olmedo," in "Ríos" (Rivers) the poetic
voice contemplates the name "Guadalupe," as "el nombre de un río de lobos" (the
name for a river of wolves).[73] Comparing the naming and controlling of river
flows that is the work of hydrologists, geologists, soldiers, and engineers who
divert, enclose, and drain aquifers dry, the poetic voice ponders if the name Guadalupe can be reappropriated and made to mean something new, asking,
"¿Imaginamos un río de lobos que cobija riachuelos, arroyos y comunidades de
vida comunicándose en una lengua que no sea la lengua del imperio" (Can we
imagine a river of wolves lacing through the mesetas and sheltering streams and
creeks and communities of life communicating in a language that isn't the language of empire?).[74] Again the poet defamiliarizes language, deterritorializing
the concept of maternal care from the domain of *guadalupanismo* to that of the
more-than-human world, with the wolves providing shelter and protection over
nature. The imagery of rivers of wolves flowing and wrapping up and sheltering
entire ecosystems comes to represent the free and natural movement within networks of autopoietic communication. Likewise, the poet looks to more-than-
human languages and indigenous cosmovisions to articulate alternative ways of
imagining the relations of the world: "Sigo buscando un caudal y una lengua que
acerque y fluya libre" (I'm still searching for a river and language flowing close
and free).[75] To embrace alternate forms of communicating and relating is to open
oneself up to new languages of possibilities and imagination. In essence, it is
"Hablar en lobos en moléculas, comprender el modo en el que el azar nos
entreteje y nos tiende variables: atender la variabilidad, la fotosíntesis y la ver-
dosidad del aire y de las hojas: recuperar las nubes de la infancia" (Speaking in
wolves in molecules, understanding how chance interweaves us and offers us
variables: attending to variability, photosynthesis, and the greenness of the air
and leaves: recovering the clouds of our childhoods).[76] A language that embraces
chance and variability is one that honors the perpetual autopoietic processes of
becoming, viewing them not as threats to be minimized in an effort to control
natural flows but as potential avenues for life to spring forth.

Returning to the motif of childhood, the poem "Respirar" (Breath) begins
like a fable, taking readers back to an Edenic place before the language of

130   SCIENCE FUSION IN CONTEMPORARY MEXICAN LITERATURE

empire, as the poetic voice narrates, "Había una vez un mundo en el que el sueño de las células sólo era devenir células y fluía en lenguas vernáculas" (Once upon a time there was a world in which cells dreamed only of becoming cells and this dream flowed along in vernacular tongues).[77] The interceding stanzas describe how through the language of empire this primeval world was disrupted as we acquiesced to cages, zoos, botanical gardens, and even offices. The following stanzas, however, describe improbable acts of resistance like the bustling ecosystem that emerges in the midst of the city in the spare lot next door. These resistances of life reverse the subtractive drives of extractivism and become "diques and represas a la lengua del imperio" (sluices and dams across the language of empire).[78] While these acts of resistance convey the persistence of life, the poet notes that just kilometers away trees are being felled and springs are being patrolled by people with guns. The back-and-forth struggle between acts of controlling violence and its converse in life and chance that the verses convey abruptly comes to an end when the poet opts for the promise of the future and the creation of life that emerges through acts of love and shared ontogeny:

> sembraré un árbol.
> Estoy aquí hablando en lo que tengo porque
> respirar contigo es una transformación que produce aliento.
> Alentar es una forma redonda y cálida de resistir.
> Devenir célula que sueña devenir célula.
>
> I'm going to plant a tree.
> I'm speaking here in what I've got because
> breathing with you is a breath-producing transformation.
> Encouragement is a round warm form of resistance
> Becoming a cell that dreams of becoming cells.[79]

Breathing as transformation, with the meanings of "aliento" as both breath and encouragement, demonstrates how life is perpetuated through engagement and cooperation. In many respects, the collective breathing and encouragement here recall the oxygen cycle, which is often the first concept of ecology that children learn. Life is nurtured through collective intra-actions, both biologically through structurally entangled autopoietic networks and socially through solidarity and communality.

According to poet and scholar José Manuel Marrero Henríquez, "Ecocriticism should explore the transbordering possibility of revealing the processes by which words breathe or, in other words, the processes by which literature proves to be the ultimate result of the natural evolution that rewards those who are able to grasp its beauty, that is, its regularities in time as well as its regularities in space."[80] In *El sueño de toda célula* the space for words to "breathe" begins in

IN SEARCH OF A NEW LANGUAGE

the cell itself. In contrast to the languages of the more-than-human world, the poet continually seeks out a new way of speaking that expresses the web of life, asking in "Partidas" (Beginnings),

> Cuál es la variante dialectal en que traducir esto:
> moléculas de agua fósforo nitrógeno sales
> minerales y cobijo.
> ¿De qué manera una madera madre atiende el crecimiento y el ritmo de sus
>   hojas sus retoños:
> plántulas a la vera?
> ¿De qué manera una madera madre
> puede enviar mensajes punzantes y turbios
> en moléculas dolorosas?
> Azar y entretejidos: espacios que se restauran y florecen.
> A veces detenerse es otra forma de fluir y amar.
> Decir
> no es suficiente:
> es preciso respirar:
> mensajes de humus y nitrógeno y aminoácidos y alegría
> de qué manera: azar:

> What is the dialectical variant in which to translate this:
> molecules of water phosphorous nitrogen salts
> minerals and shelter.
> How can a wood mother attend to the growth and the rhythm of her leaves
>   her shoots: seedlings on the riverbank?
> How can a wood mother
> send sharp and murky messages
> in painful molecules?
> Chance and interweavings: spaces that recover and blossom.
> To stop can be another way to flow and love.
> Saying
> is not enough:
> we have to breathe:
> messages of humus and nitrogen and amino acids and joy
> how: chance:

In this final poem of the book, we can see how collective breathing sustains new beginnings. By stopping the impulses of extraction that try to control life itself, the poet instead makes way for chance and all the indeterminate ways autopoiesis may perpetuate life. The poet reprimands that "Saying / is not enough," as human language alone cannot fully communicate the autopoietic experience of living. To breathe, however, is to participate in a greater act of communication within an intra-active and continually emerging network of entangled molecules, phenomena, and autopoietic organisms.

Whether through the effective power of chance and indeterminacy as in Jorge Volpi and Ignacio Padilla's fiction, the dualisms that distance humans from the more-than-human world in Sabina Berman's novels, or the complementarity of language as in Alberto Blanco's poetry, the poems of *El sueño de toda célula* engage many common themes found in ciencia-fusión. Above all, the emphasis of Guerrero's collection on relational becoming, articulated through the auto-poietic activity of cells becoming cells, communicates the intra-active and entangled nature of materiality that is portrayed throughout the genre. Like-wise, in the following chapter on the poetry of Elisa Díaz Castelo, we will see how the same concepts of intra-activity and autopoiesis both reflect and illumi-nate the embodied human experience of and within both space and time, revealing the material-discursive entanglement of the human and the material. As we have seen, such entanglements proliferate in *El sueño de toda célula*, where just as the dream of every cell is simply to become cells, Guerrero argues that to make spaces to breathe and nurture life is to experience autopoietic flow, unimaginable in the language of empire. Like Maestra Olmedo who used scien-tific knowledge in the spirit of care and taught her students to see themselves as part of greater networks of life both within and outside of the organism, *El sueño de toda célula* opens up alternatives to extractivism and the ecological and social crises of today. While it recalls the past to speak to the present, at its core Guerrero's book is about imagining future possibilities where acts of resistance and care—from the seemingly small act of breathing to the collective activism of the people of Ayutla—join into ever greater autopoietic flows that, like the river of wolves that casts a protective web over the land, open a space for the multiplicities of chance and continual becoming.

CHAPTER 6

Dimensions of Embodied Experience

SPACE AND TIME IN ELISA DÍAZ CASTELO'S *PRINCIPIA*

Upon the death of friend and colleague Michele Besso in 1955, Albert Einstein sent a letter of condolence to the grieving family, writing, "Now he has departed from this strange world a little ahead of me. That means nothing. For us believing physicists the distinction between past, present, and future only has the meaning of an illusion, though a persistent one."[1] Just weeks after penning these words, Einstein himself would experience time's cruel arrow, suffering internal bleeding from a ruptured abdominal aortic aneurism. Refusing yet another surgery so as to avoid what he called a "tasteless" death, the great thinker who demonstrated that simultaneity is an illusion relative to the observer, declared, "I have done my share; it is time to go."[2] Einstein's death marked the final departure of the scientist and public figure who, through his groundbreaking contributions to relativity and quantum mechanics, fused together the familiar three dimensions of space with the fourth dimension of time, revealing a strange universe counterintuitive to human experience. Undoubtedly, there is the temptation to approach everything Einstein said as a profound yet folksy physics lesson and to see, for example, his letter to the Besso family as an affirmation that we live in what is called a "block universe," where essentially all times exist at all times and the passage of time itself is entirely illusory.[3] To do so, however, is to remove these quotes from their own time and space, where Einstein was not submitting a scientific paper but grappling with death, loss, and that out-of-body experience of mourning where one feels displaced in space and time. Far from a physics lesson, Einstein here is expounding on the experience of living, utilizing scientific concepts to console a mourning family by situating life and death within a greater universe, transposing features of a strange more-than-human world to alleviate the agony of losing someone who will no longer be with us in the space and time in which we go on living.

It is difficult not to recall the very same ideas that Einstein addresses in his letter to the Besso family—love, death, memory, and the human experience in the universe—while reading the twenty-five poems that make up Elisa Díaz Castelo's *Principia* (2018), where she likewise connects the intimate and personal to the more-than-human universe revealed through evolving scientific knowledge. In the hands of Díaz Castelo, contemplating past relationships becomes akin to looking up at the years-old light of stars in the night sky, memories of a grandmother's home propel the ticking of time in an expanding universe, the lifeless body of the family's dog is a black hole whose crushing gravity consumes the lived memories of times past, and where intangible love, remembrance, longing, nostalgia, and the actions that were never taken become the mysterious dark matter that gives substance to a mostly empty universe. In the poem "Geometría descriptiva" (Descriptive Geometry) the poetic voice summarizes what Díaz Castelo accomplishes in all the poems of the collection, transfiguring the two-dimensional confines of the written word on paper across vast distances in space and time, fusing the human experience with an immensely more-than-human universe:

> Quiero romper de estas dos dimensiones
> la tercera, frotar una con otra hasta que ardan,
> sólo eso: revestir cierta tarde de ceniza,
> someterla a sus sombras,
> darle la vuelta al tiempo.[4]

> I want to break off from these two dimensions
> the third, rub them together until they burn,
> just that: coat a certain afternoon in ashes,
> submit it to its shadows,
> turn time around.

In this chapter I continue to build upon the concept of autopoiesis and its connections to cognitive science and literature in order to explore the many ways that Díaz Castelo brings together scientific discourse with sentimental themes in *Principia*. In particular, I focus on Díaz Castelo's treatment of the body and embodied consciousness which allow her to bring together themes of memory, family, love, and death with analogous concepts and phenomena in the physical world. In this way Díaz Castelo entangles matter, mind, and language to portray an embodied experience that is biosemiotically relational, illustrating how subjectivity both emerges from and is integral to the more-than-human universe with its continuous intra-activity of forces, bodies, and matter in space and time.

In a relatively short but prolific period, Díaz Castelo, born in Mexico City in 1986, has published two critically acclaimed poetry collections, *Principia* and *El reino de lo no lineal* (*The Realm of the Nonlinear*, 2020), in addition to the historical dramatic poem *Proyecto Manhattan* (*Manhattan Project*, 2021).[5] Known for crossing boundaries between genres and cultures, Díaz Castelo's poetry combines scientific and medical discourse with accessible verse, classical myths with pop culture, and the systematic with the sentimental. Díaz Castelo explains that, for her, "la poesía y la ciencia se sustentan en premisas similares. Para empezar, comparten dos principios: el asombro y la curiosidad" (poetry and science are based upon similar premises. For one thing, they share two starting principles: astonishment and curiosity).[6] The poet explains how both of her parents were doctors and from a young age she was drawn to scientific discourse, fascinated by the language the two spoke. It was, in her retelling,

> como una especie de idioma secreto como que cuando yo era niña eran palabras vaciadas de significado y finalmente creo que esa aproximación al lenguaje como sonido es una aproximación muy poética inherentemente, ¿no? Y cuando empecé a buscar ... a escribir sobre temas distintos o cómo ir hacia otros lenguajes, de inmediato pensé en la ciencia porque la ciencia ya tenía en mi memoria esa calidad sonora, esa calidad de sonido puro, maleable, que yo podía trabajar con la palabra, con la materia de la palabra.[7]

> like a kind of secret language as when I was a child, they were words emptied of their meaning and eventually I believe that that approximation to language as sound is inherently a very poetic approximation, right? And when I began to search for ... to write about different topics or how to go toward other languages, I immediately thought about science because science already had in my memory that sonorous quality, that quality of pure sound, malleable, that I could work with the word, with the substance of the word.

While she was initially drawn to the sound and timbre of scientific and medical language, Díaz Castelo's poetry also engages and transposes scientific concepts to inform and enrich her expression of what it is to exist in the world. Transcending long-standing distinctions between the cultures of science and the arts, in *Principia* the poetic and the scientific fuse together to convey the poet's experience, connecting the personal and intimate to the grand scale of the universe, from its infancy in the Big Bang to a distant future where the Sun, and ultimately every star, will cease to burn.

Díaz Castelo's poetry departs from a proposition of the complementarity between science and poetry that originates from a sense of astonishment that drives the impulse to explore and understand the more-than-human universe. While Alejandro Rodríguez notes how Díaz Castelo's poetry "confronta el lenguaje científico y lo saca de su zona de confort" (confronts scientific language and takes it out of its comfort zone) to then place it in the realm of the metaphorical, allegorical, and artistic,[8] Emilio Tejeda asserts that the poet's most

136 SCIENCE FUSION IN CONTEMPORARY MEXICAN LITERATURE

impressive feat is how personal experiences and emotions acquire new meaning within the contrast between the scientific and the quotidian.[9] In a similar way, Myriam Moscona observes that in *Principia*, "Las extrañezas de sus componentes íntimos construyen un universo donde lo emotivo y lo desaforado se sujetan al conocimiento, nos sacuden y hacen que apretemos los dientes" (The peculiarities of its intimate components construct a universe where the emotive and the immeasurable become affixed to knowledge, shaking us and making us grit our teeth).[10] Perhaps it is fellow poet Isabel Zapata who summarizes *Principia* best when she states that the collection takes on the entire universe in a journey in which, more than reason or emotions, it is bodies that speak, "el cuerpo humano con sus huesos que lanzan preguntas, pero también habla el cuerpo de los astros y de las plantas y de otras cosas que ni siquiera tienen nombre" (the human body with its bones that throw out questions, but also celestial bodies speak as well as bodies of plants and other things that do not even have a name).[11] Through these different bodies Díaz Castelo's poetry fuses death, memory, and the passing of time with images, concepts, and theories from physics, medicine, biology, and chemistry to articulate the embodied experience both in and of the universe.

From its very title, *Principia* establishes a dialogue with Isaac Newton's *Philosophiæ Naturalis Principia Mathematica* (1687), which revolutionized our understanding of the fundamental forces in the universe and formed the foundation of the laws of classical mechanics that endure to this day. Díaz Castelo's collection opens with an epigraph from *Principia Mathematica* where Newton states, "And to us it is enough that gravity does really exist, and act according to the laws which we have explained, and abundantly serves to account for all the motions of the celestial bodies, and of our sea."[12] Departing from Newton's explanation of how the unseen can be proven through the empirical observation of phenomena, revealing greater depths to reality than previously known, Díaz Castelo organizes *Principia* into two sections, "Sobre el sistema del mundo" (Of the System of the World) and "Sobre el movimiento de los cuerpos" (Of the Movement of Bodies). Like Newton, Díaz Castelo takes up the study of bodies and the emergence of phenomena from what is both seen and unseen, with the lyrical voice declaring in the poem "Credo" (Creed) her belief in things both visible and invisible, empirical and theorized, beginning with a series of quotidian objects observed in her urban surroundings:

Creo en los aviones, en las hormigas rojas,
en la azotea de los vecinos y en su ropa interior
que los domingos se mece, empapada,
de un hilo. Creo en los tinacos corpulentos,
negros, en el sol que los cala y en el agua
que no veo pero imagino, quieta, oscura,
calentándose.

Creo en lo que miro
en la ventana, en el vidrio
aunque sea transparente.[13]

I believe in airplanes, in red ants,
in the neighbors' terrace and in their underwear
that on Sundays swings, dripping,
from a line. I believe in corpulent water tanks,
black, in the sun that permeates them and in the water
that I do not see but imagine, still, dark,
getting heated up.
I believe in what I see
in the window, in the glass
even if it is transparent.

In these verses the interplay between opaque rooftop water tanks, so ubiqui-
tous in Mexico, upon which the sun's energy interacts, heating up the water
hidden inside, and the act of observing through a window, no less real in its
transparency than the objects on the other side of the glass, establishes a spatial
matrix from which the first-person lyrical subject contemplates the materiality
of both presence and absence that infuses *Principia*. The poet, repeating "creo"
(I believe), transitions these first principles from the everyday and what she has
experienced firsthand such as "... la geografía móvil de las sábanas / y en la piel
que ocultan ..." (... the moving geography of bedsheets / and the flesh they
hide ...)[14] to a greater universe to which the poetic subject is integral, rejecting
solipsistic and subjective idealism, declaring, "Creo en lo que no puedo ver: /
creo en los exnovios, / en los microbios y en las microondas" (I believe in what I
cannot see: / I believe in ex-boyfriends, / in microbes and in microwaves).[15] In
these verses, the poet's creed, a confession of faith, affirms all matter and phenomena as emerging from a complex web of intra- and interconnectivities in
time and space, revealed through the nexus between the personal experience of
the embodied mind and the evolving knowledge that science produces.

The Experience of the Mind-Body

Although Díaz Castelo shares with her seventeenth-century referent a preoccupation with bodies and the laws that govern natural phenomena, the concept of
subjectivity that *Principia* depicts is far different from the Cartesian thinking
subject, the mind discrete from the objects it contemplates of Isaac Newton's day.
In contrast, in *Principia* subjectivity is part of larger autopoietic processes,
emerging from the interplay of countless forces, bodies, and matter that unfold
throughout space and time. In this light, autopoiesis, the characteristic of living
systems that are capable of producing and maintaining themselves by creating

138   SCIENCE FUSION IN CONTEMPORARY MEXICAN LITERATURE

their own components, explains how all living beings cocreate their internal biology as well as external sociocultural systems through continual processes of self-realization.[16] In *Principia* the human mind-body is continually remaking and realizing itself, both being constituted of other materials, bodies, and forces in space and time while simultaneously interacting with and upon other forces, materials, and bodies. As with the logical progression in the poem "Credo," the organization of *Principia* reveals a movement of bodies that interact with and among each other through scales of time and space that continually expand outward only to return to the point of departure. As such, the first poem, "Escoliosis," begins within the familiar confines of the human body, but with bones that possess an agential vitality of their own that acts against the wills and ideals of the poetic subject. The first lines of the poem place the body in contrast to the lyrical first person, declaring,

> En la búsqueda de la forma
> se me distrajo el cuerpo. Es eso,
> nada más, asimetría[17]

> In search of the form
> my body got distracted. That's it
> nothing more, asymmetry

Recalling the eternal beauty of the Platonic Form against a temporal, material body working against itself, scoliosis here becomes the means through which the poet's body expresses its own drives and desires as an agential yet material body, already tired at the age of twelve, rebelling against itself:

> mi esqueleto
> quiso escapar un poco
> de sí mismo.[18]

> my skeleton
> wanted to escape just a bit
> from itself.

The scientific explanation of scoliosis dissolves as the poetic voice presents various metaphors, drawing from images of both living and nonliving things, observing how the name "scoliosis" is given

> a esa migración de vertebras,
> a estos goznes mal nacidos,
> hueso ambiguo[19]

> to that migration of vertebrae,
> to these bastardly rogue hinges,
> ambiguous bone

DIMENSIONS OF EMBODIED EXPERIENCE

While the metaphors establish a link between the animate and inanimate, the body's bones exhibit voice in the poem, at times indirectly, at others directly, as in the following lines where the poet muses that it is as if

dijera de pronto el cuerpo *mejor no,*
olvídalo, quiero crecer para abajo,
hacia la tierra . . . [20]

all of a sudden the body said *no, let's not,*
forget it, I want to grow downwards,
towards the earth . . .

In this desire to move toward the earth in which "lo que era tronco quiso ser raíz" (what was trunk wanted to be root),[21] scoliosis becomes less a curvature of the spine and more an expression of the body moving in an untimely way toward its own death. The poet uses the verb "desfasar" (to be out of step/synch) multiple times to express the body's wish to return to the rancid earth from a young age, an aberrant desire to stop the process of being born and living.

Despite the poet's struggle to transcend the body by giving primacy to a soul out of sync with the corporeal, the "deformed" body asserts its own symmetry through its own desire, "perfectamente alineado desde entonces / con el deseo de morir y de seguir viviendo" (perfectly aligned since then / with the desire to die and to continue living).[22] The same question of symmetry is expressed through the visual appearance of the poem itself. The first four stanzas of "Escoliosis" all contain lines of similar, though not identical, visual length except for small groupings of verses that give the impression of a curve or bend in the overall shape of the stanza. It is in one such curve that the poet comes to an epiphany about the body:

Si las vértebras, si la osamenta quiere, se desvive,
rota por no dejar el suelo. Si se quiere volver
. . . .
Paralelamente.
No es eso,
no es
eso
no
eso no,
no es ahí, donde ahí acaba,
donde empieza el dolor empieza el cuerpo.[23]

If the vertebrae, if the bones wish, going out of their way,
broken for not leaving the ground. If wanting to return
. . . .
In parallel form.

It's not that,
it's not
that
no
that no,
it's not there, where there ends,
where pain begins the body also begins.

It is spatially and conceptually in the curvature of the spine where the poet comes to the realization that the mind cannot exist in parallel to the body. And the body, made of its material components that are drivers of the poet's reality, refutes the possibility of a dualistic existence affirmed through death as telos. Instead, the continuous chiasmatic crossing over between the perception and experience of pain constitutes a shared assemblage of minerals, bones, neurons, and flesh where life begins. Consciousness arises from the very body that it contemplates. As Nicholas Humphrey observes, "To be conscious is essentially to have sensations of 'what is happening to me': in other words, of what is happening at the boundary between me and not-me."[24]

In "Escoliosis" human consciousness arises from the entire body as the seemingly agential drives of bones invert the traditional mind-body paradigm so that the "mind" is ultimately subordinate to the will of the body from which it arises. Speaking to the vital force of the material, Jane Bennett observes that "human power is itself a kind of thing-power. At one level this claim is uncontroversial: it is easy to acknowledge that humans are composed of various material parts (the minerality of our bones, or the metal of our blood, or the electricity of our neurons). But it is more challenging to conceive of these materials as lively and self-organizing, rather than as passive or mechanical means under the direction of something nonmaterial, that is, an active soul or mind."[25] The poet concludes by reinforcing the primacy of the corporeal over any supposedly autonomous mind, declaring, ". . . Es el cuerpo / que me ha dicho que no" (. . . It is the body / that has told me no).[26] As with the image of unseen water residing within the tank in "Credo," here Díaz Castelo reconfigures the relationship between long-standing assumptions about form and content, revealing bones that, hidden in the interior of body, are in reality a primary force driving the poet's experience. As literary critic Howard Mancing affirms, "The single most important idea to have come from the cognitive sciences is that *all intelligence, all thought, is embodied*."[27] In effect, the poem "Escoliosis" lyrically portrays this fact, with the thoughts of a mind emanating not from a separate entity that contemplates a distinct body but rather as both emerging from and reflecting upon the autopoietic system that is the human mind-body.

More than just tissue of the skeletal system, the motif of bones appears throughout several poems in *Principia*: bones that direct the scoliotic body, teeth

DIMENSIONS OF EMBODIED EXPERIENCE 141

that separate *Homo sapiens* from other primates, or the materiality of bones revealed by an X-ray. In Díaz Castelo's poetry, the image of bones is multifaceted. At times they are the mineralized remains of the past that still speak in the present, in others they are the living tissue that asserts its existence more forcefully than a supposedly immaterial mind. Internally living or exteriorly lifeless, they possess a vitality that acts upon and directs human experience and knowledge. As with "Escoliosis," in "Credo" the poet glides through images, freely associated, with each metaphor connecting to the next in a causal and logical chain that spatially and temporally zooms in and out. The poet's belief in condoms leads to the moving geography of bedsheets and the flesh they hide, to her belief in bones, the content within the form of the human body that she believes in:

> sólo porque a Santi se le rompió el húmero
> y lo miré en su arrebato blanco, astillado
> por el aire y la vista como un pez
> fuera del agua . . . [28]

> only because Santi broke his humerus
> and I looked at it in its white rage, shattered
> through air and sight like a fish
> out of water . . .

While the poetic voice gives various examples of things in which she believes that she can neither imagine nor understand, the decontextualized bone that angrily reveals itself through injury is something the poet must see to believe. The metonymic associations of water tanks, the periodic table, condoms, sheets, and so many other material objects prevalent in the poem recall the unseen contents that drive the exposed forms, much like the constitutive power of bones and the embodied consciousness that arises through autopoietic processes. As with the poet's belief in her own breath only because she can see evidence of its existence in its condensation in the air on a cold day, embodied self-awareness is the product of the organism's interactions with its domain of operation through examples of what Maturana defines as countless structural couplings.

As if to drive the idea of life as emerging from seemingly infinite structural couplings, the result of "recurrent interactions leading to the structural congruence between two (or more) systems,"[29] one of the more striking features of the poems in *Principia* is the way in which Díaz Castelo utilizes lyrical enjambement, with sentences that spread across lines only to end or begin in the middle of the next. The incomplete syntax suggests a flowing of thought that accentuates the interconnectivity of all things. It is hard not to perceive yet another level of metaphor in this technique as the etymology of both the English word "enjambement" and the Spanish "encabalgamiento" brings to mind a movement or crossing over of legs, of bodies, and, in the case of "Credo," of bones. Bones

142 SCIENCE FUSION IN CONTEMPORARY MEXICAN LITERATURE

are living tissue, of course, but in *Principia* they also are an articulation between the past and present, a hidden interior driving force, a hidden or absent presence giving substance to human life.

The Embodied Experience in Space

Continuing the interplay of interiority and exteriority of the human body and the bones within, the poem "Radiografías" (X-rays) tells, in eight numbered sections of varying length, the very intimate experience of a medical procedure through the recurring motifs of the human body as both presence and absence. By juxtaposing medical and scientific language of how an X-ray image is created with recollections and feelings of unease in a clinical environment, "Radiografías" functions as a meditation on mortality and the ephemeral human body as it negotiates space both with the outside and within itself. Similar to the way in which the poetic voice recognizes elements of her own corporeal being only through interaction with other entities in "Credo," here the poet uses the tangible and material equipment of the X-ray machine as an access into a deeper and invisible reality:

> De la fría excitación de las partículas, de orbitales y átomos,
> conozco sólo la intemperie en el cuerpo, el borde
> del cañón a quemarropa, la batita ridícula
> con la abertura adelante, y la voz sin diámetro del hombre
> que se ha puesto su sotana de plomo, *no te muevas*.[30]

> Of the cold excitation of particles, of orbitals and atoms,
> I only know the elements in the body, the edge
> of the barrel at point blank, the ridiculous little gown
> with the opening in the front, and the voice without diameter of the man
> that has put on his cassock of lead, *don't move*.

The vulnerable patient, barely covered by a flimsy gown that threatens to expose her flesh, here becomes a victim of the radiographer who wields the imaging tube like a weapon used in a robbery. Yet the more profound exposure comes from the unseen X-ray radiation that reveals an intimate interiority, both physically through the imaging of bones and emotionally through manifesting and making visual a spatiotemporal projection of the poet's own mortality.

In "Radiografías" the almost sacred power that the radiographer wields stands in contrast to the relatively straightforward science behind a traditional radiograph, or X-ray image. While we typically think of light as a thing out there that literally or symbolically stimulates sight or illumination, it is helpful to remember that what we refer to commonly as visual light is simply electromagnetic radiation that falls within the portion of the electromagnetic spectrum that the

DIMENSIONS OF EMBODIED EXPERIENCE

human eye can perceive. Like the more familiar ultraviolet, infrared, microwaves, or radio waves, X-rays are the same electromagnetic radiation, but at higher frequencies.[31] Much of the energy of the X-rays passes through the less dense soft tissues of the human body but is absorbed in greater degree by the denser bones made in large part of calcium and other minerals. The result is the denser tissue appearing as the familiar white image on a dark field, a process expressed in "Radiografías" as the "la traducción de órganos / a sombras" (the translation of organs / to shadows)[32] that occurs before the threshold of the visible:

> Mirada que no se deja ver,
> *cámara obscura*, inspectora de sombras
> blancas, donde el cuerpo recóndito
> da fe de sus volúmenes inversos:
> los órganos son palomas
> guarecidas en la cúpula del hueso.
> Se muestra el paisaje interior, el cuerpo
> revelado, íntimo, visceral y un poco absurdo,
> tener tanta cosa adentro y la luz
> vertida hasta el fondo.[33]

> Look that does not let itself be seen,
> *camera obscura*, inspector of white
> shadows, where the remote body
> attests to its inverse volumes:
> organs are birds
> sheltered in the cupola of bone.
> The interior landscape is shown, the body
> revealed, intimate, visceral and a little absurd,
> having so much stuff inside and the light
> spilled all the way down.

In the search for a diagnosis, the poet submits herself to a violation of her intimacy as manifested through the visual images of the X-ray. Perhaps more threatening than the images themselves is the revelation of "so much stuff" in a "remote" body that seems to remind the poet of her own unfamiliarity with the most hidden-away interiority of her body revealed only in a radiograph. The humanlike anatomy of the radiographic machine, the "cabezal, el brazo articulado, del cronorruptor y el diafragma" (the headpiece, the articulated arm, of the timer switch and the diaphragm),[34] is equally unfamiliar to the poet as the substance of her own body.

Recalling the childhood memory of holding her hand against a flashlight, the poet recalls how, seeing the glowing flesh, she imagines her body is inhabited by

144 SCIENCE FUSION IN CONTEMPORARY MEXICAN LITERATURE

strange and luminous elements.[35] Her childlike innocence is dispelled as she admits,

> Por supuesto, era la sangre, atravesada
> por la luz, me lo dijo mi padre, y aparte
> se me transparentaba la piel y me dio pena
> no haber sabido antes que cargamos
> cinco litros de sangre y tantos huesos y más dientes
> de lo que caben en la boca.[36]

> Of course, it was blood, crossed through
> by the light, my father told me, and besides that
> my skin was transparent and it made me sad
> not knowing before that we carry around
> five liters of blood and so many bones and more teeth
> than can fit in our mouths.

Just as her childlike understanding of the workings of the human body changes over time, the poet comes to understand that the luminescent glow emanates not from within but rather from the interaction between her organs and the waves of light passing through her body in a manner not dissimilar to what we have previously seen in Alberto Blanco's thought experiment involving the lit candle in "Teoría de conjuntos" (Set Theory). Here the poet reorients her understanding of the human mind-body as it exists only through its relationship with worlds both within and outside of itself:

> Ahora, tocada
> por el diámetro del cañón,
> imagino mi cuerpo encendido
> como una alberca en la noche.
> Sólo entonces, con la luz adentro,
> toma forma el agua, se sostiene a sí misma,
> es algo más que vidrio disuelto.
> Quizá solamente visto,
> desgranado en vericuetos y órganos, el cuerpo
> existe plenamente.[37]

> Now, touched
> by the diameter of the barrel,
> I imagine my body lit up
> like a pool at night.
> Only then, with the light within,
> does water take shape, sustain itself,
> is something more than dissolved glass.

DIMENSIONS OF EMBODIED EXPERIENCE

Perhaps only when seen,
threshed in dark paths and organs, the body
exists fully.

Therefore, we see in "Credo" and "Escoliosis" that when held in a new light—
here, in the most literal sense by the electromagnetic radiation of the X-ray—the
interplay and inversion between exteriority and interiority defamiliarizes and
reframes the embodied experience in a more complete and enlightening way.
The transparent waters, hidden within plain sight, are given volume and substance only when the radiation from the pool light bends and refracts as it
passes through them, dancing in contrast with the darkness of the night. Like
the pool lit up at night that illuminates the water that has been there all along,
the constituent matter of the body is on full display and ceases to be obscured
within the external form when illuminated through the X-ray.

Similar to the "moving geography" of the bedsheets from "Credo" that is an
outward manifestation of something happening underneath, in "Radiografías"
topographical imagery traces the internal contours of a source of pain from within:

Aquí las lagunas, las cumbres. Aquí
la geografía del dolor, que él nombra
sin asombro ni deleite.[38]

Here the lagoons, the summits. Here
the geography of pain, that he names
with neither surprise nor pleasure.

The break, the tumor, or the injury that necessitates X-ray imaging casts a light on
the interior of the body which, while hidden away and largely unknown to the
poet, is a place of negotiation, a three-dimensional manifold that projects into a
space within. The body, laid bare and homeomorphically turned inside out,
becomes "un árbol de huesos, un enjambre de órganos" (a tree of bones, a hive of
organs).[39] Viewed in this way, the concept of interiority dissolves as the notion of
a boundary between the internal system and an external world is proven illusory.
Even the human mind-body, understood as an autopoietic system, is not an
enclosed, separate space or inert entity that interacts with an outside world. As
Stacy Alaimo argues, the "interconnection, interchanges, and transits between
human bodies and nonhuman natures" proves that the more-than-human material world and human bodies are in reality inseparable.[40] Through structural coupling both with exterior matter and within what we would consider the
boundaries of itself, the mind-body perpetually gives rise to itself through structural coupling, a process that Ira Livingston explains in the following way:

Boundaries in particular cannot be understood only as the discrete limits of an
autopoetic system in space and time, just as closure and openness cannot be

146 SCIENCE FUSION IN CONTEMPORARY MEXICAN LITERATURE

fully understood in terms of the semipermeable membranes that separate the inside from the outside of living things. Boundary negotiations (in bodies, for example) do not take place only where skin meets air or where food is being digested; such negotiations are going on everywhere "inside" as well, at the cellular and the molecular and the atomic levels. But because of the ideological legacy of discrete selves with interiors, it is easy to fall back into treating auto-poetic systems as solipsistic interiors instead of as all edges, all interfaces.[41]

The negotiations or structural couplings that occur at the microscopic level where cells metabolize and synthesize molecules are mostly the antecedents to the externally visible macroscopic movements, actions, and interactions of the human mind-body that interacts with the world. When the context of a human life is shown as originating from within as in Díaz Castelo's poetry, the space between the mind and the body collapses into one autopoietic system coupling with other systems, molecules, and forces with innumerable boundaries that radically challenge long-held ideas of subjectivity and objectivity. As such, "Dualisms such as the classic Cartesian mind-body split—or the nature-nurture debate—become nonsubjects, incoherent ideas that cannot even be meaningfully discussed in the contextualized—and contextualizing—discourse of embodied cognition."[42]

This idea further develops in the poem "Esto otro que también me habita (y no es el alma o no necesariamente" (This Other Stuff That Also Dwells in Me [and It Is Not the Soul or Not Necessarily]). Through its content and title, Díaz Castelo's poem corresponds with Colombian Darío Jaramillo Agudelo's "Poemas de amor, 1" (Poems of Love, 1), where the latter poet ponders his own identity, the hidden parts of the self, and what could be called a soul, an intangible tension between the poet and the man where it remains ambiguous who is "Ese otro que también me habita, / acaso propietario, invasor quizás o exiliado en este cuerpo ajeno o de ambos" (That other that also dwells in me, / maybe owner, invader perhaps, or exiled in this foreign body or of us both).[43] In Díaz Castelo's poem, Jaramillo's "ese otro" (that other) is replaced with "esto otro" (this other stuff),[44] made up of the

> Animalejos
> insidiosos o inocuos,
> pero, ante todo, diminutos
> o, por lo menos, discretos. De varias patas
> o ninguna, redondos o alargados, con
> o sin ojos, con o sin dientes, asexuados
> o calientes, procreativos. Sobre todo
> invisibles o bien ocultos, invertebrados
> (por suerte), inveterados. Desde siempre
> nos habitan, huéspedes, y nosotros, anfitriones,
> no podríamos vivirnos solos, mantenernos.

Somos ellos: son nosotros. No hay dualismo
ni monismo. Todo parasitario,
todos parásitos: hay
tantas células de microbios
como células humanas en el cuerpo.[45]

Creepy-crawlies
insidious or innocuous,
but, first of all, miniscule
or, at least, discreet. With various legs
or none, round or long, with
or without eyes, with or without teeth, asexual
or horny, procreative. Above all else
invisible or well hidden, invertebrates
(fortunately), deeply rooted. Since forever
they dwell in us, guests, and we, hosts,
we ourselves could not live alone, maintain ourselves.
We are them: they are us. There is no dualism
nor monism. All parasitic,
all parasites: there are
as many cells of microbes
as human cells in the body.

The poet's meditation on the multitude of microorganisms that make up who we are underscores an intraconnectivity that problematizes the limits of the human as it diffuses its essence among the multitude of structural couplings between the body and the microbes within. What is more, while the poet notes that there are as many microbial cells as human cells in the body, if she were to include bacteria in her counting, the numbers would skew to an astounding ratio of ten microorganisms for every human cell.[46] Of course, Díaz Castelo apparently sees no need to beat this conceptual horse as the parasitic and symbiotic relationships between these organisms is already clear: human life would be impossible without the autopoietic structural coupling between microbe and human.

As occurs with the X-ray, contemplating the interior space of the body and the dwellers "de este cuerpo para ellos universo" (of this body for them a universe),[47] the poet is reminded of her own mortality and the ephemeral nature of human life when considered on the grander scale of the more-than-human universe:

Pero esto que también me habita
algún día se mudará de cuerpo:
me moriré, me comerán de adentro
para afuera, clostridia, coliformes
(se muere siempre

de adentro para afuera,
del centro al diámetro,
de la sangre al nombre).
Esto que también me habita
soy yo, parte por parte,
perviviendo
con la irresoluta sentencia
de la vida eterna o al menos
diminuta, rapaz y carroñera,
después de la muerte.[48]

But this that also dwells in me
one day will move bodies:
I will die, they will eat me from the inside
out, Clostridia, Coliform
(one always dies
from the inside out,
from the center to the diameter,
from the blood to the name).
This that also dwells in me
is me, piece by piece,
living on
with the irresolute sentence
of life eternal or at least
diminutive, predatory, and eating carrion,
life after death.

The blending of the poet's own death with the life of the microbes that, if not eternal, will at least extend beyond her life, deepens the entanglement between her and this other. The repetition of the prepositions "de" (from) and "a" (to), and the adverb "afuera" (outward) portray a constant movement of both death and life springing forth from the interiority. As the poet's death will fuel the life cycles of these microorganisms, she will live on through them, as they metabolize her remains. Framed in this way, human life arises from and devolves into a larger flow in space and time. Given that she cannot exist outside of these cycles and without continually coupling with these microorganisms that have and will transcend her existence, what it means to be human is radically altered. Recalling the ambiguity that bifurcates the identity of the poetic voice in Darío Jaramillo's "Poemas de amor, 1," what it means to be human is radically altered to the point it becomes nonsensical to draw clear spatial and structural limits between the human subject and an external world. As the title of Díaz Castelo's poem suggests, these microorganisms may not necessarily constitute a soul, but they are of us and they/we will live on long after our earthly bodies wither away.

The Human Mind-Body in Deep Time

The humbling perspective of the poet's life depending on colonies of microbes or the foretelling image of her future fossilized remains through the X-ray image underscores the theme of remapping, reorienting, and resituating the human within a greater universe that runs throughout *Principia*. In the same way that the preceding poems reposition the human in space, in *Principia* time takes on scales as grand as the history of the universe or as intimate as the frozen memories of a special day spent with loved ones. Even in poems where it is not an explicit theme, a deeper time than the passing minutes, hours, or even years of a human life serves as subsurface onto which individual events and actions unfold. Considering time on the scale of billions of years, in "Oda a los ancestros" (Ode to the Ancestors), the poet makes clear from the first verses that the ancestors in question are not her grandfather, nor his father, nor their spinster aunt who would milk the cows. Instead, echoing back to the verses of "Radiografías" where the lyrical I observes that we humans have more teeth than can fit in our mouths, here the poet pivots away from her recent ancestors, stating with a mid-verse caesura, "Tengo / demasiados huesos en la boca" (I have / too many bones in my mouth).[49] The absurdity of having too many teeth here becomes a motif throughout *Principia* that connects modern-day humans to our ancestors whose dietary patterns allowed for larger jaws. Furthermore, the concept of too many bones in one's mouth also functions as a metonymic device and catalyst for what is to come, an overflowing of stories to be told about ancestors whose presence is asserted through the remains of their own bones. The ode's introductory verses about her familial ancestors can be seen as a strophe, not in form, but rather in an overall structure of presenting the topic and themes of relational bonds across time. In the ensuing verses, which serve as the odic apostrophe, the poet's conception of ancestry expands exponentially. She speaks of her ancestor Lucy, the famous collection of fossilized bone of a female of the hominin species *Australopithecus afarensis*, and her "allegado" (next of kin) and Ardi, an even older and more complete collection of bones of a female from the species *Ardipithecus ramidus*.[50] From these early hominins, the poet quickly begins traveling back through time, establishing an ancestral lineage that stretches beyond our scientifically established family *Hominadae*. The poet closes the poem with what we can consider the thematic epode, as the final verses sing the miracle of the origins of life itself:

Celebro, al fin,
a esa primera célula organizada,
a la primera huérfana
y la última, a ella, inmaculada madre unicelular,
sin pecado concebida, bendita

entre toda la materia estéril.
A ella, he olvidado su nombre,
Melusina, Laura, Isabel, Perséfona, María,
y bendito es el fruto de su vientre.[51]

I celebrate, finally,
that first organized cell,
the first orphan
and the last, her, immaculate unicellular Mother,
conceived without sin, blessed is she
among all the barren matter.
Her, I have forgotten her name,
Melusine, Laura, Elizabeth, Persephone, Mary,
and blessed is the fruit of her womb.

Here the poet connects all humans to a mythical mother: the first single-celled living creature that emerged from nonliving matter. These final verses are constructed through a conceptual as well as intratextual mise en abyme. Lyrically, this section is scaffolded upon the words and imagery of the Hail Mary prayer, here replacing the Immaculate Mother with our evolutionary primogenitor. Within that frame, the poet embeds word for word verses from Octavio Paz's *Piedra de Sol* (*Sunstone*), declaring, "he olvidado su nombre, / Melusina, Laura, Isabel, Perséfona, María" (I have forgotten her name, / Melusine, Laura, Elizabeth, Persephone, Mary).[52] Clearly, *Principia* abounds with such lyrical and conceptual references to Díaz Castelo's artistic family tree of influences, from the polysemic bodies of Max Rojas to the humor and scientific imagery of Gerardo Deniz. In "Oda a los ancestros," the two verses from *Piedra de Sol* tap into the Paz's imagery of the mythic female progenitor, ephemerally present in the act of love, that diverges into her symbolic offspring in various mythological traditions. From communion with her, true being is given life, an eternal return that mirrors the cyclical nature of time in the Aztec tradition. It is from Paz's primordial mother, the "virgen lunar, madre del agua madre / cuerpo del mundo, casa de la muerte" (lunar virgin, mother of the mother of waters / body of the world, house of death),[53] that life emerges. Similarly, Díaz Castelo transposes Paz's syncretic Guadalupian mother with the coming together of nonliving, barren matter that seems to lyricize the Oparin-Haldane hypothesis, which describes how life arose from inorganic molecules through the process of abiogenesis, with the building blocks of amino acids and nucleotides conglomerating and being radiated in what is known popularly as the primordial soup. Framing the origins of life on Earth within the concept of miracle and myth, the mother celebrated here is a paradoxical orphan, born of no mother, yet mother to all. Of course, it is the barren matter itself that is the primordial and symbolic mother to this first living thing. The scale of time that frames Díaz Castelo's ode places the human within

DIMENSIONS OF EMBODIED EXPERIENCE

its evolutionary milieu, a family that features strange creatures and emerges from its nonbiological material foundations. Jane Bennett remarks, "In the long and slow time of evolution, then, mineral material appears as the mover and shaker, the active power, and the human beings, with their much-lauded capacity for self-directed actions, appear as *its* product."[54] In the same way, in "Oda a los ancestros" the poet traces humanity's true family through time where, at its farthest reaches, our family tree devolves from organic life, with our familial roots sprouting from the minerals and matter of the Earth.

EMBODIED COGNITION IN SPACETIME

A sense of longing is at the heart of many of the poems in *Principia*: longing for the past, nostalgia for times gone by, longing to know what would have been if a different path had been taken or what will become of a memory that is slowing fading with time. Finding analogues between the four dimensions of spacetime and the embodied cognitive experience of time and place in past, present, and future, many of the poems in *Principia* convey a poetic voice that contemplates memories of loved ones or unrealized possibilities in futures to come and futures past. Above all, the concept of death—in its literal sense as the end of life as well as in a more encompassing understanding of things lost forever or of unrealized words and actions—motivates the poetic voice to contemplate her place in the universe. If to live is to autopoietically make something out of matter, the poet questions the nature of actions past, ideas, possibilities, or memories that do not have mass or occupy a physical body. The poet laments the death of a loved one in "Acta de defunción" (Death Certificate), recognizing that in the precise moment where life ended "El corazón había perdido su gravedad" (The heart had lost its gravity).[55] With its mass and energy dispersing back into the universe, the poet is left with memories of another time and place, of a metonymic heart that no longer exerts a physical gravitational attraction yet seems to pull the poet's thoughts back in time. In this way, throughout *Principia* the poet entangles the experiences and emotions of the embodied mind with the often nonintuitive nature of spacetime to delve into this paradoxical relationship between presence and absence.

In the poem "Sobre la luz que no vemos y otras formas de desaparecer" (Of the Light That We Do Not See and Other Ways to Disappear), light traveling through the expanse of space is analogous to memories of loved ones left behind in the past. The titular light that we do not see is a clear reference to the "dark night sky paradox," also known as Olbers's Paradox, which for many years remained one of the great unsolved questions in cosmology. The paradox addresses the simple question that if the universe is relatively homogenous and populated with an infinite or near-infinite number of stars, then the night sky when viewed from Earth should be completely illuminated by the light of countless stars in every direction. We now know that the expansion of space-time explained in Big Bang cosmogony caused the early radiation of the universe to lengthen into wavelengths that are longer than visible light through a process known as redshift.[56] In a similar manner the poet frames her meditation by acknowledging that there are stars as far as the eye can see, but there are many more moving away at distances so far that their light cannot reach us. She remembers those whom she calls "mis ausentes" (my absent ones),[57] not those who have died, but rather the ex-boyfriends whom she depicts carrying out their lives in ways and places she can only imagine, "disfrazados de incógnitos, se saben de memoria / calles que nunca he visto . . ." (dressed incognito, they know from memory / streets that I have never seen . . .).[58] Like the light of a distant star that is in reality a glimpse of the past, the poet sees them in a present that is no longer shared:

> y cuando los recuerdo
> no son quienes son,
> son quienes eran, los verdaderos,
> no esos farsantes que existen
> a mis espaldas, sino
> espectros de años abajo,[59]

> and when I recall them
> they are not who they are
> they are who they were, the true ones,
> not those frauds that exist
> behind my back, but rather
> specters of years below,

The antithetic balance between who they are and who they were, with fluid movement between fraud and truth, suggests that from the embodied now of the poet, the remembered absent ones are more real than who they are in their own presents. Similar to how the lyrical voice declares in "Primogénita" (First-born) that "Es imposible hablar del espacio sin incurrir en errores (gramaticales)" (It is impossible to speak of space without making (grammatical) mistakes),[60] relativity instructs us that the idea of a homogenous and unifying "present" throughout the universe is a fallacy, based more on our experiences than any real feature of time in the universe. Carlo Rovelli describes this feature of time in terms of presence and absence, stating, "The idea that a well-defined now exists throughout the universe is an illusion, an illegitimate extrapolation of our own experience. It is like the point where the rainbow touches the forest. We think that we can see it—but if we go to look for it, it isn't there."[61] Given that the autopoietic organism brings forth its cognitive world, creating its own pragmatic understanding of its relation to external reality,[62] the events distant in spacetime

DIMENSIONS OF EMBODIED EXPERIENCE

from the embodied mind appear to be happening now only from the position of the observer and not what is being observed or contemplated. One of the central tenants of relativity—that every measurement must take into the account the measurer's subjectivity—greatly influenced Mikhail Bakhtin when he conceptualized and developed the concept of the chronotope in literary studies.[63] Mancing likens the Bakhtinian chronotope to Maturana and Varela's insights into the organism-environment inseparability of structural coupling, as the autopoietic process emerges from its particular context in space and time.[64]

In comparison to these absent ones, the poet lauds the congruency of the dead whose existence is more coherent with their bones made of stone and from whom "no les amanece nunca" (dawn never comes).[65] The interplay of perspectives between past and present is given another level when the poet closes the poem by affirming her preference for the consistency of the dead, shifting the perspective from the self to that of an absent one:

> no andan por ahí pintándose los labios,
> saludando de beso en la mejilla
> no andan por ahí recordando sus sueños
> y olvidándome un poco, y pensando
> que esta que soy ahora no es la misma
> no andan por ahí llamándome farsante,
> recordando a la otra y olvidando
> mis lunares, uno a uno, estrellas
> que se alejan, cuya luz ya no alcanza.[66]

> they do not go around putting on lipstick,
> saying hello with a kiss on the cheek
> they do not go around remembering their dreams
> and forgetting me a little, and thinking
> that this one that I am now is not the same
> they do not go around calling me a fraud,
> remembering the other and forgetting
> my moles, one by one, stars
> that move away, whose light no longer reaches.

The anaphoric "no andan . . ." (they do not go around . . .) introduces a repetitive movement between the poetic I and the object of contemplation. The referentiality becomes difficult to follow as it becomes less and less clear who really are the absent ones. Compared to the consistency of the dead who are simply absent, the poet and those far away from each other in space and time share a strange existence where contemporaneous information about the other lies beyond the limits of their knowledge. Like the stars whose acceleration away from us causes their light to not be visible in the night, information about the absent ones is not available in a conceptual transference of the cosmological horizon that the poet reverses to include herself as absent in the now of others. In explaining her inspiration for connecting the psychological with the cosmological, Díaz Castelo expands the idea of a horizon of information beyond temporal transference of knowledge to include memory of events past. She casts the fading nature of memory in a positive light: "Si la memoria fuera estática, homogénea y eterna, tal como ese universo que postulaba la paradoja de Olbers, entonces los recuerdos recubrirían cada centímetro de nuestro paisaje psíquico" (If memory were static, homogenous and eternal, like that universe postulated in Olbers's Paradox, then memories would cover every centimeter of our psychological landscape).[67] Much like the curse that plagued Funes the Memorious from Borges's famous story about the man who remembered everything, Díaz Castelo states, "Al igual que ese cielo nocturno saturado de estrellas, nuestra conciencia estaría colmada de recuerdos tan brillantes que nos deslumbrarían" (Just like that night sky saturated with stars, our consciousness would be overflowing with memories so bright that they would blind us).[68] Díaz Castelo, then, portrays the flow of mind as analogous to spacetime with memories of events, phenomena, and actors as matter and energy.

From Empty Houses to Empty Pools: Bodies, Intra-actions, and the Flow of Mind

Despite the many ways that nineteenth- and twentieth-century physics upended our understanding of time and space, Rovelli points out that one remaining feature, conversely, has proven true, that "the world is nothing but change."[69] While we tend to think of the world as made up of things, Rovelli argues that the only way to see the world that is compatible with relativity is to understand that "the world is not a collection of things, it is a collection of events."[70] In other words, the basic units of matter and energy exist not only in a *where* but also in a *when* as they are constituents of temporally delimited events. This insight is essential in understanding how Díaz Castelo brings scientific knowledge to explore and more deeply express emotional and sentimental themes throughout *Principia* and, in particular, several of the poems placed in the second section of the book, "Sobre el movimiento de los cuerpos" (Of the Movement of Bodies). From the bodies moving away from each other in spacetime of "Sobre la luz que no vemos . . ." to the power of attraction and repulsion in the form of gravitational force in "Puntos de Lagrange" (Lagrange Points) and "Zona habitable" (Habitable Zone), these poems feature the connectivity of all matter and phenomena throughout space and time. Beyond matters of attraction between lovers and loved ones, of longing for events past, the poetic voice seeks out a conceptual metaphor that will connect the embodied consciousness to the universe as a whole.

In "Materia oscura" (Dark Matter) she searches to answer what binds the universe together, comparing the elusive dark matter with the intangible things that give meaning to life. For decades, the question of dark matter, the mysterious stuff that according to traditional estimates makes up more than 80 percent of the matter in the universe yet does not interact with electromagnetism in any way, has remained a relative mystery.[71] It is invisible to us, we cannot directly detect it, yet it has gravity that it exerts on the motion of stars and galaxies. The poet establishes, "No se explica su gravedad, la cercanía de los cuerpos, su querer estar juntos por la masa presente" (One cannot explain its gravity, the proximity of bodies, its wanting to be together through the present mass).[72] While the odd-numbered sections of the poem ostensibly refer to cosmological dark matter, the even-numbered sections blur the distinction between the nonvisible matter of the cosmos and the intangible relationships and affective possibilities that make up such a large part of the world we cognitively bring forth:

> porque casi nada es visible alégrate
> pero ya lo sabíamos tanto que no vemos y sin embargo
> descubierta en el año no descubierta teorizada
> pero cuya materia se puede deducir
> necesitamos algo que nos mantenga
> no quiero decir *juntos*
> algo que no vemos nos acerca
> algo que no sucede nos ha sucedido
> algo sucedió del otro lado de la posibilidad
> las cosas que no pasaron en ningún sitio
> las cosas que pasaron en ningún sitio
> las palabras que desdijimos lo olvidado
> no los hechos concretos lo subsecuente[73]

> because almost nothing is visible be glad
> but we already knew it so much that we do not see and yet
> discovered in the year not discovered theorized
> but whose matter can be deduced
> we need something to hold us
> I hesitate to say *together*
> something that we do not see brings us together
> something that does not occur has occurred to us
> something occurred from the other side of possibility
> the things that did not happen nowhere
> the things that did happen nowhere
> the words that we took back the forgotten
> not the concrete actions what came next

Visually these verses lack the punctuation and capitalization of the prose from the adjacent sections, with logical fits and starts and the repetition and reformulation of phrases flowing in a stream of consciousness. The overall effect is to mimic the flow of mind, the cognitive projection of reality. The paradox of something that exists yet somehow does not exist conveys a more nuanced portrayal of reality here when considered through the lens of autopoiesis. As Maturana and Varela point out, cognition is an effective action in which "every act of knowing brings forth a world."[74] Just as the poet corrects herself to say that dark matter has not been discovered but rather theorized, the existence of events that never came to pass or the intangible emotions that cannot be observed or measured tie together different events, people, and places in the poet's life. In several instances the poet repeats the idea of not wanting to say the word "juntos" (together) where there is no other choice to explain the impossibility of words to express these integral connectivities where no tangible connection can be observed.

Akin to the dark matter of the cosmos, the poetic voice identifies these thoughts, emotions, unrealized possibilities, and forgotten moments as what truly fills the universe and maintains the entanglement between bodies distant in space and time. Often cosmological dark matter is explained to general audiences through human-centered metaphors that the poet employs in the seventh section, stating that in one theory—reminiscent of the display from our visit to the Túnel de la ciencia—this matter is made up of gaseous filaments that form throughout the universe in a web whose nodes are the luminous galaxies, "Una telaraña invisible de delgados hilos, una estructura que existe sólo en la teoría y se parece a la red de neuronas en el cerebro, a hilos de saliva, al vapor que exhalamos una mañana fría" (An invisible spiderweb of thin threads, a structure that exists only in theory and that resembles the web of neurons in the brain, threads of saliva, the steam that we exhale on a cold morning).[75] The self-intertextuality, or poetic callbacks, such as the visible breath bring to mind the tension between content and form that appears from the very first poems of the collection. Furthermore, the imagery of the neurons in the brain, where thought is processed and the action of cognition is realized, drives home the tension between observable matter in corporeal structures or electrical signals and a greater intangible whole that is memory and self-awareness. Still the poetic voice returns time and again to the concepts of connectivity, togetherness, and mutual interdependence. In the last verses of the final section, the poetic speaker addresses an interlocutor, revealing the entire poem to be one side of a dialogue with an absent/present other:

un día dejarás de ser
pero eso ya sucedió
le sucedió a otros escúchame

DIMENSIONS OF EMBODIED EXPERIENCE

es sólo aquello que no vemos
lo que nos lleva de la mano y existimos[76]

one day you will cease to be
but that already happened
it happened to others listen to me
it is only that which we do not see
that takes us by the hand and we exist

The idea of ceasing to be and the blurring between one's death and the existence of another in memory has its inversion in that our existence itself is due to the nonobservable bonds, assemblages, and networks we create. Maturana and Varela describe this co-ontogenic relationship as the result of mutual structural and linguistic couplings, "a world brought forth into existence with other people."[77] In essence, autopoiesis describes how the system produces and maintains itself, but always as within a larger network of matter, energy, and other autopoietic beings and systems. Ira Livingston describes how the concept of self that is embedded in autopoiesis reveals a deeper interconnectivity: "The self, the *auto* of *autopoiesis*, is able to be misrecognized as something discrete and circularly self-contained, like an egg, but look closer and it seems to be instead a node in a branching structure, and the node, in turn, opens out into rhizomic, multiple, tangled networks, and what had seemed so involuted and singular turns out to be something torn up, plural, patched together, all over the place, rags, or, in Yiddish, *schmatte*."[78] In this way, the dark matter of "Materia oscura" is an allegory for the invisible, tangled networks that bind us to each other in ways that are not empirically observable. Moreover, the existence of things that no longer are such as loves lost in the past or things that never were or will be such as dreams unfulfilled is the dark matter that makes up the world brought forth by the embodied mind. Neural processes that occur through specific biological materials can be observed, yet how this stuff gives rise to our consciousness remains, like dark matter and energy, one of the great mysteries to be solved.

The main themes that drive *Principia*—presence/absence, longing, the embodied cognitive experience of spacetime, and the allegorical universe—all converge in the poem "Alberca vacía" (Empty Pool). I agree with poet Isabel Zapata when she states that after going around in countless circles, she finally identified the central idea of *Principia* through this very poem: "una alberca vacía es alberca, aunque carezca de agua" (an empty pool is a pool even if it has no water).[79] While simple on its face, this phrase encapsulates Díaz Castelo's conceptualization of the relationship between the intimate universe and its more-than-human counterpart, as a pool cannot be solely water nor its shape alone, but rather a coming together of form and content in a particular space and time. The repeated metaphor that the universe is an empty pool begins each stanza. At times it is a space of virtual nostalgia where children pretend to swim, trying to recognize

158 SCIENCE FUSION IN CONTEMPORARY MEXICAN LITERATURE

the water in its absence. At others, it fills with matter as when lifeless leaves ephemerally coalesce to form constellations as they slowly decompose. Above all, the empty pool is a contradiction just like its walls that are painted blue yet do not hold water. Before the image of the empty pool, the poetic voice laments, "Qué desnivel absurdo, cada escalón / para llegar a ningún sitio" (What an absurd incline, each rung / to get to nowhere).[80] Drained of its water, the empty pool seems to cease being a pool. With a pessimistic tone, the poetic voice calls it "un lugar sin lugar, sitio a medias, / tumba de agua, de años luz" (a place without place, a halfway finished site, / tomb of water, of light years).[81] The empty pool leaves dissatisfaction, as the poet sees in its emptiness only what she thought was purpose:

> Y hay algo y lo sabemos
> de entrada roto sobre el sitio.
> No es que no haya nada dentro
> del espacio al que los límites dan forma,
> sólo no lo queremos. Es el contorno
> enardecido, impecable, que abarca
> ese no estar ahí del agua,[82]

> And there's something and we know it
> from the start broken about the place.
> It is not that there is nothing inside
> of the space to which the limits give shape,
> only we do not want it. It is the contour
> fired up, flawless, that encompasses
> that not being thereness of the water,

As in "Materia oscura" where the poetic voice states "el espacio es tiempo que no pasó en ningún sitio" (space is time that did not happen anywhere),[83] the poet's desire is an affective drive that mentally brings forth a world that is not, because to return to a past memory is to conceive the universe as a collection of things that take up space and endure over time. Rovelli points out that this conception—which feels intuitive in our embodied experience—is simply not compatible with the union of space and time in relativity: "We cannot think of the *physical world* as if it were made up of things, of entities. It simply doesn't work. What works instead is thinking about the world as a network of events."[84]

The final stanza of "Alberca vacía" establishes a parallel with the epigraph from Edmund Spenser's *The Faerie Queene* that opens the second section of *Principia* declaring, "For all that moveth doth in change delight." Here contemplation of the pool as form devoid of content leads the poet to the realization that the universe as pool is no more a thing out there as a human-centered subjectivity that fills it with memories of events and phenomena past. Rather,

DIMENSIONS OF EMBODIED EXPERIENCE

"El universo es eso: esa forma / de quitarse la forma: esa forma" (that form / of taking off form: that form),[85] that is both the matter it once held as well as "esas ganas de / no creer en la gravedad de las cosas" (that want / to not believe in the gravity of things).[86] Contemplating the empty pool and the "not being there-ness of the water" reminds the poet of

> la incisión de la falta y el ansia
> por estar dentro y saberlo,
> que no hay un adentro, o no ése
> sino otro.[87]

> the incision of lack and longing
> for being inside and knowing it,
> that there is no inside, or not that one
> but another.

To see the universe as an empty pool, then, is not to simply contemplate an existing form that holds what is or is not already there. Rather, it is to recognize that it is not a thing out there, but rather a continual and mutually constitutive becoming in spacetime. It is made up of both tangible molecules as well as the affective flow of embodied autopoietic systems, with reality emerging from the intra-action of matter and forces. The poet's contemplation of the pool as empty space that continually takes on forms is similar to Barad's asseveration that phenomena and objects do not precede their interactions but rather emerge as a result of intra-actions. These material-discursive apparatuses, like the autopoietic self, are virtual and contingent in a continuous process of emerging through a "mutual constitution of entangled agencies."[88]

In closing, I would like to establish another circuitous connection between this final chapter and the poetry of Alberto Blanco from the first to illustrate how and to what effects ciencia-fusión entangles scientific and literary discourses. Both Díaz Castelo and Blanco have composed works that share the same title such as "Radiografías," which correspondingly take up the interplay of absence and presence, and "Credo," in which they similarly affirm the existence of the intangible and the affective capacity of representation. However, it is often in poems with very different titles where we see most clearly how the two poets, and by extension other writers of ciencia-fusión, literarily employ knowledge from the natural sciences in a strikingly similar fashion to enrich a deeper understanding of the universe and our place within it. Both Blanco's "Canto a no yo" and Díaz Castelo's "Esto otro que también me habita" ponder subjectivity, incorporating insights from physics and biology, respectively. The two poems are constructed around the concept of change; in "Canto" it is change at the molecular and subatomic levels, whereas in "Esto otro" it is at the microbiological. Moreover, both poems unambiguously insert themselves

160 SCIENCE FUSION IN CONTEMPORARY MEXICAN LITERATURE

into dialogue with other poets and poetics, with Blanco corresponding with Whitman's "Song of Myself" and Díaz Castelo with Jaramillo Agudelo's "Poemas de amor, 1." As such, these poems, like all the other works that we have considered here, function in the nexus between science and literature. What is more, both poems refute the concept of a stable human subject somehow existing outside of diachronic processes, changes, and intra-activity.

In the face of such shifting concepts of subjectivity, both Blanco and Díaz Castelo ponder the relationship between we humans and the idea of the greater universe out there. While there are differences in the two poets' conceptualizations, both use metaphors of space and time to depict the countless relations, intraconnections, and entanglements between and within us, others, and the universe. In "Teoría de la gravedad" (Theory of Gravity), Blanco expounds upon how Einstein's general theory of relativity upended our understanding of gravity as a force of attraction between objects as explained in Newton's *Principia Mathematica*. In general relativity, gravity is actually posited as the curvature of spacetime caused by the uneven distribution of mass. The poetic voice in Blanco's poem explains how it is not really forces of attraction that keep us and it all together, but rather

> Es la forma del espacio,
> y sé que no parece una explicación.
> Pero, es la forma del espacio,
> nada más.[89]

> It is the shape of space,
> and I know that doesn't seem like an explanation.
> But, it is the shape of space,
> nothing more.

Rather than an exterior force that causes bodies to be attracted to each other, gravity is a curvature of spacetime brought about by those bodies themselves. In this light, Díaz Castelo's metaphor of the universe as empty pool and Blanco's theory of gravity are not entirely about the shape of a universe out there. Instead, like much of the work of ciencia-fusión, these metaphors and literary interventions—here through a visualization of the gravitational curvature created by material bodies and an empty pool that holds tangible matter as well as intangible potentialities—all speak of bodies that matter, emerging from and constituting an intra-active more-than-human universe.

Conclusions

KNOWING AND BELONGING
IN AN ENTANGLED UNIVERSE

Unlike the more familiar nuclear fission whose released energy for years has been harnessed for uses both destructive and productive, the dream of producing stable nuclear fusion at an industrial scale has thus far proven elusive. In contrast to nuclear fission, a reaction in which the nucleus of an atom splits into two or more nuclei, fusion occurs when two atomic nuclei combine to form a single heavier nucleus, releasing enormous amounts of energy, potentially providing a virtually limitless source of clean and renewal energy for humanity.[1] In the preceding pages we have contemplated potentialities of a different type of fusion through which the authors of ciencia-fusión meld and entangle science and literature in new discourses that reorient the human and nonhuman as emerging from and integral to nonhuman physical matter, forces, and phenomena. It would seem that these texts harness metaphoric energy from literary fusions to provide a deeper understanding not only of the universe itself but also of innovative ways with which to confront the sociocultural and ecological issues of the present. Of course, there is no literal, reductive connection between nuclear fusion and the merging of science and literature that we have studied. Nonetheless, there is great value in holding the two in yet another metaphoric relationship because doing so casts light on the creative potentialities that literary and scientific fusions produce.

As we have seen, far from simply fusing traditions, knowledges, and domains into some resulting homogenous product, ciencia-fusión creates novel ways of considering long-standing questions precisely through its embrace of productive tensions as evidenced in its plentiful deployment of paradox and complementarity. We can observe one such example in Jorge Fernández Granados's poem "Principio de incertidumbre" (Uncertainty Principle), which encapsulates many of the characteristics we have identified in ciencia-fusión. Here the poet transposes the binary aspects of the Observer Effect and Heisenberg's Uncertainty

162 SCIENCE FUSION IN CONTEMPORARY MEXICAN LITERATURE

Principle to the realm of the social and human. Through a pair of verses that come across as a sort of aphorism, the poetic voice ponders the question of distance regarding knowledge making and belonging:

si alejarse es preciso para mirar y entender
aproximarse es preciso para pertenecer[2]

if distancing oneself is necessary to look and understand
getting close is necessary to belong

The poetic voice sets up a duality through parallel verses both expressing the need for what seem to be the contradictory actions of approaching and distancing, metaphorically establishing logical connections between the social and the physical. The thematic structure of the poem is a fusion itself, merging Heisenberg's Uncertainty Principle, which establishes epistemological limits to knowing all measurable aspects of an object in space and time, with the ontological implications of the Observer Effect, which reflects how the experimenter necessarily is part of, and therefore alters, any experiment they carry out. The poet's principle of uncertainty, therefore, brings questions of knowing and being together to express what at first seem to be contradictory impulses: that one cannot fully contemplate and fully participate at the same time. Furthermore, the poet explicitly expresses how these transpositions of scientific knowledge easily function within the realm of human culture:

la *verdad*   esa medusa
ante la cual la (última) cercanía o la (demasiada) distancia son el error
desde donde amamos o juzgamos
         a la impuntual la perdediza
realidad
         (o lo que así nombramos)
en otras palabras la creencia que nace de una contradicción y (por cierto) no
         es muy distinta a nosotros mismos[3]

the *truth*   that medusa
before which the (last) closeness of the (too far) distance are the error
from which we love or judge
         the unpunctual the easily lost
reality
         (or what we call as such)
in other words the belief that is born from a contradiction and (by the way)
         is not very different from ourselves

The poet's slippery grasp of morphing and manifold truth and reality is built upon the contradictions inherent in attempting to understand reality from within. Like the medusa—both the invertebrate jellyfish and the mythological

CONCLUSIONS

Gorgon whose gaze turned men to stone—transforming claims of knowledge are evolving reflections upon a world in process that we cannot measure and fully comprehend. Moreover, in our errant belief that we can observe and understand from afar, we inadvertently turn ourselves and all of reality to stone, a poor reflection of the ever-changing process of becoming of which we are part.

Instead, ciencia-fusión challenges us to consider a much more dynamic reality from within, as can be appreciated holding the preceding verses with the poet's assertion in an opening stand-alone verse that "presenciar es participar" (to witness is to participate).[4] Bound in this frame, the poem communicates a more robust conceptualization of humanity and the universe representative of much of the work of ciencia-fusión. The multiple meanings of the verb *presenciar*—to "witness" as well as to simply "be present"—provide insights into the same entanglement of the human and the material as well as the literary and scientific, which we have seen in previous chapters. Similar to the depiction of contemplating reality from within in Fernández Granados's "Principio de incertidumbre," Barad marks a clear distinction between the activity of "reflection," holding and reflecting upon objects at a distance, and the activity of "diffraction," which describes the interference patterns produced by waves that come into coherent contact with other waves or obstacles. Like two stones dropped into a pond at a distance apart from each other, all waves in the universe ultimately overlap and interact with each other. Barad sees diffraction patterns as intra-active difference, identifying them as "the fundamental constituents that make up the world."[5] A methodology of diffraction does not fix what is the object and what is the subject in advance, and therefore "is respectful of the entanglement of ideas and other materials in ways that reflexive methodologies are not."[6] For Barad, such diffractive thinking is an "onto-epistem-ology" that, while "marking difference from within and as part of an entangled state," affirms that "knowing is a material practice of engagement as part of the world in its differential becoming."[7] As in Fernández Granados's poem, to be present is to witness, and any act of witnessing or knowing is an act of engagement and belonging to an expanding universe. It would be hard not to argue that all of the works of ciencia-fusión surveyed in this book exhibit what Barad calls diffractive thinking as these authors use science and literature to take up conceptualizations of the universe, life, and what it means to be human.

As we have seen, the relationship between what we now conceive of as science and literature predates even the words themselves. At the same time that literature has at times clarified and at others challenged scientific concepts, scientific knowledge has transformed and disrupted notions of discourse, narrative, and even literature and literary studies.[8] It is important to note that authors of ciencia-fusión overtly feature such destabilizing interfaces not through a lens of suspicion, but instead through an embrace and utilization of these inherent tensions to create works of art that, like that of metaphoric fusion, become more than the simple sum of their constituent parts. In ciencia-fusión insights from

164 SCIENCE FUSION IN CONTEMPORARY MEXICAN LITERATURE

chemistry, biology, physics, and other natural sciences bring a deeper understanding of both literature and the world it engages with. In Jorge Volpi's *En busca de Klingsor* we see how concepts of indeterminacy, chance, chaos, and scale in the scientific illuminate and problematize normative understandings of historiography and the act of narration itself. Depictions of life as enlightened by work in biology and chemistry through the activity of autopoiesis reveal greater inter- and intraconnectivity as we see in Maricela Guerrero's *El sueño de toda célula* and Sabina Berman's Karen novels. In these works, scientific knowledge meets the environmental humanities, challenging readers to reorient humanity's place within greater networks while framing its impact on the more-than-human world within new conceptualizations that transcend the nature-culture divide. At the same time, far from depicting science as a benign pursuit of knowledge apart from culture, Berman and Guerrero show how science and technology can function at the service of human avarice, having been used to extract, destroy, and kill both human and more-than-human life. Similarly, Ignacio Padilla depicts in *El androide y otras quimeras* a darker side to the Scientific Revolution and intersections between science and commerce throughout the centuries. In ciencia-fusión, depictions of science are as multifaceted and heterogeneous as the corresponding ways that science impacts and moves within culture. Undoubtedly, these authors are reverential of but not deferential to the knowledge-making practices of science. Perhaps Alberto Blanco best expresses ciencia-fusión's approach in his poetic epigraph to *La raíz cuadrada del cielo*:

La
ciencia
me enseñó
Que
el sol no es
el centro del universo;
El sol
me enseñó
que la ciencia tampoco.[9]

As
science
taught me
That
the sun is not
the center of the universe;
The sun
taught me
that science isn't either.

CONCLUSIONS   165

In the symbolism of the sun in the preceding poem and throughout Blanco's science poetry, metaphorical and metonymic transferal is not simply a literary or rhetorical device or even a feature of human language and thought. Rather, transference and movement from one domain to another is a feature of nature through biological processes and effective and communicatory actions in all forms of more-than-human life. In this manner, ciencia-fusión explores metaphoric movement in the world at the same time that it applies and transposes metaphors from scientific discourse to human experiences through themes of movement, interconnectivity, and perpetually enacted relations. While metaphoric transpositions feature in the works of narrative we have examined, we particularly see in the lyrical form how poets such as Blanco, Guerrero, and Díaz Castelo use linguistic and conceptual metaphors to express embodied experiences that emerge from and are simultaneously integral to a more-than-human universe. Through a depiction of humanity as material-discursive enactment in Blanco's *Antes de nacer* and Guerrero's life-giving flows of and among plant and animal life in *El sueño de toda célula*, the indeterminant nature of poetic language and imagery allows us to reconceptualize the interconnective entanglements of the material and the human in new ways. Future studies could further explore how such formal and rhetorical features pertaining to genre impact the development of ciencia-fusión. While we have taken up several examples of ciencia-fusión in poetry and narrative, there are a number of works of theater by Mexican playwrights such as Luis Guerrero's *Números imaginarios* (*Imaginary Numbers*) and Mario Cantú Toscano's *Golem* (*Golem*) that remain to be considered. Whether in poetry or narrative, all the works we have taken up embrace the uncertain, indeterminant, and relativistic universe that science reveals; they employ metaphor in a way that is careful to not reductively apply these concepts to human ethics and society. One would be hard-pressed to find popularly held tropes such as general and special relativity reduced to moral relativity in works of ciencia-fusión. In fact, at the heart of the novels, stories, poems, and plays is a deeper and nuanced engagement in ethics. Furthermore, in their emphasis on the limits of knowledge and subjectivity, these authors subvert totalization whenever it appears in political, cultural, moral, and, not surprisingly, both literary and scientific discourse.

A final characteristic that sets these works of ciencia-fusión apart is how they all approach the question of the human within the universe with the explicit acknowledgment of the material-discursive entanglements that blur conventional limits of subjectivity. By incorporating and transposing more recent scientific discoveries, these works challenge many of the dualistic paradigms associated with humanism in order to reorient humans and human conditions within greater frameworks of materiality. Not coincidentally, they all feature potentialities where distinctions between subject/object and human/nonhuman fuse together. Díaz Castelo's empty pool, the blank spaces in Blanco's double-helix verses, the absently present bodies of Padilla's gendered automata, the vast ocean in Berman's novels, Volpi's indeterminate historical text, and Guerrero's cell as a blank leaf or vacant lot next door all show reality as open and outstretching spacetime being constituted through human and nonhuman intra-actions in a process of continual becoming. Through connectivity, indeterminacy, intra-action, and autopoiesis, these works depict a universe in constant flux that—while material in nature—is not simply a substantialist space or a summation of things, but rather a flowing network of events, processes, and phenomena. Human cognition and its material-discursive underpinnings both emerge from and consequently further imagine analogous potentialities. In the poem "Si" (If) in the collection *El acelerador de partículas* (*The Particle Accelerator*), Julio Trujillo ponders questions of materiality and immateriality:

> Si una persona es una cosa
> una idea no lo es.
>
> . . . .
>
> Si es cosa la mitad de la mitad de un átomo
> la música no lo es.[10]

> If a person is a thing
> an idea is not.
>
> . . . .
>
> If a half of a half of an atom is a thing
> music is not.

By portraying a reality that is neither wholly substantialist nor completely functionalist, ciencia-fusión reveals a universe and human experience that is intra-active, both material and discursive, where every effective action, act of knowing, and way of being has ethical consequences. Through the entanglement of complementary concepts and knowledge from literary and scientific traditions, these works resignify and reimagine long-held conceptualizations of the universe and humanity's place in it. These literary fusions bring together the human and the material to render reality and all human activity as a continual process of becoming, an exploration not only of forces and matter, but also of what in this universe it truly means to matter.

Acknowledgments

In hindsight, this book started many years ago when Keri, my best friend and spouse, gave me a book on quantum mechanics for my birthday, which started my habit of reading science books at bedtime. A graduate student at the time, I deceived myself into thinking that reading about science would allow me to shift gears from the literary and cultural studies that filled my days and evenings. Little did I suspect that those two worlds would collide when Juan Carlos González Espitia suggested I pick up Jorge Volpi's *En busca de Klingsor*, thus setting me off on a long journey to writing *Science Fusion*.

Like that one suggestion from a great professor, so many teachers and mentors have touched my life in ways for which I can never fully express my gratitude. Coach Mac, Bob Eckard, Arturo Ortiz, María Mabrey, Lucille Charlebois, Alicia Rivero, and Stuart Day are just a few of the teachers and professors who have shared their knowledge, passion, and love for literature from the Spanish-speaking world.

I would like to thank two journals for permission to reprint previously published material. Much of chapter 2 was previously published in "The Scale of History in Jorge Volpi's *En busca de Klingsor*" in *Hispania* 101, no. 3 (2018): 232–242. An earlier version of chapter 3 was published as "Of Automatons and Androcentric Desire: Control and Commodification in Ignacio Padilla's *El androide y otras quimeras*" in *Ometeca* 25 (2020–2021): 49–66.

I am grateful to work at a university that supports faculty as both teachers and scholars. I thank Derrick Miller, David Webster, Kemille Moore, and Michelle Scatton-Tessier for their generous support and encouragement. The support I received from the UNCW College of Arts and Sciences Research Reassignment and Summer Research Initiative facilitated much of the research and writing that went into making this book a reality.

I extend my sincerest thanks to the talented Feliks Christian Primigg who generously shared his photographs of Juan O'Gorman's mural at UNAM's Biblioteca Central.

I also work with some great colleagues who also happen to be dear friends. In particular, thank you, Paco Brignole, Sergi Rivero Navarro, and Christina Lord for many conversations that sparked ideas that informed this book. Thank you, Diana Perez, for sharing lots of laughs and an endless supply of old man candy to keep my writing going. I also thank all of you WLC friends for sharing your insights, wisdom, and laughter with me. I am also forever grateful to Oswaldo Estrada, who provided me the spark to jump back into research after a long period coordinating a program. I am also thankful to María Zalduondo, Ron Friis, and Emile Harley, who generously shared work and insights that have furthered this project.

I do not know how to fully express my gratitude and appreciation for the amazing people and editorial board at Bucknell University Press. I never imagined that publishing a book could be such a positive experience. I send a special thank-you to Suzanne Guiod for welcoming my project from the very start, giving always constructive advice, and shepherding this project throughout the process. I am incredibly grateful to Aníbal González for his enthusiasm and am honored by his support for including this project in a book series that has been so important to my research over the years. In addition, I thank the anonymous external readers who provided me with much appreciated and insightful feedback that enriched the development of this book. I am beyond grateful for the care, attention, and knowledge that they brought to the review process.

Above all, I want to acknowledge and thank my family and friends for always being supportive, loving, and understanding as this book was being written. Mom, Dad, Lauren, and Leigh, thank you for teaching me to love fully, to be kind, and to laugh out loud. I am also grateful to Bert, Kyle, Sometimes Monday, and my L-R and WPPC friends. And finally, Keri, Gale, and Lily, thank you for truly making these the golden years. I am beyond blessed to share this life with you. I love you so much.

Notes

INTRODUCTION

1. Túnel de la Ciencia, "Historia del Túnel de la Ciencia," last revised 2017, http://www.tuneldelaciencia.unam.mx/home/historia-del-tunel-de-la-ciencia.

2. An image of this display can be found at http://www.tuneldelaciencia.unam.mx/exposicion/estructura-del-universo.

3. Carlos Monsiváis, *Los rituales del caos* (Mexico City: Ediciones Era, 1995), 113. This quote is from the essay "El metro: Viaje hacia el fin del apretujón," which reflects many of the characteristics of ciencia-fusión given the way Monsiváis ponders how in Mexico City's Metro system a crushing humanity is made to fit into a small space, breaking down the molecular structure of the universe as more than one object must occupy the same space at the same time.

4. Rafael Catalá, *Cienciapoesía* (Minneapolis: Prisma Books, 1986), 13.

5. Niels Bohr explains the challenge of moving from the domain of mathematical deduction to explicatory conceptual models of quantum mechanics, remarking, "We must be clear that when it comes to atoms, language can be used only as in poetry. The poet, too, is not nearly so concerned with describing facts as with creating images and establishing mental connections." Quoted in Jim Baggott, *The Quantum Story: A History of 40 Moments* (Oxford: Oxford University Press, 2011), 47.

6. José Gordon, *El inconcebible Universo: sueños de unidad* (Mexico City: Sexto Piso / Instituto Cultural de León, 2017), 9.

7. See C. P. Snow, *Two Cultures and the Scientific Revolution* (Cambridge: Cambridge University Press, 1998).

8. Edward O. Wilson, *Consilience: The Unity of Knowledge* (New York: Knopf, 1998), viii.

9. Mónica Prandi, "Ciencia-Ficción: Dos modos de entender el mundo. Entrevista a Jorge Volpi," *Letra Urbana* 22 (October 25, 2013), https://letraurbana.com/articulos/ciencia-ficcion-dos-modos-de-entender-el-mundo-entrevista-a-jorge-volpi/.

10. Joe Moran, *Interdisciplinarity: The New Critical Idiom* (London: Routledge, 2006), 160. Viewing science as a discursive practice inspired a proliferation of social constructionist approaches to the history of science in the later decades of the twentieth

century. Seminal works such as Bruno Latour and Steve Woolgar's polemical *Laboratory Life: The Construction of Scientific Facts* certainly highlighted the discursive and nonempirical nature of much scientific work. While even Latour has walked back much of what he said earlier in his career, there is no doubt that social constructionism continues to impact philosophies and histories of science. For a nuanced and balanced criticism of constructivism, see André Kukla, *Social Constructivism and the Philosophy of Science* (London: Routledge, 2000).

11. Victoria Carpenter, "Literature and Science: To Each Its Own?," in *Interface between Literature and Science: Cross-Disciplinary Approaches to Latin American Texts*, ed. Victoria Carpenter (Newcastle upon Tyne: Cambridge Scholars, 2015), 1.

12. Jerry Hoeg, *Science, Technology, and Latin American Narrative in the Twentieth Century and Beyond* (Cranbury, NJ: Associated University Press, 2000), 10. Hoeg's formulation of the Social Imaginary is largely based on the work of Cornelius Castoriadis, who argued that the imaginary of society "creates for each historical period its singular way of living, seeing and making its own existence." Castoriadis, *The Imaginary Institution of Society*, trans. Kathleen Blamey (Cambridge, MA: MIT Press, 1997), 145.

13. Gerardo Herrera Corral, *El Higgs, el universo líquido y el Gran Colisionador de Hadrones* (Mexico City: Fondo de Cultura Económica, 2014), 14.

14. Abril Perezyera, "Gerardo Herrera Corral, experto del Cinvestav prevé explicar el cosmos a través de poesía," *SDP Noticias*, February 26, 2014, https://www.sdpnoticias.com/estilo-de-vida/experto-herrera-gerardo-corral.html.

15. Nina Engelhardt and Julia Hoydis, "Introduction: Connectivities Between Literature and Science in the Twenty-First Century," in *Representations of Science in Twenty-First-Century Fiction: Human and Temporal Connectivities*, ed. Engelhardt and Hoydis (Cham, Switzerland: Palgrave, 2019), 3.

16. Miguel de Asúa, *Ciencia y Literatura: Un relato histórico* (Buenos Aires: Eudeba, 2011), 6–7.

17. Miguel de Asúa, *Ciencia y Literatura*, 7.

18. Bruno Latour, *We Have Never Been Modern*, trans. Catherine Porter (Cambridge, MA: Harvard University Press, 1993), 115–116.

19. Antonio Barrera-Osorio, *Experiencing Nature: The Spanish American Empire and the Early Scientific Revolution* (Austin: University of Texas Press, 2006), 3.

20. Asúa, *Ciencia y Literatura*, 7–8.

21. Mary Louise Pratt, *Imperial Eyes: Travel Writing and Transculturation* (London: Routledge, 1992), 29.

22. María del Pilar Blanco and Joanna Page, "Introduction: Reimagining Science in Latin America," in *Geopolitics, Culture, and the Scientific Imaginary in Latin America*, ed. Blanco and Page (Gainesville: University Press of Florida, 2020), 1.

23. We are reminded of Warwick Anderson's statement that "there is a broader sense in which any critical account of how science travels and interacts, whatever its assumptions and theories, is *implicitly* postcolonial." Anderson, "From Subjugated Knowledge to Conjugated Subjects: Science and Globalisation, or Postcolonial Studies of Science?," *Postcolonial Studies* 12, no. 4 (2009): 390.

24. Alicia Rivero, "El papel de la ciencia en la literatura hispánica moderna. Introducción," *La Torre: Revista general de la Universidad de Puerto Rico* 3, no. 9 (1998): 525.

NOTES TO PAGES 6–8

25. Rafael Catalá, "Literatura y ciencia en las culturas de habla hispana," *Torre: Revista General de la Universidad de Puerto Rico* 3, no. 9 (1998): 529–550.

26. Evelyn Fishburn and Eduardo L. Ortiz, "Introduction," in *Science and the Creative Imagination in Latin America*, ed. Fishburn and Ortiz (London: Institute for the Study of the Americas, 2005), 1.

27. Carpenter, "Literature and Science," 4.

28. Carpenter, "Literature and Science," 4.

29. For examples of similar scholarship regarding science in peninsular Spanish literature, see Isabel Jaén and Julien Jacques Simon, eds., *Cognitive Approaches to Early Modern Spanish Literature* (New York: Oxford University Press, 2016), and Óscar Iván Useche, *Founders of the Future: The Science and Industry of Spanish Modernization* (Lewisburg, PA: Bucknell University Press, 2022).

30. Oscar A. Pérez, *Medicine, Power, and the Authoritarian Regime in Hispanic Literature* (New York: Routledge, 2022), 3.

31. David Dalton, *Mestizo Modernity: Race, Technology, and the Body in Postrevolutionary Mexico* (Gainesville: University Press of Florida, 2018), 2.

32. See Claude Fell, *José Vasconcelos: Los años del águila (1920–1925)* (Mexico City: UNAM, 1989).

33. Brais Outes-León, "Energía, termodinámica, y el imaginario tecnológico en *La raza cósmica* de José Vasconcelos," *Revista de Estudios Hispánicos* 53, no. 1 (2019): 262.

34. Dalton, *Mestizo Modernity*, 36.

35. Alongside transculturation (Ángel Rama) and hybridity (Néstor García-Canclini), heterogeneity is frequently employed as a defining characteristic of Latin American literature as articulated by Antonio Cornejo-Polar in *Escribir en el aire: Ensayo sobre la heterogeneidad en las literaturas andinas* (Lima: Horizonte, 1994). Interestingly, we can perceive the same distrust of scientific thought invading the artistic sphere that Vasconcelos expressed in Cornejo-Polar's last public writing where the Peruvian critic spoke of the danger of using the metaphor of hybridity, which, originating in biology, could produce what he calls "productos infértiles" (infertile products). Cited in David Sobrevilla, "Transculturación y Heterogeneidad: Avatares de dos categorías literarias en América Latina," *Revista de Crítica Literaria Latinoamericana* 27, no. 54 (2001): 26.

36. Catalá, "Literatura," 531.

37. Michael F. Capobianco and Gloria S. Meléndez, "Of Poets, Prophets, and Engineers: Nezahualcoyotl and Nezahualpilli," *Ometeca* 3–4 (1996): 509–510.

38. Miguel León-Portilla, *Aztec Thought and Culture: A Study of the Ancient Nahuatl Mind*, trans. Jack Emory Davis (Norman: University of Oklahoma Press, 1963), 92–93.

39. Isabel Jaén and Julien Jacques Simon, "Introduction," in Jaén and Simon, *Cognitive Approaches to Early Modern Spanish Literature*, 4.

40. Elías Trabulse, "El tránsito del hermetismo a la ciencia moderna: Alejandro Fabián, Sor Juana Inés de La Cruz y Carlos de Sigüenza y Góngora (1667–1690)," *Calíope: Journal of the Society for Renaissance & Baroque Hispanic Poetry* 4, no. 1–2 (1998): 56–57.

41. Peter Beardsall, "Writing at the Interface: Toward an Overview of the Relationship between Science and Literature," in Carpenter, *Interface between Literature and Science*, 20.

42. Stephanie Kirk, "Gender and Authority in Sor Juana's Sonnet to Sigüenza y Góngora," *Romance Notes* 58, no. 2 (2018): 232.

43. David Galicia Lechuga, "La ciencia en la obra de sor Juana," *Revista Digital Universitaria* 16, no. 12 (December 2015): 11, http://www.revista.unam.mx/vol.16/num12/art96/index.html.

44. Elías Trabulse, "El universo científico de Sor Juana Inés de la Cruz," *Colonial Latin America Review* 4, no. 2 (1995): 46.

45. José F. Robles, *Polemics, Literature, and Knowledge in Eighteenth-Century Mexico: A New World for the Republic of Letters* (Liverpool: Liverpool University Press, 2021), 2.

46. Robles, *Polemics, Literature, and Knowledge*, 17.

47. Laura Suárez y López-Guazo, "The Mexican Eugenics Society: Racial Selection and Improvement," in *The Reception of Darwinism in the Iberian World: Spain, Spanish America, and Brazil*, ed. Thomas F. Glick, Miguel Angel Puig-Samper, and Rosaura Ruiz (Boston: Kluwer, 2001), 144.

48. See Natalia Priego, "Un país en busca de su identidad: Reflexiones sobre el cientificismo de 'Los Científicos' en el México de don Porfirio," in *Paradigmas, Culturas y Saberes: La Transmisión Del Conocimiento Científico En Latinoamérica*, ed. Natalia Priego and Sonia Lozano (Frankfurt: Vervuert, 2007), 37–60.

49. Catalá, "Literatura," 536.

50. Ignacio Sánchez Prado, "El mestizaje en el corazón de la utopía: *La raza cósmica* entre Aztlán y América Latina," *Revista Canadiense de Estudios Hispánicos* 33, no. 2 (2009): 395.

51. Jorge Quintana-Navarrete, "Biopolítica y vida inorgánica: La plasmogenia de Alfonso Herrera," *Revista Hispánica Moderna* 72, no. 1 (2019): 79–80.

52. Quintana-Navarrete, "Biopolítica y vida inorgánica," 81.

53. Quintana-Navarrete, "Biopolítica y vida inorgánica," 94.

54. Sara Calderón, "Narrative Techniques in Jorge Volpi's Fictions," in *The Mexican Crack Writers: History and Criticism*, ed. Héctor Jaimes (Cham, Switzerland: Palgrave Macmillan, 2017), 65.

55. Daniel Sifuentes Espinoza, "Alfonso Reyes y la ciencia y tecnología. Un caso: 'La pólvora en infiernitos," *Ciencia UANL* 18, no. 75 (2015): 15.

56. Alfonso Reyes, *El deslinde* (Mexico City: Colegio de México, 1944), 78.

57. Sebastián Pineda Buitrago, *La musa crítica: Teoría y ciencia literaria de Alfonso Reyes* (Mexico City: El Colegio Nacional, 2007), 27.

58. Pineda Buitrago, *La musa crítica*, 34.

59. John Skirius, *El ensayo hispanoamericano del siglo XX* (Mexico City: Fondo de Cultura Económica, 1994), 10.

60. Carlos Chimal, "Levedad, rapidez, precisión. Octavio Paz y la ciencia," *Letras Libres* 259 (June 1998): 90.

61. Octavio Paz, *Corriente alterna* (Mexico City: Siglo XXI, 2000), 79.

62. Chimal, "Levedad, rapidez, precisión," 90.

63. José Emilio Pacheco, "Lumbre en el aire," in *Tarde o temprano* (Barcelona: Tusquets, 2010), 573; Pacheco, "La gota," in *Tarde o temprano*, 429.

64. Gerardo Deniz, *Erdera* (Mexico City: Fondo de Cultura Económica, 2006), 329. Readers will undoubtedly find a very clear interconnectivity between this poem and the Wagnerian subtext of Jorge Volpi's *En busca de Klingsor*.

65. Arturo Azuela, *El matemático* (Mexico City: Plaza y Valdés, 1988), 135–142.

66. George Lakoff and Mark Johnson, *Metaphors We Live By* (Chicago: University of Chicago Press, 1980), 3.

NOTES TO PAGES 13–15

67. Lakoff and Johnson, *Metaphors We Live By*, 235, emphasis original.

68. Lakoff and Johnson, *Metaphors We Live By*, 194, emphasis original.

69. Antonio Barcelona, "Introduction: The Cognitive Theory of Metaphor and Metonymy," in *Metaphor and Metonymy at the Crossroads: A Cognitive Perspective*, ed. Barcelona (Berlin: De Gruyter, 2003), 3–4.

70. David R. Gruber, "Material Foundations of Scientific Metaphors: A New Materialist Metaphor Studies," *Configurations: A Journal of Literature, Science, and Technology* 31, no. 1 (Winter 2023): 6.

71. Gruber, "Material Foundations of Scientific Metaphors," 34.

72. Rosi Braidotti, *The Posthuman* (Cambridge: Polity, 2013), 16.

73. Braidotti, *Posthuman*, 51.

74. Ignacio M. Sánchez Prado, "El giro (post)humanista. A manera de introducción," *Revista de Crítica Literaria Latinoamericana* 34, no. 68 (2008): 7–8.

75. Sánchez Prado, "El giro (post)humanista," 17.

76. Francesca Ferrando, "Posthumanism, Transhumanism, Antihumanism, Metahumanism, and New Materialisms: Differences and Relations," *Existenz* 8, no. 2 (2013): 27.

77. Aníbal Quijano, "Coloniality of Power and Eurocentrism in America," *International Sociology* 15, no. 2 (2000): 221–222.

78. Mabel Moraña, *Inscripciones críticas. Ensayos sobre cultura latinoamericana* (Santiago: Cuarto Propio, 2014), 93–94.

79. Moraña, *Inscripciones críticas*, 308.

80. Walter Mignolo and Catherine E. Walsh, *On Decoloniality: Concepts, Analytics, Praxis* (Durham, NC: Duke University Press, 2018), 241.

81. Lucy Bollington and Paul Merchant, "Introduction: Reworking the Human's Limits," in *Latin American Culture and the Limits of the Human*, ed. Lucy Bollington and Paul Merchant (Gainesville: University Press of Florida, 2020), 2.

82. Bollington and Merchant, "Introduction," 2.

83. In his excellent book on world literature, cosmopolitanism, and models of national culture, Ignacio Sánchez Prado speaks of Jorge Volpi's "co-optation of the language of European colonial knowledge" in *En busca de Klingsor* and further situates how Volpi uniquely treats science and literature in a period in which with increasing frequency "science replaces the social sciences in providing the protagonists with existential meaning." Ignacio Sánchez Prado, *Strategic Occidentalism: On Mexican Fiction, the Neoliberal Book Market, and the Question of World Literature* (Evanston, IL: Northwestern University Press, 2018), 97, 109.

84. Juan E. de Castro, *The Spaces of Latin American Literature: Tradition, Globalization, and Cultural Production* (New York: Palgrave Macmillan, 2008), xviii.

85. Julia Prieto, "Doing Poetry with Science: Unthinking Knowledge in Sarduy, Perlongher, and Eielson," in Blanco and Page, *Geopolitics, Culture, and the Scientific Imaginary in Latin America*, 231.

86. Mignolo and Walsh, *On Decoloniality*, 148.

87. Ian Buchanan, *Assemblage Theory and Method* (London: Bloomsbury, 2021), 4.

88. Gilles Deleuze and Félix Guattari, *A Thousand Plateaus: Capitalism and Schizophrenia*, trans. Brian Massumi (Minneapolis: University of Minnesota Press, 1987), 406.

89. Manuel DeLanda, *A New Philosophy of Society: Assemblage Theory and Social Complexity* (New York: Continuum, 2006), 5.

90. Diana H. Coole and Samantha Frost, "Introducing New Materialisms," in *New Materialisms: Ontology, Agency, and Politics*, ed. Coole and Frost (Durham, NC: Duke University Press, 2010), 13.

91. Jane Bennett, *Vibrant Matter: A Political Ecology of Things* (Durham, NC: Duke University Press, 2010), 6.

92. Bennett, *Vibrant Matter*, 13.

93. Serenella Iovino and Serpil Oppermann, "Introduction: Stories Come to Matter," in *Material Ecocriticism*, ed. Iovino and Oppermann (Bloomington: Indiana University Press, 2014), 3.

94. Héctor Hoyos, *Things with a History: Transcultural Materialism and the Literatures of Extraction in Contemporary Latin America* (New York: University of Columbia Press, 2019), 13.

95. Tara Daly, *Beyond Human: Vital Materialisms in the Andean Avant-Gardes* (Lewisburg, PA: Bucknell University Press, 2019), 2.

96. Karen M. Barad, *Meeting the Universe Halfway: Quantum Physics and the Entanglement of Matter and Meaning* (Durham, NC: Duke University Press, 2007), 89.

97. Barad, *Meeting the Universe Halfway*, 89.

98. Barad, *Meeting the Universe Halfway*, 33.

99. Barad, *Meeting the Universe Halfway*, 89.

100. Humberto R. Maturana and Francisco J. Varela, *Autopoiesis and Cognition: The Realization of the Living* (Boston: Reidel, 1980), xvii.

101. Catherine Connor-Swietlicki, "Why Autopoiesis and Memory Matter to Cervantes, Don Quixote, and the Humanities," in Jaén and Simon, *Cognitive Approaches to Early Modern Spanish Literature*, 53.

102. Alberto Blanco, "La teoría de Newton," in *La raíz cuadrada del cielo* (Monterrey: Universidad Autónoma de Nuevo León, 2016), 30, lines 37–40.

CHAPTER 1 — ENTANGLED MATTER

1. Kimberly A. Eherenman, "Las formas del instante: Entrevista con Alberto Blanco," *Fractal: Revista Trimestral* 7, no. 25 (April–June 2002) https://mxfractal.org/F25blanco.html, emphasis original.

2. Javier Galindo Ulloa, "El silencio en la poesía de Alberto Blanco," *Tema y Variaciones de Literatura* 48 (2017): 91.

3. Eherenman, "Las formas del instante."

4. Alberto Blanco, *Antes de nacer* (Mexico City: Editorial Penélope, 1983), page E, line 1.

5. Blanco, *Antes de nacer*, page E, line 4.

6. Evodio Escalante, "De la vanguardia militante a la vanguardia blanca: Los nuevos trastornadores del lenguaje en la poesía mexicana de nuestros días: David Huerta, Gerardo Deniz, Alberto Blanco y Coral Bracho," in *Perfiles: Ensayos sobre literatura mexicana reciente*, ed. Federico Patán (Boulder, CO: Society of Spanish and Spanish American Studies, 1992), 31.

7. Juan Armando Rojas Joo, *Posmodernidad y multiforma en la obra de dos poetas mexicanos contemporáneos: Alberto Blanco y Coral Bracho* (Madrid: Pliegos, 2018), 13.

8. Teresa Chapa, "La poesía de Alberto Blanco: Innovación y renovación *en Amanecer de los sentidos*," *Revista de Literatura Mexicana Contemporánea* 2, no. 4 (October 1996): 32.

9. Irma Chávez Robinson, "El Budismo Zen, El Yin Yang y La Ecología En La Obra de Alberto Blanco" (PhD diss., Florida State University, 2006), 3.

NOTES TO PAGES 25–31

10. Christopher Domínguez Michael, *Diccionario crítico de la literatura mexicana (1955–2005)* (Fondo de Cultura Económica, 2007), 59.

11. Domínguez Michael, *Diccionario crítico*, 60.

12. Ronald J. Friis, *White Light: The Poetry of Alberto Blanco* (Lewisburg, PA: Bucknell University Press, 2021), 15.

13. Friis, *White Light*, 239.

14. Fritjof Capra, *The Tao of Physics: An Exploration of the Parallels between Modern Physics and Eastern Mysticism* (Boston: Shambhala, 1985), 25.

15. Eherenman, "Las formas del instante."

16. Eherenman, "Las formas del instante."

17. Lakoff and Johnson, *Metaphors We Live By*, 3.

18. Capra, *Tao of Physics*, 160.

19. See Niels Bohr, *Atomic Physics and Human Knowledge* (New York: John Wiley, 1958).

20. Jan Faye, "Copenhagen Interpretation of Quantum Mechanics," in *The Stanford Encyclopedia of Philosophy* (Winter 2019 ed.), ed. Edward N. Zalta, https://plato.stanford.edu/archives/win2019/entries/qm-copenhagen/.

21. Friis, *White Light*, 18. Friis points out that, in addition to the balancing of opposites in the Zen Buddhist tradition, Blanco draws upon many traditions including Hegelian dialectics, Bakhtinian dialogism, and Octavio Paz's dialectal vision of the world (18).

22. Escalante, "De la vanguardia," 39.

23. Alberto Blanco, "No sé cuándo empecé a hacer collage . . ." (2020), https://www.albertoblancocollage.com/bio.

24. Blanco, *Antes de nacer*, 81–82.

25. Barad, *Meeting the Universe Halfway*, 333.

26. Barad, *Meeting the Universe Halfway*, 31, emphasis original.

27. Barad, *Meeting the Universe Halfway*, 33.

28. Barad, *Meeting the Universe Halfway*, 33, emphasis original.

29. Barad, *Meeting the Universe Halfway*, 89.

30. Eherenman, "Las formas del instante."

31. I use the term "quantum jump" as opposed to the more popularly held expression "quantum leap," which is seldom used in scientific discourse. I suspect that many readers, like myself, have a hard time disassociating the latter term from the title of the television show *Quantum Leap* from the late eighties and early nineties, which introduced my generation to the idea of a quantum leap as somehow related to time travel and wisecracking holograms.

32. Chapa, "La poesía," 29.

33. Denis Noble, *The Music of Life: Biology beyond Genes* (Oxford: Oxford University Press, 2006), 15–22.

34. Noble, *Music of Life*, 21.

35. Noble, *Music of Life*, 104.

36. Wendy Wheeler, "The Biosemiotic Turn: Abduction, or, the Nature of Creative Reason in Nature and Culture," in *Ecocritical Theory: New European Approaches*, ed. Axel Goodbody and Kate Rigby (Charlottesville: University of Virginia Press, 2011), 276.

37. Alberto Blanco, "Declaración de principios," in *Raíz cuadrada*, 13, lines 1–5.

38. Blanco, "Declaración de principios," 13, line 7.

39. Alfred North Whitehead and Bertrand Russell, *Principia Mathematica* (Cambridge: Cambridge University Press, 1925), 1–379.

40. Blanco, "Declaración de principios," 13, line 19.

41. Carlos Zamora-Zapata, "Crítica contextual: *El corazón del instante* de Alberto Blanco: Ensayo de un método" (PhD diss., University of Kentucky, 2014), 142.

42. Friis, *White Light*, 221.

43. Pacheco, "La gota," in *Tarde o temprano*, 429.

44. Rojas Joo, *Posmodernidad y multiforma*, 156.

45. Katie Mack, *The End of Everything (Astrophysically Speaking)* (New York: Scribner, 2020), 21, emphasis original.

46. Brian Greene, *The Fabric of the Cosmos* (New York: Knopf, 2004), 284. Greene goes on to say, "These numbers are staggering. An expansion factor of 10^{30}—a conservative estimate—would be like scaling up a molecule of DNA to roughly the size of the Milky Way galaxy, and in a time interval that's much shorter than a billionth of a billionth of a billionth of the blink of an eye" (285).

47. Anthony F. Aveni, *Skywatchers: A Revised and Updated Version of Skywatchers of Ancient Mexico* (Austin: University of Texas Press, 2001), 131.

48. Blanco, "Teoría de Newton," 30–31, lines 23–40.

49. For a fascinating study on how discoveries regarding electromagnetism impacted the social imaginary, see Kieran M. Murphy, *Electromagnetism and the Metonymic Imagination* (University Park: University of Pennsylvania Press, 2020).

50. Werner Heisenberg, *Nuclear Physics*, trans. Frank Gaynor and Amethe von Zeppelin (New York: Taylor & Francis, 1952), 30.

51. Greene, *Fabric of the Cosmos*, 96.

52. Blanco, "Teoría de la incertidumbre," in *Raíz cuadrada*, 46, lines 1–12.

53. Blanco, "Teoría de la incertidumbre," 47, lines 28–41.

54. Barad, *Meeting the Universe Halfway*, 26, emphasis original.

55. Barad, *Meeting the Universe Halfway*, 89.

56. Blanco, "Teoría de la incertidumbre," 48, lines 49–60.

57. Blanco, "Teoría de conjuntos," in *Raíz cuadrada*, 59.

58. Set theory, in its most intuitive and naïve form, functions as grouping of sets and properties such as the intersectionality in a Venn diagram. Set theory is made through formal axioms that, together, "imply the existence of a set-theoretic universe so rich that all mathematical objects can be construed as sets." Joan Bagaria, "Set Theory," in *The Stanford Encyclopedia of Philosophy* (Winter 2021 ed.), ed. Edward N. Zalta, https://plato.stanford.edu/archives/win2021/entries/set-theory/.

59. Friis, *White Light*, 204.

60. Barad, *Meeting the Universe Halfway*, 33.

61. There are similarities between set theory and assemblages, mapping, and even Barad's concept of agential "cuts," as each axiom would necessarily extend or exclude certain components or members.

62. Walt Whitman, *Leaves of Grass* (Minneapolis: Lerner, 2018), 38, line 3.

63. Blanco, "Canto a no yo," in *A la luz de siempre* (Mexico City: Fondo de Cultura Económica, 2018), 183, lines 1–7.

64. Whitman, *Leaves of Grass*, 38, line 6.

65. Whitman's work has been of great interest to scholars working under the umbrella of new materialisms. Jane Bennett extends the concept of vital materialism to the treatment

NOTES TO PAGES 41–48

of subjectivity and flows in Whitman's *Leaves of Grass* in *Influx and Efflux: Writing Up with Walt Whitman* (Durham, NC: Duke University Press, 2020). Similarly, Teresa Requena-Pelegrí examines the concept of transcorporeality in Whitman in "Masculinities, Nature, and Vulnerability: Towards a Transcorporeal Poetics in Washington Irving and Walt Whitman," in *Men, Masculinities, and Earth*, ed. Paul M. Pulé and Martin Hultman (Cham, Switzerland: Palgrave Macmillan, 2021), 135–149.

66. Blanco, "Canto a no yo," 184, line 8.

67. Blanco, "Canto a no yo," 184, lines 20–23.

68. Blanco, "Canto a no yo," 184, lines 29–30.

69. Blanco, "Canto a no yo," 184, lines 31–35.

70. Friis, *White Light*, 155.

71. Blanco, "Canto a no yo," 184–185, lines 36–42.

72. Barad, *Meeting the Universe Halfway*, 178.

73. Blanco, "El hombre," in *A la luz de siempre*, 177, line 1.

74. Juan Armando Rojas Joo, "The Lightning Bolt: The Allegory of Creation in Alberto Blanco's Afterglow," in *De Aztlán Al Río de La Plata: Studies in Honor of Charles M. Tatum*, ed. Sergio M. Martínez (Newark, DE: Juan de la Cuesta, 2016), 309.

75. Blanco, "El hombre," 179, line 15.

76. Blanco, "El hombre," 179, lines 16–18.

77. I use the term "abstract machine" in the spirit laid forth by Deleuze and Guattari in *A Thousand Plateaus*, where we find that "the diagrammatic or abstract machine does not function to represent, even something real, but rather constructs a real that is yet to come, a new type of reality. Thus when it constitutes points of creation or potentiality it does not stand outside history but is instead always 'prior to' history." Deleuze and Guattari, *A Thousand Plateaus*, 141.

78. Alberto Blanco, "Química," *Milenio* (Mexico), *Laberinto: Revista Cultural*, March 25, 2022, https://www.milenio.com/cultura/laberinto/quimica-por-alberto -blanco.

79. Arthur Kornberg, *For the Love of Enzymes: The Odyssey of a Biochemist* (Cambridge, MA: Harvard University Press, 1989), 287, emphasis original. One can see in a fuller quote how this reductionist model would provoke Blanco's sensibilities. Kornberg states, "The form and function of the brain and nervous system are simply chemistry. I am astonished that otherwise intelligent and informed people, including physicians, are reluctant to believe that mind *is* matter and *only* matter. Perhaps the repeated failures of science to analyze social, economic and political systems has perpetuated the notion that individual human behavior cannot be explained by physical laws" (287).

80. Blanco, "Química."

81. Noble, *Music of Life*, 78.

CHAPTER 2 — QUANTUM MECHANICS, HISTORY, AND THE QUESTION OF SCALE IN JORGE VOLPI'S *EN BUSCA DE KLINGSOR*

1. Jim Baggott, *The First War of Physics: The Secret History of the Atom Bomb, 1939–1949* (New York: Pegasus, 2010), 345.

2. Jorge Volpi, *Leer la mente: El cerebro y el arte de la ficción* (Mexico City: Alfaguara, 2011), 73.

3. Volpi, *Leer la mente*, 79.

4. There has been recent scholarship that argues that *En busca Klingsor* is not focused solely on epistemological questions. Brian Whitener sees *Klingsor* as part of an ontological turn in the novel, as a reflection of the crises of finance and state in the 1990s brought about by the ascendency of neoliberalism, arguing that "*Klingsor* is a novel that in a moment of political and economic breakdown, a moment of unprecedented indeterminacy, attempts to find means of creating (indeed of ensuring) a moral or social order." Whitener, "Ontology and Crises of State and Finance in Jorge Volpi's *En busca de Klingsor*," *Journal of Latin American Cultural Studies* 24, no. 1 (2015): 55.

5. Heisenberg, *Nuclear Physics*, 30, emphasis original.

6. Robert Goebel, "Un germanista en busca de Klingsor," *Revista de Literatura Mexicana Contemporánea* 7, no. 14 (2001): 33. For an overview of the Uncertainty Principle in Latin American literature, see Alicia Rivero, "Heisenberg's Uncertainty Principle in Contemporary Spanish American Fiction," in Fishburn and Ortiz, *Science and the Creative Imagination in Latin America*, 129–150.

7. Joaquín Aguirre Romero and Yolanda Delgado Batista, "Jorge Volpi: Las respuestas absolutas siempre son mentiras," *Espéculo* 11 (1999), https://webs.ucm.es/info/especulo/numero11/volpi.html.

8. See Tomás Regalado López, "El Crack vs la crítica: encuentros, mediaciones, contrastes," in *McCrack: McOndo, el Crack y los destinos de la literatura latinoamericana*, ed. Pablo Brescia and Oswaldo Estrada (Valencia: Albatros, 2018), 87–101.

9. Isabel Obiols, "El mexicano Jorge Volpi gana el Biblioteca Breve en la 'resurrección' del premio," *El país*, April 15, 1999, https://elpais.com/diario/1999/04/15/cultura/924127206_850215.html.

10. Tomás Regalado López, *Historia personal del Crack: Entrevistas críticas* (Valencia: Albatros, 2018), 96.

11. Exploring the complex role and reception of the Crack writers in Mexican, Latin American, and world literature falls outside of the purview of this chapter. For extended analysis on this group of writers, see Jaimes, *Mexican Crack Writers*; Regalado López, *Historia personal del Crack*; and Brescia and Estrada, *McCrack*.

12. Aníbal González, "Science, Art, and Magic: Totalization and Totalitarianism in Jorge Volpi's *In Search of Klingsor*," in Jaimes, *Mexican Crack Writers*, 75.

13. Adriana López Labourdette, "Laberintos del saber. Una lectura de *En busca de Klingsor* como escenificación de la poscolonialidad," in *En busca de Volpi: Ensayos sobre su obra*, edited by José Manuel López de Abiada, Félix Jiménez Ramírez, and Augusta López Bernasocchi (Madrid: Verbum, 2004), 190.

14. Aguirre Romero and Delgado Batista, "Jorge Volpi."

15. Ingrid Simson, "El principio de la paradoja en la literatura latinoamericana: de Jorge Luis Borges a Jorge Volpi," in *La narración paradójica: "Normas narrativas" y el principio de la "transgresión,"* ed. Nina Grabe, Sabine Lang, and Klaus Meyer-Minnemann (Madrid: Iberoamericana, 2006), 118–119; Manuel Grau, "En busca de Klingsor y la teoría de los juegos," in López de Abiada, Jiménez Ramírez, and López Bernasocchi, *En busca de Volpi*, 162.

16. It is difficult to overstate the impact that Gödel's Incompleteness Theorems have had in the fields of logic and mathematics. Their central feature is the idea that all axiomatic propositions in number theory have undecidable propositions. Panu Raatikainen explains that essentially "the first incompleteness theorem states that in any consistent formal system F within which a certain amount of arithmetic can be carried

NOTES TO PAGES 52–55

out, there are statements of the language of *F* which can neither be proved nor disproved in *F*. According to the second incompleteness theorem, such a formal system cannot prove that the system itself is consistent (assuming it is indeed consistent)." Raatikainen, "Gödel's Incompleteness Theorems," in *The Stanford Encyclopedia of Philosophy* (Spring 2015 ed.), ed. Edward N. Zalta, https://plato.stanford.edu/archives/spr2015/entries/goedel-incompleteness.

17. Jorge Volpi, *En busca de Klingsor* (1999; Barcelona: Seix Barral, 2002), 89.

18. Volpi, *En busca*, 334.

19. Joaquín Lahsen argues that Volpi's novel does much more than fictionalize the advances of which the Uncertainty Principle is most emblematic, observing that "Klingsor estaría asociado a la Teoría del Todo–el Santo Grial de las ciencias naturales, que explicaría el comportamiento del Universo, desde átomos hasta planetas, incluyendo, por supuesto, a los seres humanos" (Klingsor would be associated with the Theory of Everything—the Holy Grail of the natural sciences, that would explain the behavior of the Universe, from atoms to planets, including, of course, human beings). Lahsen, "Transposición científica de *En busca de Klingsor* de Jorge Volpi: Teoría del todo," *Latin Americanist* 58, no. 2 (2014): 78. Lahsen's detailed reasoning on how Klingsor is associated with the equally elusive Theory of Everything, a theoretical framework that would unite general relativity and quantum field theory, underscores the impossibility of the moral and philosophical crises provoked by the first half of the twentieth century. In a similar manner, Fernando Morales Gamboa sees the main theme of the novel as "la contradicción y tensión que se produce entre lo racional y lo irracional, entre la ciencia y el mito, entre la razón y la verdad. La figura de Klingsor, su marca onomástica mitológica, pero a la vez su profundo conocimiento científico, configuran una paradoja que simboliza la crisis de la Modernidad, o más bien, de la Ilustración" (the contradiction and tension that is produced between the rational and irrational, between science and myth, between reason and truth. The figure of Klingsor, with his mythological onomastic hallmark, but at the same time his profound scientific knowledge, form a paradox that symbolizes the crisis of Modernity, or rather, of the Enlightenment). Morales Gamboa, "La crítica de la Razón y la Modernidad desde el género policial en *En busca de Klingsor* de Jorge Volpi," *Espéculo* 34 (2006), https://webs.ucm.es/info/especulo/numero34/klvolpi.html.

20. Aguirre Romero and Delgado Batista, "Jorge Volpi."

21. Ignacio Álvarez, "Paradoja y contradicción: Epistemología y estética en *En Busca de Klingsor*, de Jorge Volpi," *Taller de letras* 33, no. 47 (2003): 49.

22. Joshua DiCaglio, *Scale Theory: A Nondisciplinary Inquiry* (Minneapolis: University of Minnesota Press, 2021), 6.

23. DiCaglio, *Scale Theory*, 7.

24. DiCaglio, *Scale Theory*, 6.

25. Volpi, *En busca*, 16.

26. Volpi, *En busca*, 18.

27. Volpi, *En busca*, 18, emphasis original.

28. Volpi, *En busca*, 26.

29. Volpi, *En busca*, 26.

30. Mihály Dés, "Como lector, tengo mi propio punto de vista sobre quién pudo haber sido Klingsor," *Lateral* 6, no. 70 (2000): 28.

31. Mikhail Bakhtin, *The Dialogic Imagination: Four Essays*, ed. and trans. Michael Holquist and Caryl Emesron (Austin: University of Texas Press, 1981), 15.

180 NOTES TO PAGES 55–63

32. Hayden White, *Metahistory: The Historical Imagination in Nineteenth-Century Europe* (Baltimore: Johns Hopkins University Press, 1973), 1–11.

33. Linda Hutcheon, *A Poetics of Postmodernism: History, Theory, Fiction* (London: Routledge, 1988), 16.

34. Hutcheon, *Poetics of Postmodernism*, 82–83, emphasis original.

35. DiCaglio, *Scale Theory*, 8–9.

36. Volpi, *En busca*, 31.

37. Danny J. Anderson, "The Novels of Jorge Volpi and the Possibility of Knowledge," *Studies in the Literary Imagination* 33, no. 1 (2000): 14.

38. Aguirre Romero and Delgado Batista, "Jorge Volpi."

39. Jorge Zamora, "*En busca de Klingsor* y *Frankenstein* aspectos de intertexto y misoginia," *Revista de Literatura Mexicana Contemporánea* 30 (2006): 33–42.

40. Volpi, *En busca*, 13.

41. Volpi, *En busca*, 18.

42. Volpi, *En busca*, 152.

43. Volpi, *En busca*, 378.

44. Volpi, *En busca*, 114.

45. Volpi, *En busca*, 213.

46. Dés, "Como lector," 28.

47. Volpi, *En busca*, 279.

48. Volpi, *En busca*, 351.

49. Volpi, *En busca*, 103.

50. Volpi, *En busca*, 103.

51. Alberto Blanco, "Segunda teoría del caos," in *Raíz cuadrada*, 45, lines 13–14.

52. An electron, to take an example, can be seen as both a particle and a wave. Max Born proposed the idea of the probability wave that explains this dual nature. Greene explains that like waves in the sea, probability waves "also have regions of high and low intensity, but the meaning he ascribed to these wave shapes was unexpected: the size of a wave at a given point in space is proportional to the probability that the electron is located at that point in space." Greene, *Fabric of the Cosmos*, 89.

53. Volpi, *En busca*, 279.

54. Volpi, *En busca*, 315.

55. Reinhart Koselleck, *Futures Past: On the Semantics of Historical Time*, trans. Keith Tribe (Cambridge, MA: MIT Press, 1985), 115.

56. Koselleck, *Futures Past*, 115.

57. Koselleck, *Futures Past*, 115.

58. Olivier Hekster, "The Size of History: Coincidence, Counterfactuality and Questions of Scale in History," in *The Challenge of Chance: A Multidisciplinary Approach from Science and the Humanities*, ed. Klaas Landsman and Ellen van Wolde (Cham, Switzerland: Springer, 2016), 217.

59. These narratological strategies are similar to what Hayden White terms "emplotments" within historiographic writing. White, *Metahistory*, 7–8.

60. Volpi, *En busca*, 112.

61. Volpi, *En busca*, 18.

62. Hekster, "Size of History," 219.

63. Mariela Insúa Cereceda, "La pesquisa de la verdad en *En busca de Klngsor* de Jorge Volpi," *Revista Chilena de Literatura* 64 (2004): 95, emphasis original.

NOTES TO PAGES 63–69

64. Gioconda Marún, "El teorema de Gödel y la literatura latinoamericana: Jorge Volpi y Guillermo Martínez," *Hispania* 92, no. 4 (2009): 700.

65. Volpi, *En busca*, 426.

66. Volpi, *En busca*, 436.

67. What actually "happens" when we measure a particle is of great debate to this day. Regardless, when a particle is observed at a given location, the probability of finding it somewhere else goes to zero. Therefore, its wave function "collapses" as its probability of being found in the location it is observed is now 100 percent.

68. Volpi, *En busca*, 178.

69. Clemens Franken, "*En busca de Klingsor* by Jorge Volpi: Una novela con formato policial híbrido, posmoderno y poscolonial," *Acta literaria* 44 (2012): 56.

70. Volpi, *En busca*, 255.

71. Eduardo Santiago Ruiz, "La física cuántica: De la metaficción a los problemas éticos en la novela *En busca de Klingsor*," *Hispanófila* 188 (2020): 113.

72. Barad, *Meeting the Universe Halfway*, 185.

73. Barad, *Meeting the Universe Halfway*, 381.

74. Hekster, "Size of History," 229, emphasis added.

75. Fernando García Ramírez, "Todo se vale a pequeña escala," *Letras libres* 6, no. 69 (September 2004), https://letraslibres.com/revista-mexico/gerardo-deniz-todo-se-vale -a-pequena-escala/.

76. Aguirre Romero and Delgado Batista, "Jorge Volpi."

CHAPTER 3 — AUTOMATONS, ANDROIDS, AND ANDROCENTRISM
IN IGNACIO PADILLA'S *EL ANDROIDE Y OTRAS QUIMERAS*

1. For a fascinating overview of the legend as well as its significance in its original milieu in contrast to contemporary interpretations, see Minsoo Kang, "The Mechanical Daughter of Rene Descartes: The Origin and History of an Intellectual Fable," *Modern Intellectual History* 14, no. 3 (2017): 633–660.

2. Gaby Wood, *Living Dolls: A Magical History of the Quest for Mechanical Life* (London: Faber and Faber, 2002), 4.

3. Ignacio Padilla, *La vida íntima de los encendedores* (Madrid: Páginas de Espuma, 2016), 87, emphasis original.

4. Alicia H. Puleo, *Ecofeminismo. Para otro mundo posible* (Madrid: Cátedra, 2017), 104.

5. Stephen Cave and Kanta Dihal, "The Automaton Chronicles," *Nature* 559 (July 26, 2018): 473.

6. René Descartes, *Discourse on Method and Meditations on First Philosophy*, trans. Donald A. Cress (Indianapolis: Hackett, 1998), 18–20.

7. Wood, *Living Dolls*, 8.

8. These terms are related but not entirely synonymous. For a brief explanation of the nuances between the terms, see William L. Hosch, "Automaton," in *Encyclopedia Britannica*, https://www. britannica.com/technology/automaton/.

9. Bruno Pardo Porto, "Sale a la luz la obra maestra de Ignacio Padilla," *ABC*, December 16, 2018, 55, https://www.abc.es/cultura/libros/abci-ignacio-padilla-y-cofre-tesoro-2018 12160106_noticia.html. Padilla playfully coined the adjective "cuéntico," which I roughly translate as "of the story," as a portmanteau of the words "cuántico" (quantum) and "cuento" (short story).

10. Pedro Ángel Palou, "Físico cuéntico, la *Micropedia* como labor de vida," in *Homenaje a Ignacio Padilla: De monstruos, dobles, autómatas y quimeras*, ed. Jorge Volpi (Madrid: Páginas de Espuma, 2018), 44.

11. Pardo Porto, "Sale a la luz," 55.

12. Jorge Fernández Granados, "Apuntes para una teoría de la física cuéntica de Ignacio Padilla," *Unidiversidad: Revista de Pensamiento y Cultura de la Benemérita Universidad Autónoma de Puebla* 30 (2018): 40.

13. Brian Stableford, *Science Fact and Science Fiction: An Encyclopedia* (New York: Routledge, 2006), 22.

14. Stableford, *Science Fact and Science Fiction*, 22.

15. Wood, *Living Dolls*, xvi.

16. Ignacio Padilla, *El androide y las quimeras* (Madrid: Páginas de Espuma, 2008), 113.

17. Roberto Pliego, "Ambidiestro: Sobre *El androide y las quimeras* de Ignacio Padilla," *Nexos: Sociedad, Ciencia, Literatura*, March 2009, https://www.nexos.com.mx/?p=12982.

18. Siridia Fuertes Trigal, "Lo fantástico del mal en el proyecto *Micropedia* de Ignacio Padilla," *Revista de Literatura Mexicana Contemporánea* 15, no. 43 (2009): 39.

19. Jessica Riskin, "Machines in the Garden," *Republics of Letters* 1, no. 2 (April 2010): 17.

20. Carolyn Merchant, *The Death of Nature: Women, Ecology, and the Scientific Revolution* (San Francisco: Harper & Row, 1980), 2.

21. Merchant, *Death of Nature*, 214.

22. Gisela Heffes, "Introducción. Para una ecocrítica latinoamericana: Entre la postulación de un ecocentrismo crítico y la crítica a un antropocentrismo hegemónico," *Revista de Crítica Literaria Latinoamericana* 40, no. 79 (2014): 15.

23. Donna J. Haraway, *Simians, Cyborgs, and Women: The Reinvention of Nature* (New York: Routledge, 1991), 154.

24. Haraway, *Simians, Cyborgs, and Women*, 149.

25. Haraway, *Simians, Cyborgs, and Women*, 181.

26. J. Andrew Brown, *Cyborgs in Latin America* (New York: Palgrave Macmillan, 2010), 1.

27. Elizabeth M. Ginway, *Cyborgs, Sexuality, and the Undead: The Body in Mexican and Brazilian Speculative Fiction* (Nashville: Vanderbilt University Press, 2020), 27.

28. Alicia Rivero, "La mujer cibernética en 'Salvad vuestros ojos' de Huidobro, 'Anuncio' de Arreola y *El eterno femenino* de Castellanos," *La Torre: Revista de la Universidad de Puerto Rico* 3, no. 9 (1998): 580.

29. Dalton, *Mestizo Modernity*, 18.

30. Brown, *Cyborgs in Latin America*, 3–4.

31. Chela Sandoval, "New Sciences: Cyborg Feminism and the Methodology of the Oppressed," in *The Cyborg Handbook*, ed. Chris Gray (New York: Routledge, 1995), 408.

32. Sara Potter, "Disturbing Muses: Gender, Technology and Resistance in Mexican Avant-Garde Cultures" (PhD diss., Washington University in St. Louis, 2013), ix.

33. Potter, "Disturbing Muses," x, emphasis original.

34. Fuertes Trigal, "Lo fantástico del mal," 32.

35. Neda Ulaby, "Edison's Talking Dolls Can Now Provide the Soundtrack to Your Nightmares," *The Two-Way*, May 5, 2015, www.npr.org/sections/thetwo-way/2015/05/05/404445211/edisons-talking-dolls-can-now-provide-the-soundtrack-to-your-nightmares/.

NOTES TO PAGES 74–81

36. Victoria Dawson, "The Epic Failure of Thomas Edison's Talking Doll," *Smithsonian Magazine*, June 1, 2015, https://www.smithsonianmag.com/smithsonian-institution/epic-failure-thomas-edisons-talking-doll-180955442/.

37. Wood, *Living Dolls*, 113.

38. Padilla, *El androide*, 15.

39. Ruth Oldenziel, *Making Technology Masculine: Men, Women, and Modern Machines in America, 1870–1945* (Amsterdam: Amsterdam University Press, 1999), 14.

40. Padilla, *El androide*, 17.

41. Padilla, *El androide*, 17.

42. Padilla, *El androide*, 17–18.

43. Padilla, *El androide*, 19.

44. Wood, *Living Dolls*, 138.

45. Padilla, *El androide*, 20.

46. Walter Benjamin, *Illuminations*, ed. and trans. Hannah Arendt (New York: Harcourt, Brace, and World, 1968), 220–223.

47. Benjamin, *Illuminations*, 18.

48. Padilla, *La vida íntima*, 84–85.

49. Padilla, *El androide*, 20.

50. Hesiod and Homer, *Hesiod, the Homeric Hymns, and Homerica*. ed. Hugh G. Evelyn-White (Project Gutenberg, 2008), 2:176–206, https://www.gutenberg.org/ebooks/348.

51. John P. Rafferty, "Mary Anning," in *Encyclopedia Britannica*, May 17, 2022, https://www.britannica. com/biography/Mary-Anning/.

52. Stephen Shapin, *The Scientific Revolution* (Chicago: University of Chicago Press, 1996), 34.

53. Merchant, *Death of Nature*, 193.

54. Padilla, *El androide*, 25.

55. Padilla, *El androide*, 26.

56. Socorro Venegas, "Chicos superpoderosos," in Volpi, *Homenaje a Ignacio Padilla*, 60.

57. Padilla, *El androide*, 28.

58. Padilla, *El androide*, 29.

59. There seems to be a clear connection to the fictional Mary Anning's contemporary Jane Eyre, who in her defiant protestation to Mr. Rochester in *Jane Eyre* challenges, "Do you think I am an automaton?—a machine without feelings? and can bear to have my morsel of bread snatched from my lips, and my drop of living water dashed from my cup? Do you think, because I am poor, obscure, plain, and little, I am soulless and heartless?" Charlotte Brontë, *Jane Eyre* (New York: Norton, 1997), 253.

60. Padilla, *El androide*, 29.

61. Edmundo Paz Soldán, "El otro, el mismo," in Volpi, *Homenaje a Ignacio Padilla*, 40.

62. See Edgar Allan Poe, "Maelzel's Chess Player," *Southern Literary Messenger* 2 (April 1836): 318–326, https://www.eapoe.org/works/essays/maelzel.htm; Ambrose Bierce, "Moxon's Master," in *Ambrose Bierce: The Devil's Dictionary, Tales & Memoirs*, ed. S. T. Joshi (New York: Library of America, 2011), 252–261; and Benjamin, "Theses on the Philosophy of History," in *Illuminations*, 253–254.

63. Padilla, *El androide*, 44.

64. Padilla, *El androide*, 45.

65. See Wood, *Living Dolls*, 67, for a reproduction of Racknitz's engraving along with Wood's explanation of the diagrams.

66. Wood, *Living Dolls*, 93, emphasis original.

67. For an excellent introduction to Padilla's painstakingly researched and incisive essays, see Tomás Regalado López, "Pesar con las manos las cosas: Ignacio Padilla y el ejercicio del ensayo," *Unidiversidad. Revista de pensamiento y cultura de la Benemérita Universidad Autónoma de Puebla* 30 (January 2018): 49–56.

68. Padilla, *La vida íntima*, 91. These are but a few of the multiple intertextual connections that Padilla establishes with García Márquez's fiction. Padilla even begins *La vida íntima de los encededores* with the following epigraph taken from *Cien años de soledad*: "Las cosas tienen vida propia—pregonaba el gitano con áspero acento—, todo es cuestión de despertarles el ánima."

69. Padilla, *La vida íntima*, 91.

70. Héctor Jaimes notes how the Crack writers knowingly place themselves within literary traditions both within and outside of Latin America beginning with the "Crack Manifesto," where "the textual tapestry implied in it brings forth the notion of influence but also of continuity within the great tradition of literary writing." Héctor Jaimes, "Introduction: The Mexican Crack Writers—Toward a New Literary Aesthetics," in Jaimes, *Mexican Crack Writers*, 2.

71. Padilla, *El androide*, 48.

72. Wood, *Living Dolls*, 95.

73. David Dalton, "Robo Sacer: 'Bare Life' and Cyborg Labor Beyond the Border in Alex Rivera's *Sleep Dealer*," *Hispanic Studies Review* 1, no. 1 (2016): 16.

74. Padilla, *El androide*, 49.

75. Padilla, *El androide*, 49.

76. Padilla, *El androide*, 50.

CHAPTER 4 — A SCIENCE OF GOOD AND EVIL

1. Jacqueline Bixler, "Sabina Berman Redux: Adaptation and the Anxiety of (Self) Influence," *Romance Notes* 55, no. 2 (2015): 229.

2. In addition to her literary publications, Berman has engaged these same themes in various columns in the mainstream press as well as on television programs. After the success of her long-running *Shalalá* on Televisión Azteca and the contentious, short-lived *John & Sabina*, Berman launched another interview series, *Largo Aliento*, in March 2021 on Canal Once, featuring segments with politicians, intellectuals, and other public figures who explore the issues of the day through the lens of nature, ecology, and sustainability.

3. Stuart Day, "La intersextualidad (dramática) de Sabina Berman," in *El narco negocia con Dios; Testosterona*, by Sabina Berman (Mexico City: El Milagro, 2013), 13.

4. Bixler, "Sabina Berman Redux," 238.

5. Sabina Berman, "'Largo Aliento,' la naturaleza como centro de la vida: Sabina Berman," interview by Gabriela Warkentin and Javier Risco, *Así las cosas*, W Radio (XEW-AM), Mexico City, March 11, 2021, https://wradio.com.mx/programa/2021/03/11/asi_las_cosas/1615489112_911627.html.

6. Valerie Plumwood, *Environmental Culture: The Ecological Crisis of Reason* (New York: Routledge, 2003), 146.

7. Plumwood, *Environmental Culture*, 146.

NOTES TO PAGES 87–92

8. Berman, "Largo Aliento."

9. For a greater look at the role of Sabina Berman and other public intellectuals in Mexico, see Debra A. Castillo and Stuart A. Day, eds., *Mexican Public Intellectuals* (New York: Palgrave, 2014).

10. Sabina Berman, *Matemáticas para la felicidad y otras fábulas* (Mexico City: Porrúa, 2017), 8–9.

11. Despite being associated with Darwin's groundbreaking work, the phrase "survival of the fittest" was not in the original *On the Origin of Species.* It was Herbert Spencer who applied the concept of natural selection to the sociological and economic fields in what would later be termed social Darwinism: "This survival of the fittest which I have here sought to express in mechanical terms, is that which Mr Darwin has called 'natural selection, or the preservation of favoured races in the struggle for life.'" Herbert Spencer, *The Principles of Biology* (1866; Project Gutenberg, 2017), chap. 7, https://www.gutenberg.org/ebooks/54612.

12. Bixler, "Sabina Berman Redux," 229.

13. Brian T. Chandler, "Of Narcos and Necros: Violence and Morality in Sabina Berman's *El narco negocia con Dios,*" *Chasqui* 50, no. 2 (2022): 147.

14. Chandler, "Of Narcos and Necros," 148.

15. Berman, *El narco,* 78.

16. Berman, *El narco,* 84.

17. Octavio Paz, *El laberinto de la soledad y otras obras* (New York: Penguin, 1997), 101–102.

18. Berman, *El narco,* 79.

19. Alfonso Varona, "Entrevista a Sabina Berman," *Latin American Theatre Review* 47, no. 1 (2013): 137.

20. Irmgard Emmelhainz, *La tiranía del sentido común: La reconversión neoliberal de México* (Mexico City: Paradiso, 2016), 19.

21. Emmelhainz, *La tiranía del sentido común,* 21.

22. Berman, "Largo Aliento."

23. Sabina Berman, "Barra de opinion: *La mujer que buceó dentro del corazón del mundo,*" interview by Estela Livera, *Desafíos,* March 11, 2011, https://www.youtube.com/watch?v=pQNa1mk_xCE.

24. Berman, "Barra de opinion."

25. Sabina Berman, *La mujer que buceó dentro del corazón del mundo* (Mexico City: Planeta Mexicana, 2010), 81.

26. Berman, *La mujer,* 248.

27. María Celina Bortolotto and May Summer Farnsworth, "Autismo, antropocentrismo y género en *La mujer que buceó dentro del corazón del mundo* (2010) de Sabina Berman," *Romance Notes* 55, no. 2 (2015): 216–217.

28. Etna Verónica Ávalos Molina, "Representaciones literarias de la discapacidad en el contexto latinoamericano del siglo XXI" (PhD diss., University of North Carolina at Chapel Hill, 2019), 97.

29. Alana Gómez Gray, "Emoción frente a neoliberalismo en la novela *La mujer que buceó dentro del corazón del mundo* de Sabina Berman," *Vanderbilt E-Journal of Luso-Hispanic Studies* 11, no. 1 (February 2021): 34.

30. Eduardo Huchín Sosa, "Narrar la diferencia," *Letras libres,* November 6, 2011, https://www.letraslibres.com/mexico/libros/narrar-la-diferencia.

NOTES TO PAGES 92–94

31. Ana Ugarte, "Hibris literaria, eco-autismo y empatía en *La mujer que buceó dentro del corazón del mundo* de Sabina Berman," *Revista de Estudios de Género y Sexualidades* 45, no. 1 (2019): 142.

32. Berman, *La mujer*, 274–275.

33. Berman, *La mujer*, 41.

34. M. Victoria García Serrano, "El binomio Descartes y Darwin en *La mujer que buceó dentro del corazón del mundo* de Sabina Berman," in *Idealismo, racionalismo y empirismo en la literatura hispánica*, ed. Jesús Pérez Magallón and Ricardo de la Fuente Ballesteros (Valladolid, Spain: Verdelís, 2015), 66. On several occasions Berman seems to conflate Descartes's dictum with ontological idealism. In an interview with *BBC News* Berman states, "Pienso, luego existo: eso es una gran mentira y es cómico; el pensamiento es una parte pequeñísima de la realidad, una parte engreída. La realidad son las cosas, los organismos, el aire, la luz, la naturaleza" (I think, therefore I exist: that is a big lie and it's funny; thought is a small part of reality, a self-centered part. Reality is things, organisms, air, light, nature). Diana Massis, "Sabina Berman: Pienso, luego existo: eso es una gran mentira y es cómico; el pensamiento es una parte pequeñísima de la realidad, una parte engreída," *BBC News*, September 4, 2021, https://www.bbc.com/mundo/noticias-58397405.

35. Freya Mathews, "The Dilemma of Dualism," in *Routledge Handbook of Gender and Environment*, ed. Sherilyn MacGregor (New York: Routledge, 2017), 54.

36. Valerie Plumwood, *Feminism and the Mastery of Nature* (New York: Routledge, 1993), 41–42.

37. Berman, *La mujer*, 40.

38. Diana Coole and Samantha Frost draw attention to how this duality is constructed upon the absence of a common materiality: "The Cartesian-Newtonian understanding of matter thereby yields a conceptual and practical domination of nature as well as a specifically modern attitude or ethos of subjectivist potency." Coole and Frost, "Introducing New Materialisms," 8. Similarly, Alicia Puleo explores how the man/nature duality extends the dyadic relationship between culture/nature and man/woman: "Con la Modernidad, a partir del siglo XVII, el saber-poder de la razón instrumental se destinó al dominio total de la antigua Terra Mater, la cual, de ser percibida como totalidad orgánica femenina, pasaría a convertirse en simple materia prima pasiva, inerte y atomística" (With Modernity, beginning in the seventeenth century, the knowledge-power of instrumental reason was destined for the total dominance over the ancient Terra Mater, which, if perceived as an organic feminine totality, would become simple raw material, passive, inert and atomistic). Puleo, *Ecofeminismo*, 92.

39. Berman, *La mujer*, 40.

40. Berman, *La mujer*, 41.

41. Mathews, "Dilemma of Dualism," 55.

42. Descartes, *Discourse on Method*, 38.

43. John Cottingham argues that Descartes's thinking on animals has been grossly mischaracterized, as the Cartesian conceptualization of beast machine is a commentary on its ability to think, not a license for it to be considered a lifeless entity. "The phrase 'bête-machine' can thus be rather misleading, since the mechanical physiology Descartes has in mind operates equally in the case of *homo sapiens.*" Cottingham, "'A Brute to the Brutes?' Descartes' Treatment of Animals," *Philosophy* 5, no. 206 (1978): 552.

44. Berman, *La mujer*, 88.

NOTES TO PAGES 94–100

45. Berman, *La mujer*, 91.

46. Luis Javier Plata Rosas, "Temple Grandin, autismo y etología," *Nexos*, August 1, 2012, https://www.nexos.com.mx/?p=14948.

47. Berman, *La mujer*, 11.

48. Berman, *La mujer*, 17.

49. Berman, *La mujer*, 93.

50. Berman, *La mujer*, 92.

51. Berman, *La mujer*, 149.

52. Notimex, "El mundo vive una esquizofrenia, derivada de creyentes y ateos: Berman," *20 Minutos*, May 20, 2014, https://www.20minutos.com.mx/noticia/b152880/el-mundo-vive-una-esquizofrenia-derivada-de-creyentes-y-ateos-berman/.

53. Berman, *La mujer*, 149.

54. Berman also uses the motif of ants and the anthill in many works before the 2010s. Priscilla Meléndez examines how Berman uses images of ants and anthills to take up the world from interior and exterior positions in "(De)Humanizing Humor: The Anthill of Life and Politics in the Theatre of Sabina Berman," *Studies in Twentieth and Twenty First Century Literature* 32, no. 2 (2008): 359–385.

55. Berman, *La mujer*, 104.

56. Berman, *La mujer*, 106.

57. Berman, *La mujer*, 232.

58. Mathews, "Dilemma of Dualism," 64.

59. Humorously, Karen judges the name Atunes Consuelo to be "el nombre más inadecuado de la industria pesquera del planeta" (the most inappropriate name in the fishing industry on the planet). Berman's fictional company is most likely a play on the longtime Mexican brand of canned tuna Atún Dolores, another suggestive proper name like the novel's Atunes Consuelo (Solace Tuna). The name Dolores, whose origin recalls the suffering of the Virgin Mary, literally translates into English as "pains."

60. Berman, *La mujer*, 186.

61. Berman, *La mujer*, 271.

62. Coole and Frost, "Introducing New Materialisms," 29.

63. Berman, *La mujer*, 233.

64. Berman, *La mujer*, 70.

65. Karen's different abilities allow her to perceive an intercorporeality akin to Susan Antebi's affirmation between bodies and reading as an embodied activity of "mutual dependency and referentiality linking bodies to one another, [suggesting] as well the role of critical reading as an embodied practice, an ongoing, transhistorical, living and textual encounter through which disability may still come to mean otherwise." Antebi, *Embodied Archive: Disability in Post-Revolutionary Mexican Cultural Production* (Ann Arbor: University of Michigan Press, 2021), 4.

66. Bennett, *Vibrant Matter*, 22–23.

67. Berman, *La mujer*, 281.

68. Berman, *La mujer*, 281.

69. Berman, *La mujer*, 281.

70. As an example, while I will address the many consequential issues the novel raises, I cannot for the life of me shake how an immensely powerful conspiracy that spans borders, sects, and centuries is somehow incapable of hacking into a file protected by the password "anomaly."

71. By lumping all thinking inspired by Darwin into one grouping, Karen glosses over the nearly countless ways Darwin has impacted religion, science, culture, and society. From Spencerian progressivism to social Lamarckism, Darwinism, from the first public reactions to *On the Origin of Species*, has diverged from any thetic dogma. Hoeg and Larsen argue that "at the behest of creationists and strict constructionists alike, much of this development has occurred in an inescapably teleological manner, modifying the original tenets and even doctrines of the concept of 'descent with modification' such that Darwin himself might scarcely recognize them as his disciplinary offspring." Jerry Hoeg and Kevin S. Larsen, "Introduction," in *Interdisciplinary Essays on Darwinism in Hispanic Literature and Film: The Intersection of Science and the Humanities*, ed. Hoeg and Larsen (Lewiston, NY: Edwin Mellen Press, 2009), 1.

72. Eduardo E. Parrilla Sotomayor, "La isla de James y el biocentrismo como utopía en *El dios de Darwin* de Sabina Berman," *Romanica Silesiana* 10 (2015): 289.

73. The narrator adds a metafictional touch by anticipating the incongruity of the third person narration for events in the plot that Karen did not witness: "Escribo esta historia en tercera persona porque Yo no la viví, me fue narrada" (15).

74. Linda Hutcheon, *A Theory of Adaptation* (New York: Routledge, 2016), 19–20.

75. Sabina Berman, *El dios de Darwin* (Barcelona: Ediciones Destino, 2014), 9.

76. Berman, *El dios de Darwin*, 474.

77. Berman, *El dios de Darwin*, 130.

78. Jean-François Lyotard, *The Postmodern Condition: A Report on Knowledge*, trans. Geoff Bennington and Brian Massumi (Minneapolis: Minnesota University Press, 1984), xxiv.

79. Varona, "Entrevista a Sabina Berman," 143.

80. Donna Haraway, *Staying with the Trouble: Making Kin in the Chthulucene* (Durham, NC: Duke University Press, 2016), 12.

81. Varona, "Entrevista a Sabina Berman," 43.

82. Berman, *La mujer*, 315. It is telling that one of the more unlikeable characters in the novel is the cantankerous John Ford, a Christopher Hitchens–type figure, who, while representing what Karen identifies as the side of Science, seems primarily motivated by publicity and self-aggrandizement to underwrite his gluttonous lifestyle.

83. Berman, *La mujer*, 316.

84. Berman, *La mujer*, 300.

85. Berman, *La mujer*, 424.

86. Charles Darwin, *The Autobiography of Charles Darwin, 1809–1882: With Original Omissions Restored*, ed. Nora Barlow (New York: Collins, 1958), 87.

87. Berman, *La mujer*, 429.

88. Charles Darwin, *The Descent of Man, and Selection in Relation to Sex* (1871; Project Gutenberg, 1999), chap. 5.

89. Samir Okasha, "Biological Altruism," in *The Stanford Encyclopedia of Philosophy* (Summer 2020 ed.), ed. Edward N. Zalta, plato.stanford.edu/archives/sum2020/entries/altruism-biological/.

90. Berman, *La mujer*, 436.

91. Whether employed inadvertently or not, Berman's treatment of the term "positive laws" is problematic in this context. The text suggests that the fictional Darwin chooses this term because these laws found in nature serve as affirmations and are antipodal to the divinely revealed Ten Commandments that focus more on negatively articulated

NOTES TO PAGES 103–111 189

prohibitions. In reality, the term "positive laws" refers to those posited by humans or institutions to specify or enforce certain actions. It could be argued that in the novel Darwin's laws are an example of natural law, given that they articulate an already present ethical system that transcends human society and institutions.

92. Bennett, *Vibrant Matter*, 117.

93. Berman, *La mujer*, 439.

94. Berman, *La mujer*, 478.

95. Berman, *La mujer*, 477.

96. Berman, *La mujer*, 478.

97. All of Berman's columns in *El Universal* can be found at https://www.eluniversal.com.mx/opinion/sabina-berman/.

98. Berman, *Matemáticas*, 9.

99. Berman, *Matemáticas*, 99.

100. Berman, *Matemáticas*, 101.

101. Mabel Moraña, "Escasez y modernidad," in *Precariedades, exclusiones y emergencias: Necropolítica y sociedad civil en América Latina*, ed. Mabel Moraña and José Manuel Valenzuela (Mexico City: Universidad Autónoma Metropolitana, 2017), 29.

102. Gilles Deleuze and Félix Guattari, *Anti-Oedipus: Capitalism and Schizophrenia*, trans. Robert Hurley, Mark Seem, and Helen R. Lane (Minneapolis: University of Minnesota Press, 1983), 246.

103. Berman, *Matemáticas*, 129.

104. Berman, *Matemáticas*, 128.

105. Françoise d'Eaubonne, *Feminism or Death: How the Women's Movement Can Save the Planet*, ed. and trans. Ruth Hottell (London: Verso, 2022), 3.

106. Barad, *Meeting the Universe Halfway*, 178–179.

CHAPTER 5 — IN SEARCH OF A NEW LANGUAGE

1. Samantha Demby, "Pandemic Intensifies Women's Struggle for Water in Oaxaca, Mexico" (North American Congress on Latin America [NACLA], July 16, 2020), https://nacla.org/news/2020/07/15/oaxaca-water-mexico-pandemic. Footage of the terrifying events is documented by Siete Días Oaxaca, "Conflicto entre Ayutla Mixes y Tamazulapam," YouTube, June 6, 2017, https://www.youtube.com/watch?v=eECthxp_ATM.

2. Yásnaya Elena Aguilar Gil, "Agua con A de Ayutla. Una denuncia," *Revista de la Universidad de México*, June 2020, https://www.revistadelauniversidad.mx/articles/f03bc7f3-df5a-460f-b2fe-ad5dd1b91fba/agua-con-a-de-ayutla.

3. Aguilar Gil, "Agua con A de Ayutla."

4. Elena Gómez del Valle, "Y a veces detenerse es otra forma de fluir y amar: *El sueño de toda célula*, de Maricela Guerrero," *Replicante: Periodismo digital / cultura crítica*, July 11, 2020, https://revistareplicante.com/y-a-veces-detenerse-es-otra-forma-de-fluir-y-amar/.

5. Ignacio Ballester Pardo, "Reseña: *El sueño de toda célula*, de Maricela Guerrero," *Bitácora de vuelos: Literatura y e-books*, February 2019, https://www.rdbitacoradevuelos.com.mx/2019/02/resena-el-sueno-de-toda-celula-de.html.

6. Ignacio Ruiz-Pérez, "Repensar la escritura: cuerpo, sexualidad y usos amorosos del siglo XXI en la poesía de Maricela Guerrero," *iMex. México Interdisciplinario. Interdisciplinary Mexico* 7, no. 13 (January 2018): 32.

7. Deleuze and Guattari, *A Thousand Plateaus*, 18.

8. Mignolo and Walsh, *On Decoloniality*, 141–145. In defining this term, Mignolo builds on Aníbal Quijano's concept of "coloniality" to articulate how often-hidden domains such as language and knowledge propel colonial power: "The colonial matrix of power (the CMP) is a complex structure of management and control composed of domains, levels, and flows. Like the unconscious in Sigmund Freud or surplus value in Karl Marx, the CMP is a theoretical concept that helps to make visible what is invisible to the naked (or rather nontheoretical) eye" (142).

9. Heffes, "Introducción," 19.

10. Laura Barbas-Rhoden, *Ecological Imaginations in Latin American Fiction* (Gainesville: University Press of Florida, 2011), 7.

11. Macarena Gómez-Barris, *The Extractive Zone: Social Ecologies and Decolonial Perspectives* (Durham, NC: Duke University Press, 2017), xvii.

12. Lesley Wylie, *The Poetics of Plants in Spanish American Literature* (Pittsburgh: University of Pittsburgh Press, 2020), 3.

13. Carolyn Fornoff, "Planetary Poetics of Extinction in Contemporary Mexican Poetry," in *Mexican Literature as World Literature*, ed. Ignacio M. Sánchez Prado (New York: Bloomsbury, 2021), 232.

14. Fornoff, "Planetary Poetics of Extinction," 235.

15. Robin Myers, "Translator's Note," in *The Dream of Every Cell / El sueño de toda célula*, by Maricela Guerrero (Berkeley: Cardboard House Press, 2022), 134–135.

16. Maricela Guerrero, Eliana Hernández, and Susana Villalba, "Poética vegetal," *Café de patio*, May 12, 2022, Humanidades ambientales, https://www.humanidadesambientales.com/cafe/15-poetica.

17. Guerrero, Hernández, and Villalba, "Poética vegetal."

18. I am referring here to Deleuze's declaration against totalizing concepts, binary thinking, and hierarchical logic: "We're tired of trees. We should stop believing in trees, roots, and radicles. They've made us suffer too much. All of arborescent culture is founded on them, from biology to linguistics." Deleuze and Guattari, *A Thousand Plateaus*, 15.

19. All translations of *El sueño de toda célula* are from Maricela Guerrero, *The Dream of Every Cell / El sueño de toda célula*, trans. Robin Myers (Berkeley: Cardboard House Press, 2022).

20. Maricela Guerrero, *El sueño de toda célula* (Mexico City: Antílope, 2018), 15.

21. Guerrero, *El sueño*, 17.

22. Guerrero, *El sueño*, 17.

23. Guerrero, *El sueño*, 16.

24. Maturana and Varela, *Autopoiesis and Cognition*, 48.

25. Guerrero, *El sueño*, 72.

26. Guerrero, *El sueño*, 87.

27. Humberto R. Maturana and Francisco J. Varela, *The Tree of Knowledge: The Biological Roots of Human Understanding* (Boston: Shambhala, 1992), 75.

28. Paul Bains, *The Primacy of Semiosis: An Ontology of Relations* (Toronto: University of Toronto Press, 2006), 102.

29. Bains, *Primacy of Semiosis*, 92.

30. Maturana and Varela, *Autopoiesis and Cognition*, 13, emphasis original.

31. Bains, *Primacy of Semiosis*, 107.

NOTES TO PAGES 117–128

32. Guerrero, *El sueño*, 39.

33. Guerrero, *El sueño*, 39.

34. Monica Gagliano, John Ryan, and Patricia I. Vieira, "Introduction," in *The Language of Plants: Science, Philosophy, Literature*, ed. Gagliano, Ryan, and Vieira (Minneapolis: University of Minnesota Press, 2017), xvii–iii.

35. Guerrero, *El sueño*, 39.

36. Guerrero, *El sueño*, 67.

37. Michael Hardt and Antonio Negri, *Empire* (Cambridge, MA: Harvard University Press, 2000), xii.

38. Gómez-Barris, *Extractive Zone*, xvii.

39. Guerrero, *El sueño*, 67–68.

40. See Niels Rivas Nielsen, "Bosquejos de lo universal: La apertura del lenguaje en *Trilce, Altazor*, y *En la masmédula*," *Alpha* 44 (July 2017): 137–151.

41. Antebi, *Embodied Archive*, 13.

42. Rebecca Janzen, *The National Body in Mexican Literature: Collective Challenges to Biopolitical Control* (New York: Palgrave Macmillan, 2015), 4.

43. Mignolo and Walsh, *On Decoloniality*, 163.

44. Guerrero, *El sueño*, 73.

45. Pratt, *Imperial Eyes*, 28.

46. Aníbal Quijano, "Coloniality of Power, Eurocentrism, and Latin America," trans. Michael Ennis, *Nepantla: Views from the South* 1, no. 3 (2000): 534–535.

47. Guerrero, *El sueño*, 73.

48. Guerrero, *El sueño*, 61.

49. Guerrero, *El sueño*, 74.

50. Mignolo and Walsh, *On Decoloniality*, 241.

51. Guerrero, *El sueño*, 74.

52. Hoyos, *Things with a History*, 226.

53. Guerrero, *El sueño*, 19.

54. Guerrero, *El sueño*, 19.

55. Guerrero, *El sueño*, 84.

56. Guerrero, *El sueño*, 69.

57. Gómez-Barris, *Extractive Zone*, 4.

58. Yásnaya Elena Aguilar Gil, *Ää: Manifiestos sobre la diversidad lingüística* (Mexico City: Almadía, 2020), 185. My translation is based on the Spanish translation of the original speech found on 183–185.

59. Guerrero, *El sueño*, 21.

60. Guerrero, *El sueño*, 21.

61. Guerrero, *El sueño*, 22.

62. Gagliano, Ryan, and Vieira, "Introduction," xviii.

63. Maturana and Varela, *Tree of Knowledge*, 208.

64. Maturana and Varela, *Tree of Knowledge*, 247.

65. Guerrero, *El sueño*, 76.

66. R. Guy Emerson, *Necropolitics: Living Death in Mexico* (London: Palgrave Macmillan, 2019), 4.

67. Guerrero, *El sueño*, 59.

68. Guerrero, *El sueño*, 71.

69. Guerrero, *El sueño*, 101–102.

70. Guerrero, *El sueño*, 102.

71. Guerrero, *El sueño*, 102.

72. Maturana and Varela, *Tree of Knowledge*, 247.

73. Guerrero, *El sueño*, 41. Guadalupe originally comes from the name of the river in Extramadura, Spain, a combination of the Arabic *wadi* (river) and the Latin *lupum* (wolf). In the fifteenth century there was a robust cult dedicated to the Marian apparition at Santa María de Guadalupe in Cáceres, Spain. Emery de Gaál Gyulai, "The Marian Connection between the Americas and Europe: Our Lady of Guadalupe, 1300–1900," *Marian Studies* 62 (2011): Article 6.

74. Guerrero, *El sueño*, 41.

75. Guerrero, *El sueño*, 42.

76. Guerrero, *El sueño*, 42.

77. Guerrero, *El sueño*, 62.

78. Guerrero, *El sueño*, 63.

79. Guerrero, *El sueño*, 64.

80. Ellen Skowronski, "Words That Breathe: An Interview with José Manuel Marrero Henríquez," *Ecozon@* 6, no. 1 (2015): 115.

CHAPTER 6 — DIMENSIONS OF EMBODIED EXPERIENCE

1. Thomas Venning, "Time's Arrow: Albert Einstein's Letters to Michele Besso," Christie's, November 14, 2017, https://www.christies.com/features/Einstein-letters-to-Michele-Besso-8422-1.aspx.

2. Albert Einstein and Alice Calaprice, *The Expanded Quotable Einstein* (Princeton, NJ: Princeton University Press, 2000), 148.

3. Carlo Rovelli reminds his readers, "I am not sure that because Einstein has penned some phrase or other we should treat it as the utterance of an oracle. Einstein changed his mind many times on fundamental questions, and it is possible to find numerous erroneous phrases of his that contradict each other. But in this instance [the letter to the Besso family], things are perhaps much simpler. Or more profound." Rovelli, *The Order of Time*, trans. Erica Segre and Simon Carnell (New York: Riverhead Books, 2018), 114.

4. Elisa Díaz Castelo, "Geometría descriptiva," in *Principia* (Mexico City: Tierra Adentro, 2018), 50, lines 22–26.

5. Díaz Castelo's work has quickly garnered critical praise and has been awarded several literary prizes including the Premio Nacional de Poesía Alfonso Vidal (the Alfonso Vidal National Poetry Prize) for *Principia* and the Premio Bellas Artes de Poesía Aguascalientes (the Aguascalientes Fine Arts Prize in Poetry) for *El reino de lo no lineal*.

6. Elisa Díaz Castelo, "Principios de incertidumbre: Poesía y ciencia," *Periódico de poesía*, Universidad Autónoma de México, July 8, 2019, https://periodicodepoesia.unam.mx/texto/principios-de-incertidumbre-poesia-y-ciencia/.

7. IPN Cultura, "Conversatorio de poesía, filosofía y tecnología | Con Elisa Díaz Castelo y Ulises Paniagua," Instituto Politécnico Nacional, Mexico, April 9, 2021, https://www.youtube.com/watch?v=RwMeQwBlra4.

8. Alejandro Rodríguez, "La ciencia hecha poesía. *Principia* de Elisa Díaz Castelo," *Figuras: Revista Académica de Investigación* 2, no. 1 (November 2020–February 2021): 119.

9. Emilio Tejeda, "Flotar entre dos equilibrios: La poesía de Elisa Díaz Castelo," *Opción* 205 (December 2018): 105.

NOTES TO PAGES 136–145

10. Myriam Moscona, back cover endorsement of *Principia*, by Elisa Díaz Castelo (Mexico City: Tierra Adentro, 2018).

11. Isabel Zapata, *"Principia*, de Elisa Díaz Castelo: Instrucciones para dejar las cosas intactas,"* Revista de la Universidad de México* 840 (September 2018): 140.

12. Isaac Newton, *The Mathematical Principles of Natural Philosophy*, trans. Andrew Motte (New York: Daniel Adee, 1846), 508.

13. Díaz Castelo, "Credo," in *Principia*, 16, lines 1–10.

14. Díaz Castelo, "Credo," 16, lines 17–18.

15. Díaz Castelo, "Credo," 17, lines 27–29.

16. Connor-Swietlicki, "Why Autopoiesis and Memory Matter," 53.

17. Díaz Castelo, "Escoliosis," in *Principia*, 14, lines 1–3.

18. Díaz Castelo, "Escoliosis," 13, lines 13–15.

19. Díaz Castelo, "Escoliosis," 13, lines 15–18.

20. Díaz Castelo, "Escoliosis," 14, lines 33–35, emphasis original.

21. Díaz Castelo, "Escoliosis," 15, line 70.

22. Díaz Castelo, "Escoliosis," 14, lines 46–47.

23. Díaz Castelo, "Escoliosis," 15, lines 48–49, 54–61.

24. Nicholas Humphrey, *A History of the Mind* (New York: Simon & Schuster, 1992), 203–204.

25. Bennett, *Vibrant Matter*, 10.

26. Díaz Castelo, "Escoliosis," 15, lines 73–74.

27. Howard Mancing, "Embodied Cognitive Science and the Study of Literature," in *Cognitive Cervantes*, ed. Julien J. Simon, Barbara Simerka, and Howard Mancing, special cluster of essays in *Cervantes: Bulletin of the Cervantes Society of America* 32, no. 1 (2012): 29, emphasis original.

28. Díaz Castelo, "Credo," 16–17, lines 19–22.

29. Maturana and Varela, *Tree of Knowledge*, 75.

30. Díaz Castelo, "Radiografías," in *Principia*, 21, lines 1–5, emphasis original.

31. In a traditional X-ray tube, the cathode emits accelerated electrons toward a positively charged anode, where the impact decelerates the electrons, releasing their energy as heat and electromagnetic radiation.

32. Díaz Castelo, "Radiografías," 21, lines 10–11.

33. Díaz Castelo, "Radiografías," 21–22, lines 13–22.

34. Díaz Castelo, "Radiografías," 21, lines 7–8.

35. The poet recalls how as a child she would contemplate her body lit from behind, red, "encarnizado, denso y rutilante / como imagino el plasma" (lines 25–26), which seems to be in communication with Gerardo Deniz's "Antistrofa," where "inútil como acercar la mano hasta una luz muy fuerte / y verla traslúcida y roja y atroz." Gerardo Deniz, "Antistrofa," in *Gerardo Deniz: Material de lectura*, ed. Pablo Mora (Mexico City: UNAM, 2011), 17.

36. Díaz Castelo, "Radiografías," 22, lines 29–34.

37. Díaz Castelo, "Radiografías," 22–23, lines 35–44.

38. Díaz Castelo, "Radiografías," 23, lines 50–53.

39. Díaz Castelo, "Radiografías," 23, lines 55–56.

40. Stacy Alaimo, *Bodily Natures: Science, Environment, and the Material Self* (Bloomington: Indiana University Press, 2010), 2.

NOTES TO PAGES 146–152

41. Ira Livingston, *Between Science and Literature: An Introduction to Autopoetics* (Urbana: University of Illinois Press, 2006), 83, emphasis original.

42. Mancing, "Embodied Cognitive Science," 39.

43. Darío Jaramillo Agudelo, "Poemas de amor, 1," in *Darío Jaramillo Agudelo: Una antología*, ed. Vicente Quirarte (Mexico City: Universidad Nacional Autónoma de México, 2016), 25.

44. By comparing the parts of speech used in Jaramillo's verse and Díaz Castelo's title, we can appreciate how Díaz Castelo plays with the idea of one's identity originating from the Other. Jaramillo's "ese otro" (that other) is a combination of the demonstrative adjective "ese" (that) with the pronoun "otro" (other), describing a separate entity at a distance from the speaker. In contrast, Díaz Castelo's "esto otro" (this other stuff) flips the construction, using the neutral demonstrative pronoun "esto" (this thing/stuff) with "other" here functioning as an adjective. The effect is to emphasize its proximity to the speaker as well as give substance to its being, with its otherness as a qualitative feature.

45. Díaz Castelo, "Esto otro que también me habita (y no es el alma o no necesariamente)," in *Principia*, 35, lines 1–16.

46. Comparing the number of cells or microorganisms underscores the parasitic and symbiotic interconnections between the human and more-than-human world. When compared by mass, the ratios change, but the importance of these couplings remains: "The human body contains trillions of microorganisms—outnumbering human cells by 10 to 1. Because of their small size, however, microorganisms make up only about 1 to 3 percent of the body's mass (in a 200-pound adult, that's 2 to 6 pounds of bacteria), but play a vital role in human health." "NIH Human Microbiome Project Defines Normal Bacterial Makeup of the Body," *NIH News*, July 31, 2012, https://www.genome.gov/27549144/2012-release-nih-human-microbiome-project-defines-normal-bacterial-makeup-of-the-body.

47. Díaz Castelo, "Esto otro que también me habita," 36, line 36.

48. Díaz Castelo, "Esto otro que también me habita," 36–37, lines 41–56.

49. Díaz Castelo, "Oda a los ancestros," in *Principia*, 26, lines 6–7.

50. Díaz Castelo, "Oda a los ancestros," 26, lines 7–21.

51. Díaz Castelo, "Oda a los ancestros," 27, lines 41–49.

52. Octavio Paz, *Piedra de Sol*, ed. Ramón Xirau (Mexico City: Universidad Nacional Autónoma de México, 2008), 9, lines 104–105.

53. Paz, *Piedra de Sol*, 9, lines 530–531. English translation from Octavio Paz, *The Collected Poems of Octavio Paz 1957–1987*, ed. and trans. Eliot Weinberger (New York: New Directions, 1987), 31.

54. Bennett, *Vibrant Matter*, 11, emphasis original.

55. Díaz Castelo, "Acta de defunción," in *Principia*, 41, line 34.

56. Redshift is an example of the Doppler effect known to most of us through sound waves. When an ambulance accelerates away from us, we notice that the pitch of its siren sounds lower and lower. We can observe the relic radiation of the early universe, known as the cosmic microwave background, although it is imperceivable to the human eye, through the use of radio telescopes.

57. Díaz Castelo, "Sobre la luz que no vemos y otras formas de desaparecer," in *Principia*, 79, line 11.

58. Díaz Castelo, "Sobre la luz," 79, lines 18–19.

59. Díaz Castelo, "Sobre la luz," 79, lines 32–37.

NOTES TO PAGES 152–159

60. Díaz Castelo, "Primogénita," in *Principia*, 43.

61. Rovelli, *Order of Time*, 44.

62. Mancing, "Embodied Cognitive Science," 27.

63. Bakhtin states, "We will give the name chronotope (literally, 'time space') to the intrinsic connectedness of temporal and spatial relations that are artistically expressed in literature. This term is employed in mathematics and was introduced as part of Einstein's theory of relativity. The special meaning it has in relativity theory is not important for our purposes; we are borrowing it for literary criticism almost as a metaphor (almost, but not entirely). What counts for us is the fact that it expresses the inseparability of space and time (time as the fourth dimension of space). We understand the chronotope as a formal and constitutive category of literature; we will not deal with the chronotope in other areas of culture." Bakhtin, *Dialogic Imagination*, 84.

64. Mancing, "Embodied Cognitive Science," 27.

65. Díaz Castelo, "Sobre la luz," 79, line 58.

66. Díaz Castelo, "Sobre la luz," 79, lines 63–69.

67. Elisa Díaz Castelo, "Formas (guiadas) de desaparecer," *Periódico de poesía*, Universidad Autónoma de México, November 16, 2020, https://periodicodepoesia.unam.mx /texto/formas-guiadas-de-desaparecer/.

68. Díaz Castelo, "Formas (guiadas) de desaparecer."

69. Rovelli, *Order of Time*, 96.

70. Rovelli, *Order of Time*, 98.

71. The 80 percent figure has been used for decades, yet recent research suggests that our rudimentary understanding of dark matter may be entirely wrong. For a brief summary for nonspecialists, consult Ian Stewart, *Calculating the Cosmos: How Mathematics Unveils the Universe* (New York: Basic Books, 2016), 267–276.

72. Díaz Castelo, "Materia oscura," in *Principia*, 69.

73. Díaz Castelo, "Materia oscura," 69–70.

74. Maturana and Varela, *Tree of Knowledge*, 27.

75. Díaz Castelo, "Materia oscura," 72.

76. Díaz Castelo, "Materia oscura," 73.

77. Maturana and Varela, *Tree of Knowledge*, 329.

78. Livingston, *Between Science and Literature*, 89. Livingston concludes this description of the autopoietic assemblage with what may be my favorite sentence in an academic monograph: "At the risk of selling my argument short, then, I am tempted to sum up the entire critical intervention of this book in the following two words: Autopoiesis? Schmattepoiesis."

79. Zapata, "*Principia*, de Elisa Díaz Castelo," 143. Díaz Castelo's metaphor of the empty pool clearly inspired Zapata when composing the essay "Maneras de desaparecer" (Ways to disappear) for her 2019 essay collection appropriately titled *Alberca vacía* (Empty pool).

80. Díaz Castelo, "Alberca vacía," in *Principia*, 83, lines 20–21.

81. Díaz Castelo, "Alberca vacía," 83, lines 27–28.

82. Díaz Castelo, "Alberca vacía," 83, lines 30–36.

83. Díaz Castelo, "Materia oscura," 71.

84. Rovelli, *Order of Time*, 99, emphasis original.

85. Díaz Castelo, "Alberca vacía," lines 52–54.

86. Díaz Castelo, "Alberca vacía," lines 57–58.

87. Díaz Castelo, "Alberca vacía," lines 37–41.

88. Barad, *Meeting the Universe Halfway*, 33.

89. Alberto Blanco, "Teoría de la gravedad," in *Raíz cuadrada*, 31–32, lines 21–24.

CONCLUSIONS

1. Matteo Barbarino, "What Is Nuclear Fusion?" (International Atomic Energy Agency, March 31, 2021), https://www.iaea.org/newscenter/news/what-is-nuclear-fusion.

2. Jorge Fernández Granados, "Principio de incertidumbre," in *Principio de incertidumbre* (Mexico City: Era, 2007), 52, lines 16–17.

3. Fernández Granados, "Principio de incertidumbre," 52, lines 6–15.

4. Fernández Granados, "Principio de incertidumbre," 52, line 1.

5. Barad, *Meeting the Universe Halfway*, 72.

6. Barad, *Meeting the Universe Halfway*, 30.

7. Barad, *Meeting the Universe Halfway*, 89.

8. Beardsall, "Writing at the Interface," 33.

9. Blanco, *Raíz cuadrada*, 9.

10. Julio Trujillo, "Si," in *El acelerador de partículas* (Mexico City: Alamdía, 2017), 63, lines 1–2, 14–15.

Bibliography

Aguilar Gil, Yásnaya Elena. *Ää: Manifiestos sobre la diversidad lingüística*. Mexico City: Almadía, 2020.

———. "Agua con A de Ayutla. Una denuncia." *Revista de la Universidad de México*, June 2020. https://www.revistadelauniversidad.mx/articles/f03bc7f3-df5a-460f-b2fe-ad5dd1b91fba/agua-con-a-de-ayutla.

Aguirre Romero, Joaquín, and Yolanda Delgado Batista. "Jorge Volpi: Las respuestas absolutas siempre son mentiras." *Espéculo* 11 (1999). https://webs.ucm.es/info/especulo/numero11/volpi.html.

Alaimo, Stacy. *Bodily Natures: Science, Environment, and the Material Self*. Bloomington: Indiana University Press, 2010.

Álvarez, Ignacio. "Paradoja y contradicción: Epistemología y estética en *En busca de Klingsor*, de Jorge Volpi." *Taller de letras* 33, no. 47 (2003): 47–60.

Anderson, Danny J. "The Novels of Jorge Volpi and the Possibility of Knowledge." *Studies in the Literary Imagination* 33, no. 1 (2000): 1–20.

Anderson, Warwick. "From Subjugated Knowledge to Conjugated Subjects: Science and Globalisation, or Postcolonial Studies of Science?" *Postcolonial Studies* 12, no. 4 (2009): 389–400.

Antebi, Susan. *Embodied Archive: Disability in Post-Revolutionary Mexican Cultural Production*. Ann Arbor: University of Michigan Press, 2021.

Asúa, Miguel de. *Ciencia y Literatura: Un relato histórico*. Buenos Aires: Eudeba, 2011.

Ávalos Molina, Etna Verónica. "Representaciones literarias de la discapacidad en el contexto latinoamericano del siglo XXI." PhD diss., University of North Carolina at Chapel Hill, 2019.

Aveni, Anthony F. *Skywatchers: A Revised and Updated Version of Skywatchers of Ancient Mexico*. Austin: University of Texas Press, 2001.

Azuela, Arturo. *El matemático*. Mexico City: Plaza y Valdés, 1988.

Bagaria, Joan. "Set Theory." In *The Stanford Encyclopedia of Philosophy* (Winter 2021 ed.), edited by Edward N. Zalta. https://plato.stanford.edu/archives/win2021/entries/set-theory/.

Baggott, Jim. *The First War of Physics: The Secret History of the Atom Bomb, 1939–1949*. New York: Pegasus, 2010.

———. *The Quantum Story: A History in 40 Moments*. Oxford: Oxford University Press, 2011.

Bains, Paul. *The Primacy of Semiosis: An Ontology of Relations*. Toronto: University of Toronto Press, 2006.

Bakhtin, Mikhail. *The Dialogic Imagination: Four Essays*. Edited and translated by Michael Holquist and Caryl Emesron. Austin: University of Texas Press, 1981.

Ballester Pardo, Ignacio. "Reseña: El sueño de toda célula, de Maricela Guerrero." *Bitácora de vuelos: Literatura y e-books*, February 2019. https://www.rdbitacoradevuelos.com.mx/2019/02/resena-el-sueno-de-toda-celula-de.html.

Barad, Karen M. *Meeting the Universe Halfway: Quantum Physics and the Entanglement of Matter and Meaning*. Durham, NC: Duke University Press, 2007.

Barbarino, Matteo. "What Is Nuclear Fusion?" International Atomic Energy Agency, March 31, 2021. https://www.iaea.org/newscenter/news/what-is-nuclear-fusion.

Barbas-Rhoden, Laura. *Ecological Imaginations in Latin American Fiction*. Gainesville: University Press of Florida, 2011.

Barcelona, Antonio. "Introduction: The Cognitive Theory of Metaphor and Metonymy." In Barcelona, *Metaphor and Metonymy at the Crossroads*, 1–28.

———, ed. *Metaphor and Metonymy at the Crossroads: A Cognitive Perspective*. Berlin: De Gruyter, 2003.

Barrera-Osorio, Antonio. *Experiencing Nature: The Spanish American Empire and the Early Scientific Revolution*. Austin: University of Texas Press, 2006.

Beardsall, Peter. "Writing at the Interface: Toward an Overview of the Relationship between Science and Literature." In Carpenter, *Interface between Literature and Science*, 11–44.

Beltrán, Rosa. *El cuerpo expuesto*. Mexico City: Alfaguara, 2014.

Benjamin, Walter. *Illuminations*. Edited and translated by Hannah Arendt. New York: Harcourt, Brace, and World, 1968.

Bennett, Jane. *Influx and Efflux: Writing Up with Walt Whitman*. Durham, NC: Duke University Press, 2020.

———. *Vibrant Matter: A Political Ecology of Things*. Durham, NC: Duke University Press, 2010.

Berman, Sabina. "Barra de opinion: *La mujer que buceó dentro del corazón del mundo*." Interview by Estela Livera. *Desafíos*, March 11, 2011. https://www.youtube.com/watch?v=pQNa1mk_xCE.

———. *El dios de Darwin*. Barcelona: Ediciones Destino, 2014.

———. *El gordo, la pájara y el narco. El suplicio del placer*. Aguascalientes: Instituto Cultural de Aguascalientes, 1994.

———. *El narco negocia con Dios; Testosterona*. Mexico City: El Milagro, 2013.

———. *Krisis. Tramoya* 52 (1997): 51–99.

———. "'Largo Aliento,' la naturaleza como centro de la vida: Sabina Berman." Interview by Gabriela Warkentin and Javier Risco. *Así las cosas*, W Radio (XEW-AM), Mexico City, March 11, 2021. https://wradio.com.mx/programa/2021/03/11/asi_las_cosas/1615489112_911627.html.

———. *Matemáticas para la felicidad y otras fábulas*. Mexico City: Porrúa, 2017.

———. *La mujer que buceó dentro del corazón del mundo*. Mexico City: Planeta Mexicana, 2010.

BIBLIOGRAPHY

Bierce, Ambrose. "Moxon's Master." In *Ambrose Bierce: The Devil's Dictionary, Tales & Memoirs*, edited by S. T. Joshi, 252–261. New York: Library of America, 2011.

Bixler, Jacqueline. "Sabina Berman Redux: Adaptation and the Anxiety of (Self) Influence." *Romance Notes* 55, no. 2 (2015): 227–239.

Blanco, Alberto. *A la luz de siempre*. Mexico City: Fondo de Cultura Económica, 2018.

———. *Antes de nacer*. Mexico City: Editorial Penélope, 1983.

———. *El corazón del instante*. Mexico City: Fondo de Cultura Económica, 1998.

———. *La raíz cuadrada del cielo*. Monterrey: Universidad Autónoma de Nuevo León, 2016.

———. "No sé cuándo empecé a hacer collage. . . ." 2020. https://www.albertoblancocollage.com/bio.

———. "Química." *Milenio* (Mexico), *Laberinto: Revista Cultural*, March 25, 2022. https://www.milenio.com/cultura/laberinto/quimica-por-alberto-blanco.

Blanco, María del Pilar, and Joanna Page, eds. *Geopolitics, Culture, and the Scientific Imaginary in Latin America*. Gainesville: University Press of Florida, 2020.

———. "Introduction: Reimagining Science in Latin America." In Blanco and Page, *Geopolitics, Culture, and the Scientific Imaginary in Latin America*, 1–22.

Bohr, Niels. *Atomic Physics and Human Knowledge*. New York: John Wiley, 1958.

Bollington, Lucy, and Paul Merchant, eds. *Latin American Culture and the Limits of the Human*. Gainesville: University Press of Florida, 2020.

———. "Introduction: Reworking the Human's Limits." In Bollington and Merchant, *Latin American Culture and the Limits of the Human*, 1–34.

Borges, Jorge Luis. *Ficciones*. New York: Vintage Español, 2012.

Bortolotto, María Celina, and May Summer Farnsworth. "Autismo, antropocentrismo y género en *La mujer que buceó dentro del corazón del mundo* (2010) de Sabina Berman." *Romance Notes* 55, no. 2 (2015): 215–226.

Braidotti, Rosi. *The Posthuman*. Cambridge: Polity, 2013.

Brescia, Pablo, and Oswaldo Estrada, eds. *McCrack: McOndo, el Crack y los destinos de la literatura latinoamericana*. Valencia: Albatros, 2018.

Brontë, Charlotte. *Jane Eyre*. New York: Norton 1997.

Brown, J. Andrew. *Cyborgs in Latin America*. New York: Palgrave Macmillan, 2010.

Buchanan, Ian. *Assemblage Theory and Method*. London: Bloomsbury, 2021.

Calderón, Sara. "Narrative Techniques in Jorge Volpi's Fictions." In Jaimes, *Mexican Crack Writers*, 51–72.

Cantú Toscano, Mario. *Golem. Semana de la Dramaturgia Nuevo León 2012–2016*. Monterrey: Consejo para la Cultura y las Artes de Nuevo León, 2016.

Capobianco, Michael F., and Gloria S. Meléndez. "Of Poets, Prophets, and Engineers: Nezahualcoyotl and Nezahualpilli." *Ometeca* 3–4 (1996): 508–514.

Capra, Fritjof. *The Tao of Physics: An Exploration of the Parallels between Modern Physics and Eastern Mysticism*. Boston: Shambhala, 1985.

Carpenter, Victoria, ed. *Interface between Literature and Science: Cross-Disciplinary Approaches to Latin American Texts*. Newcastle upon Tyne: Cambridge Scholars, 2015.

———. "Literature and Science: To Each Its Own?" In Carpenter, *Interface between Literature and Science*, 1–9.

Carroll, Lewis. *Through the Looking-Glass and What Alice Found There*. New York: Open Road Media, 2015.

Castillo, Debra A., and Stuart A. Day, eds. *Mexican Public Intellectuals*. New York: Palgrave, 2014.

Castoriadis, Cornelius. *The Imaginary Institution of Society*. Translated by Kathleen Blamey. Cambridge, MA: MIT Press, 1997.

Castro, Juan E. de. *The Spaces of Latin American Literature: Tradition, Globalization, and Cultural Production*. New York: Palgrave Macmillan, 2008.

Catalá, Rafael. *Cienciapoesía*. Minneapolis: Prisma Books, 1986.

———. "Literatura y ciencia en las culturas de habla hispana." *Torre: Revista General de la Universidad de Puerto Rico* 3, no. 9 (1998): 529–550.

Cave, Stephen, and Kanta Dihal. "The Automaton Chronicles." *Nature* 559 (July 26, 2018).

Chandler, Brian T. "Of Narcos and Necros: Violence and Morality in Sabina Berman's *El narco negocia con Dios*." *Chasqui* 50, no. 2 (2022): 147–162.

Chapa, Teresa. "La poesía de Alberto Blanco: Innovación y renovación en *Amanecer de los sentidos*." *Revista de Literatura Mexicana Contemporánea* 2, no. 4 (October 1996): 27–32.

Chávez Robinson, Irma. "El Budismo Zen, El Yin Yang y La Ecología En La Obra de Alberto Blanco." PhD diss., Florida State University, 2006.

Chimal, Carlos. "Levedad, rapidez, precisión. Octavio Paz y la ciencia." *Letras Libres* 259 (June 1998): 89–91.

Connor-Swietlicki, Catherine. "Why Autopoiesis and Memory Matter to Cervantes, Don Quixote, and the Humanities." In Jaén and Simon, *Cognitive Approaches to Early Modern Spanish Literature*, 53–73.

Coole, Diana H., and Samantha Frost. "Introducing New Materialisms." In Coole and Frost, *New Materialisms*, 1–43.

———, eds. *New Materialisms: Ontology, Agency, and Politics*. Durham, NC: Duke University Press, 2010.

Cornejo-Polar, Antonio. *Escribir en el aire: Ensayo sobre la heterogeneidad en las literaturas andinas*. Lima: Horizonte, 1994.

Cottingham, John. "'A Brute to the Brutes?' Descartes' Treatment of Animals." *Philosophy* 5, no. 206 (1978): 551–559.

Cuesta, Jorge. *Canto a un dios mineral*. Edited by Adolfo Castañón. Mexico City: UNAM, 2007.

Dalton, David S. *Mestizo Modernity: Race, Technology, and the Body in Postrevolutionary Mexico*. Gainesville: University Press of Florida, 2018.

———. "Robo Sacer: 'Bare Life' and Cyborg Labor Beyond the Border in Alex Rivera's *Sleep Dealer*." *Hispanic Studies Review* 1, no. 1 (2016): 15–29.

Daly, Tara. *Beyond Human: Vital Materialisms in the Andean Avant-Gardes*. Lewisburg, PA: Bucknell University Press, 2019.

Darwin, Charles. *The Autobiography of Charles Darwin, 1809–1882: With Original Omissions Restored*. Edited by Nora Barlow. New York: Collins, 1958.

———. *The Descent of Man, and Selection in Relation to Sex*. 1871. Project Gutenberg, 1999.

———. *On the Origin of Species*. 1859. Minneapolis: First Avenue, 2018.

Dawkins, Richard. *The Selfish Gene*. New York: Oxford University Press, 1976.

Dawson, Victoria. "The Epic Failure of Thomas Edison's Talking Doll." *Smithsonian Magazine*, June 1, 2015. https://www.smithsonianmag.com/smithsonian-institution/epic-failure-thomas-edisons-talking-doll-180955442/.

BIBLIOGRAPHY

Day, Stuart. "La intersextualidad (dramática) de Sabina Berman." In Berman, *El narco negocia con Dios*, 9–21.

d'Eaubonne, Françoise. *Feminism or Death: How the Women's Movement Can Save the Planet*. Edited and translated by Ruth Hottell. 1974. London: Verso, 2022.

DeLanda, Manuel. *A New Philosophy of Society: Assemblage Theory and Social Complexity*. New York: Continuum, 2006.

Deleuze, Gilles, and Félix Guattari. *Anti-Oedipus: Capitalism and Schizophrenia*. Translated by Robert Hurley, Mark Seem, and Helen R. Lane. Minneapolis: University of Minnesota Press, 1983.

———. *A Thousand Plateaus: Capitalism and Schizophrenia*. Translated by Brian Massumi. Minneapolis: University of Minnesota Press, 1987.

Demby, Samantha. "Pandemic Intensifies Women's Struggle for Water in Oaxaca, Mexico." North American Congress on Latin America (NACLA), July 16, 2020. https://nacla.org/news/2020/07/15/oaxaca-water-mexico-pandemic.

Deniz, Gerardo. *Erdera*. Mexico City: Fondo de Cultura Económica, 2006.

———. *Gerardo Deniz: Material de lectura*. Edited by Pablo Mora. Mexico City: UNAM, 2011.

Dés, Mihály. "Como lector, tengo mi propio punto de vista sobre quién pudo haber sido Klingsor." *Lateral* 6, no. 70 (2000): 28–29.

Descartes, René. *Discourse on Method and Meditations on First Philosophy*. Translated by Donald A. Cress. Indianapolis: Hackett, 1998.

Díaz Castelo, Elisa. *El reino de lo no lineal*. Mexico City: Fondo de Cultura Económica, 2020.

———. "Formas (guiadas) de desaparecer." *Periódico de poesía*, Universidad Autónoma de México, November 16, 2020. https://periodicodepoesia.unam.mx/texto/formas-guiadas-de-desaparecer/.

———. *Principia*. Mexico City: Tierra Adentro, 2018.

———. "Principios de incertidumbre: Poesía y ciencia." *Periódico de poesía*, Universidad Autónoma de México, July 8, 2019. https://periodicodepoesia.unam.mx/texto/principios-de-incertidumbre-poesia-y-ciencia/.

———. *Proyecto Manhattan*. Mexico City: Ediciones Antílope, 2020.

DiCaglio, Josh. *Scale Theory: A Nondisciplinary Inquiry*. Minneapolis: University of Minnesota Press, 2021.

Domínguez Michael, Christopher. *Diccionario crítico de la literatura mexicana (1955–2005)*. Mexico City: Fondo de Cultura Económica, 2007.

Eherenman, Kimberly A. "Las formas del instante: Entrevista con Alberto Blanco." *Fractal: Revista Trimestral* 7, no. 25 (April–June 2002). https://mxfractal.org/F25blanco.html.

Einstein, Albert, and Alice Calaprice. *The Expanded Quotable Einstein*. Princeton, NJ: Princeton University Press, 2000.

Elizondo, Salvador. *Salvador Elizondo: Material de lectura*. Edited by John Bruce-Novoa and Rolando Romero. Mexico City: UNAM, 2009.

Emerson, R. Guy. *Necropolitics: Living Death in Mexico*. London: Palgrave Macmillan, 2019.

Emmelhainz, Irmgard. *La tiranía del sentido común: La reconversión neoliberal de México*. Mexico City: Paradiso, 2016.

Engelhardt, Nina, and Julia Hoydis. "Introduction: Connectivities between Literature and Science in the Twenty-First Century." In Engelhardt and Hoydis, *Representations of Science in Twenty-First-Century Fiction*, 1–17.

———, eds. *Representations of Science in Twenty-First-Century Fiction: Human and Temporal Connectivities*. Cham, Switzerland: Palgrave, 2019.

Escalante, Evodio. "De la vanguardia militante a la vanguardia blanca: Los nuevos trastornadores del lenguaje en la poesía mexicana de nuestros días: David Huerta, Gerardo Deniz, Alberto Blanco y Coral Bracho." In Patán, *Perfiles*, 27–45.

Faye, Jan. "Copenhagen Interpretation of Quantum Mechanics." In *The Stanford Encyclopedia of Philosophy* (Winter 2019 ed.), edited by Edward N. Zalta. https://plato.stanford.edu/archives/win2019/entries/qm-copenhagen/.

Fell, Claude. *José Vasconcelos: Los años del águila (1920–1925)*. Mexico City: UNAM, 1989.

Fernández Granados, Jorge. "Apuntes para una teoría de la física cuántica de Ignacio Padilla." *Unidiversidad: Revista de Pensamiento y Cultura de la Benemérita Universidad Autónoma de Puebla* 30 (2018): 38–43.

———. *Principio de incertidumbre*. Mexico City: Era, 2007.

Ferrando, Francesca. "Posthumanism, Transhumanism, Antihumanism, Metahumanism, and New Materialisms: Differences and Relations." *Existenz* 8, no. 2 (2013): 26–32.

Fishburn, Evelyn, and Eduardo L. Ortiz. "Introduction." In Fishburn and Ortiz, *Science and the Creative Imagination in Latin America*, 1–12.

———, eds. *Science and the Creative Imagination in Latin America*. London: Institute for the Study of the Americas, 2005.

Fornoff, Carolyn. "Planetary Poetics of Extinction in Contemporary Mexican Poetry." In Sánchez Prado, *Mexican Literature as World Literature*, 231–245.

Franken, Clemens. "*En busca de Klingsor* by Jorge Volpi: Una novela con formato policial híbrido, posmoderno y poscolonial." *Acta literaria* 44 (2012): 53–72.

Friis, Ronald J. *White Light: The Poetry of Alberto Blanco*. Lewisburg, PA: Bucknell University Press, 2021.

Fuertes Trigal, Siridia. "Lo fantástico del mal en el proyecto *Micropedia* de Ignacio Padilla." *Revista de Literatura Mexicana Contemporánea* 15, no. 43 (2009): 31–41.

Gaál Gyulai, Emery de. "The Marian Connection between the Americas and Europe: Our Lady of Guadalupe, 1300–1900." *Marian Studies* 62 (2011): Article 6.

Gagliano, Monica, John Ryan, and Patricia I. Vieira. "Introduction." In Gagliano, Ryan, and Vieira, *Language of Plants*, vii–xxxiii.

———, eds. *The Language of Plants: Science, Philosophy, Literature*. Minneapolis: University of Minnesota Press, 2017.

Galicia Lechuga, David, "La ciencia en la obra de sor Juana." *Revista Digital Universitaria* 16, no. 12 (December 2015): 3–13. http://www.revista.unam.mx/vol.16/num12/art96/index.html.

Galindo Ulloa, Javier. "El silencio en la poesía de Alberto Blanco." *Tema y Variaciones de Literatura* 48 (2017): 85–98.

García Canclini, Néstor. *Culturas híbridas: estrategias para entrar y salir de la modernidad*. Mexico City: Debolsillo, 2009.

García Márquez, Gabriel. *Cien años de soledad*. New York: Vintage Español, 2009.

———. *Todos los cuentos*. Bogotá: Oveja Negra, 1994.

García Ramírez, Fernando. "Todo se vale a pequeña escala." *Letras libres* 6, no. 69 (September 2004). https://letraslibres.com/revista-mexico/gerardo-deniz-todo-se-vale-a-pequena-escala/.

García Serrano, M. Victoria. "El binomio Descartes y Darwin en *La mujer que buceó dentro del corazón del mundo* de Sabina Berman." In Pérez Magallón and de la

BIBLIOGRAPHY

Fuente Ballesteros, *Idealismo, racionalismo y empirismo en la literatura hispánica*, 63–72.

Ginway, Elizabeth M. *Cyborgs, Sexuality, and the Undead: The Body in Mexican and Brazilian Speculative Fiction*. Nashville, TN: Vanderbilt University Press, 2020.

Girondo, Oliverio. *En la masmédula*. 1954. Madrid: Del Centro, 2017.

Glick, Thomas F., Miguel Angel Puig-Samper, and Rosaura Ruiz, eds. *The Reception of Darwinism in the Iberian World: Spain, Spanish America, and Brazil*. Boston: Kluwer, 2001.

Goebel, Robert. "Un germanista en busca de Klingsor." *Revista de Literatura Mexicana Contemporánea* 7, no. 14 (2001): 32–41.

Gómez-Barris, Macarena. *The Extractive Zone: Social Ecologies and Decolonial Perspectives*. Durham, NC: Duke University Press, 2017.

Gómez del Valle, Elena. "Y a veces detenerse es otra forma de fluir y amar: *El sueño de toda célula*, de Maricela Guerrero." *Replicante: Periodismo digital / cultura crítica*, July 11, 2020. https://revistareplicante.com/y-a-veces-detenerse-es-otra-forma-de-fluir-y-amar/.

Gómez Gray, Alana. "Emoción frente a neoliberalismo en la novela *La mujer que buceó dentro del corazón del mundo* de Sabina Berman." *Vanderbilt E-Journal of Luso-Hispanic Studies* 11, no. 1 (February 2021): 33–49.

González, Aníbal. "Science, Art, and Magic: Totalization and Totalitarianism in Jorge Volpi's *In Search of Klingsor*." In Jaimes, *Mexican Crack Writers*, 73–86.

Goodbody, Axel, and Kate Rigby, eds. *Ecocritical Theory: New European Approaches*. Charlottesville: University of Virginia Press, 2011.

Gordon, José. *El inconcebible Universo: sueños de unidad*. Mexico City: Sexto Piso / Instituto Cultural de León, 2017.

Grabe, Nina, Sabine Lang, and Klaus Meyer-Minnemann, eds. *La narración paradójica: "Normas narrativas" y el principio de la "transgresión."* Madrid: Iberoamericana, 2006.

Grau, Manuel. "*En busca de Klingsor* y la teoría de los juegos." In López de Abiada, Jiménez Ramírez, and López Bernasocchi, *En busca de Volpi*, 149–162.

Gray, Chris, ed. *The Cyborg Handbook*. New York: Routledge, 1995.

Greene, Brian. *The Fabric of the Cosmos*. New York: Knopf, 2004.

Gruber, David R. "Material Foundations of Scientific Metaphors: A New Materialist Metaphor Studies." *Configurations: A Journal of Literature, Science, and Technology* 31, no. 1 (Winter 2023): 1–34.

Guerrero, Luis. *Números imaginarios. Semana de la Dramaturgia Nuevo León 2012–2016*. Monterrey: Consejo para la Cultura y las Artes de Nuevo León, 2016.

Guerrero, Maricela. *The Dream of Every Cell / El sueño de toda célula*. Translated by Robin Myers. Berkeley: Cardboard House Press, 2022.

———. *El sueño de toda célula*. Mexico City: Antílope, 2018.

———. *Peceras*. Mexico City: Filodecaballos, 2013.

———. *Se llaman nebulosas*. Mexico City: Tierra Adentro, 2010.

Guerrero, Maricela, Eliana Hernández, and Susana Villalba. "Poética vegetal." *Café de patio*, May 12, 2022. Humanidades ambientales. https://www.humanidadesambientales.com/cafe/15-poetica.

Haraway, Donna J. *Simians, Cyborgs, and Women: The Reinvention of Nature*. New York: Routledge, 1991.

———. *Staying with the Trouble: Making Kin in the Chthulucene*. Durham, NC: Duke University Press, 2016.

Hardt, Michael, and Antonio Negri. *Empire*. Cambridge, MA: Harvard University Press, 2000.

Heffes, Gisela. "Introducción. Para una ecocrítica latinoamericana: Entre la postulación de un ecocentrismo crítico y la crítica a un antropocentrismo hegemónico." *Revista de Crítica Literaria Latinoamericana* 40, no. 79 (2014): 11–34.

Heisenberg, Werner. *Nuclear Physics*. Translated by Frank Gaynor and Amethe von Zeppelin. New York: Taylor & Francis, 1952.

Hekster, Olivier. "The Size of History: Coincidence, Counterfactuality and Questions of Scale in History." In Landsman and van Wolde, *Challenge of Chance*, 215–232.

Herrera, Alfonso. *Nociones de biología*. In *Herrera's "Plasmogenia" and Other Collected Works: Early Writings on the Experimental Study of the Origin of Life*, edited by Henderson James Cleaves et al., 7–162. New York: Springer, 2014.

Herrera Corral, Gerardo. *El Higgs, el universo líquido y el Gran Colisionador de Hadrones*. Mexico City: Fondo de Cultura Económica, 2014.

Hesiod and Homer. *Hesiod, the Homeric Hymns, and Homerica*. Edited by Hugh G. Evelyn-White. Project Gutenberg, 2008. https://www.gutenberg.org/ebooks/348.

Hoeg, Jerry. *Science, Technology, and Latin American Narrative in the Twentieth Century and Beyond*. Cranbury, NJ: Associated University Press, 2000.

Hoeg, Jerry, and Kevin S. Larsen, eds. *Interdisciplinary Essays on Darwinism in Hispanic Literature and Film: The Intersection of Science and the Humanities*. Lewiston, NY: Edwin Mellen Press, 2009.

———. "Introduction." In Hoeg and Larsen, *Interdisciplinary Essays on Darwinism in Hispanic Literature and Film*, 1–4.

Hosch, William L. "Automaton." In *Encyclopedia Britannica*, September 18, 2013. https://www.britannica.com/technology/automaton/.

Hoyos, Héctor. *Things with a History: Transcultural Materialism and the Literatures of Extraction in Contemporary Latin America*. New York: University of Columbia Press, 2019.

Huchín Sosa, Eduardo. "Narrar la diferencia." *Letras libres*, November 6, 2011. https://www.letraslibres.com/mexico/libros/narrar-la-diferencia.

Humphrey, Nicholas. *A History of the Mind*. New York: Simon & Schuster, 1992.

Hutcheon, Linda. *A Poetics of Postmodernism: History, Theory, Fiction*. London: Routledge, 1988.

———. *A Theory of Adaptation*. New York: Routledge, 2006.

Inés de la Cruz, Sor Juana. *Primero sueño*, 1692. Edited by Alejandro Soriano Vallès. Toluca, Mexico: Secretaría de Cultura, 2019.

Insúa Cereceda, Mariela. "La pesquisa de la verdad en *En busca de Klngsor* de Jorge Volpi." *Revista Chilena de Literatura* 64 (2004): 91–101.

Iovino, Serenella, and Serpil Oppermann. "Introduction: Stories Come to Matter." In Iovino and Oppermann, *Material Ecocriticism*, 1–17.

———, eds. *Material Ecocriticism*. Bloomington: Indiana University Press, 2014.

IPN Cultura. "Conversatorio de poesía, filosofía y tecnología | Con Elisa Díaz Castelo y Ulises Paniagua." Instituto Politécnico Nacional, Mexico, April 9, 2021. https://www.youtube.com/watch?v=RwMeQwBlra4.

BIBLIOGRAPHY

Jaén, Isabel, and Julien Jacques Simon, eds. *Cognitive Approaches to Early Modern Spanish Literature.* New York: Oxford University Press, 2016.

———. "Introduction." In Jaén and Simon, *Cognitive Approaches to Early Modern Spanish Literature,* 1–10.

Jaimes, Héctor. "Introduction: The Mexican Crack Writers—Toward a New Literary Aesthetics." In Jaimes, *Mexican Crack Writers,* 1–9.

———, ed. *The Mexican Crack Writers: History and Criticism.* Cham, Switzerland: Palgrave Macmillan, 2017.

Janzen, Rebecca. *The National Body in Mexican Literature: Collective Challenges to Biopolitical Control.* New York: Palgrave Macmillan, 2015.

Jaramillo Agudelo, Darío. *Darío Jaramillo Agudelo: Una antología.* Edited by Vicente Quirarte. Mexico City: Universidad Nacional Autónoma de México, 2016.

Kang, Minsoo. "The Mechanical Daughter of Rene Descartes: The Origin and History of an Intellectual Fable." *Modern Intellectual History* 14, no. 3 (2017): 633–660.

Kirk, Stephanie. "Gender and Authority in Sor Juana's Sonnet to Sigüenza y Góngora." *Romance Notes* 58, no. 2 (2018): 231–239.

Kornberg, Arthur. *For the Love of Enzymes: The Odyssey of a Biochemist.* Cambridge, MA: Harvard University Press, 1989.

Koselleck, Reinhart. *Futures Past: On the Semantics of Historical Time.* Translated by Keith Tribe. Cambridge, MA: MIT Press, 1985.

Kukla, André. *Social Constructivism and the Philosophy of Science.* London: Routledge, 2000.

Lahsen, Joaquín. "Transposición científica de *En busca de Klingsor* de Jorge Volpi: Teoría del todo." *Latin Americanist* 58, no. 2 (2014): 75–95.

Lakoff, George, and Mark Johnson. *Metaphors We Live By.* Chicago: University of Chicago Press, 1980.

Landsman, Klaas, and Ellen van Wolde, eds. *The Challenge of Chance: A Multidisciplinary Approach from Science and the Humanities.* Cham, Switzerland: Springer, 2016.

Latour, Bruno. *Laboratory Life: The Construction of Scientific Facts.* Princeton, NJ: Princeton University Press, 1986.

———. *We Have Never Been Modern.* Translated by Catherine Porter. Cambridge, MA: Harvard University Press, 1993.

León-Portilla, Miguel. *Aztec Thought and Culture: A Study of the Ancient Nahuatl Mind.* Translated by Jack Emory Davis. Norman: University of Oklahoma Press, 1963.

Livingston, Ira. *Between Science and Literature: An Introduction to Autopoetics.* Urbana: University of Illinois Press, 2006.

López de Abiada, José Manuel, Félix Jiménez Ramírez, and Augusta López Bernasocchi, eds. *En busca de Volpi: Ensayos sobre su obra.* Madrid: Verbum, 2004.

López Labourdette, Adriana. "Laberintos del saber. Una lectura de *En busca de Klingsor* como escenificación de la poscolonialidad." In López de Abiada, Jiménez Ramírez, and López Bernasocchi, *En busca de Volpi,* 187–202.

Lyotard, Jean-François. *The Postmodern Condition: A Report on Knowledge.* Translated by Geoff Bennington and Brian Massumi. Minneapolis: University of Minnesota Press, 1984.

MacGregor, Sherilyn, ed. *Routledge Handbook of Gender and Environment.* New York: Routledge, 2017.

Mack, Katie. *The End of Everything (Astrophysically Speaking)*. New York: Scribner, 2020.

Mancing, Howard. "Embodied Cognitive Science and the Study of Literature." In Simon, Simerka, and Mancing, *Cognitive Cervantes*, 25–69.

Martínez, Sergio M., ed. *De Aztlán Al Río de La Plata: Studies in Honor of Charles M. Tatum*. Newark, DE: Juan de la Cuesta, 2016.

Marún, Gioconda. "El teorema de Gödel y la literatura latinoamericana: Jorge Volpi y Guillermo Martínez." *Hispania* 92, no. 4 (2009): 696–704.

Massis, Diana. "Sabina Berman: Pienso, luego existo: eso es una gran mentira y es cómico; el pensamiento es una parte pequeñísima de la realidad, una parte engreída." *BBC News*, September 4, 2021. https://www.bbc.com/mundo/noticias-58397405.

Mathews, Freya. "The Dilemma of Dualism." In MacGregor, *Routledge Handbook of Gender and Environment*, 54–70.

Maturana, Humberto R., and Francisco J. Varela. *Autopoiesis and Cognition: The Realization of the Living*. Boston: Reidel, 1980.

———. *The Tree of Knowledge: The Biological Roots of Human Understanding*. Boston: Shambhala, 1992.

Meléndez, Priscilla. "(De)Humanizing Humor: The Anthill of Life and Politics in the Theatre of Sabina Berman." *Studies in Twentieth and Twenty First Century Literature* 32, no. 2 (2008): 359–385.

Merchant, Carolyn. *The Death of Nature: Women, Ecology, and the Scientific Revolution*. San Francisco: Harper & Row, 1980.

Mignolo, Walter, and Catherine E. Walsh. *On Decoloniality: Concepts, Analytics, Praxis*. Durham, NC: Duke University Press, 2018.

Monsiváis, Carlos. *Los rituales del caos*. Mexico City: Ediciones Era, 1995.

Morales Gamboa, Fernando. "La crítica de la Razón y la Modernidad desde el género policial en *En busca de Klingsor* de Jorge Volpi." *Espéculo* 34 (2006). https://webs.ucm.es/info/especulo/numero34/klvolpi.html.

Moran, Joe. *Interdisciplinarity: The New Critical Idiom*. London: Routledge, 2006.

Moraña, Mabel. "Escasez y modernidad." In Moraña and Valenzuela, *Precariedades, exclusiones y emergencias*, 25–36.

———. *Inscripciones críticas. Ensayos sobre cultura latinoamericana*. Santiago: Cuarto Propio, 2014.

Moraña, Mabel, and José Manuel Valenzuela, eds. *Precariedades, exclusiones y emergencias: Necropolítica y sociedad civil en América Latina*. Mexico City: Universidad Autónoma Metropolitana, 2017.

Moscona, Myriam. Back cover endorsement. *Principia*, by Elisa Díaz Castelo, Mexico City: Tierra Adentro, 2018.

Murphy, Kieran M. *Electromagnetism and the Metonymic Imagination*. University Park: University of Pennsylvania Press, 2020.

Myers, Robin. "Translator's Note." In *The Dream of Every Cell / El sueño de toda célula*, by Maricela Guerrero, 133–135. Berkeley: Cardboard House Press, 2022.

Newton, Isaac. *The Mathematical Principles of Natural Philosophy*. Translation of *Philosophiæ Naturalis Principia Mathematica* (1687) by Andrew Motte. New York: Daniel Adee, 1846.

"NIH Human Microbiome Project Defines Normal Bacterial Makeup of the Body." *NIH News*, July 31, 2012. https://www.genome.gov/27549144/2012-release-nih-human-microbiome-project-defines-normal-bacterial-makeup-of-the-body.

BIBLIOGRAPHY

Noble, Denis. *The Music of Life: Biology beyond Genes.* Oxford: Oxford University Press, 2006.

Notimex. "El mundo vive una esquizofrenia, derivada de creyentes y ateos: Berman." *20 Minutos*, May 20, 2014. https://www.20minutos.com.mx/noticia/b152880/el-mundo-vive-una-esquizofrenia-derivada-de-creyentes-y-ateos-berman/.

Obiols, Isabel. "El mexicano Jorge Volpi gana el Biblioteca Breve en la 'resurrección' del premio." *El país*, April 15, 1999. https://elpais.com/diario/1999/04/15/cultura/924127206_850215.html.

Okasha, Samir, "Biological Altruism." In *The Stanford Encyclopedia of Philosophy* (Summer 2020 ed.), edited by Edward N. Zalta,. plato.stanford.edu/archives/sum2020/entries/altruism-biological/.

Oldenziel, Ruth. *Making Technology Masculine: Men, Women, and Modern Machines in America, 1870–1945.* Amsterdam: Amsterdam University Press, 1999.

Outes-León, Brais. "Energía, termodinámica, y el imaginario tecnológico en *La raza cósmica* de José Vasconcelos." *Revista de Estudios Hispánicos* 53, no. 1 (2019): 261–282.

Pacheco, José Emilio. *Tarde o temprano.* Barcelona: Tusquets, 2010.

Padilla, Ignacio. *El androide y las quimeras.* Madrid: Páginas de Espuma, 2008.

———. *La vida íntima de los encendedores.* Madrid: Páginas de Espuma, 2016.

———. *Lo volátil y las fauces.* Madrid: Páginas de Espuma, 2018.

Palou, Pedro Ángel. "Físico cuéntico, la *Micropedia* como labor de vida." In Volpi, *Homenaje a Ignacio Padilla*, 43–51.

Pardo Porto, Bruno. "Sale a la luz la obra maestra de Ignacio Padilla." *ABC*, December 16, 2018. https://www.abc.es/cultura/libros/abci-ignacio-padilla-y-cofre-tesoro-201812160106_noticia.html.

Parrilla Sotomayor, Eduardo E. "La isla de James y el biocentrismo como utopía en *El dios de Darwin* de Sabina Berman." *Romanica Silesiana* 10 (2015): 282–291.

Patán, Federico, ed. *Perfiles: Ensayos sobre literatura mexicana reciente.* Boulder, CO: Society of Spanish and Spanish American Studies, 1992.

Paz, Octavio. *The Collected Poems of Octavio Paz 1957–1987.* Edited and translated by Eliot Weinberger. New York: New Directions, 1987.

———. *Corriente alterna.* Mexico City: Siglo XXI, 2000.

———. *El laberinto de la soledad y otras obras.* New York: Penguin, 1997.

———. *Piedra de Sol.* Edited by Ramón Xirau. Mexico City: Universidad Nacional Autónoma de México, 2016.

Paz Soldán, Edmundo. "El otro, el mismo." In Volpi, *Homenaje a Ignacio Padilla*, 39–42.

Pérez, Oscar A. *Medicine, Power, and the Authoritarian Regime in Hispanic Literature.* New York: Routledge, 2022.

Pérez Magallón, Jesús, and Ricardo de la Fuente Ballesteros, eds. *Idealismo, racionalismo y empirismo en la literatura hispánica.* Valladolid, Spain: Verdelís, 2015.

Perezyera, Abril. "Gerardo Herrera Corral, experto del Cinvestav prevé explicar el cosmos a través de poesía." *SDP Noticias*, February 26, 2014. https://www.sdpnoticias.com/estilo-de-vida/experto-herrera-gerardo-corral.html.

Pineda Buitrago, Sebastián. *La musa crítica: Teoría y ciencia literaria de Alfonso Reyes.* Mexico City: El Colegio Nacional, 2007.

Plata Rosas, Luis Javier. "Temple Grandin, autismo y etología." *Nexos*, August 1, 2012. https://www.nexos.com.mx/?p=14948.

BIBLIOGRAPHY

Pliego, Roberto. "Ambidiestro: Sobre *El androide y las quimeras* de Ignacio Padilla." *Nexos: Sociedad, Ciencia, Literatura*, March 2009. https://www.nexos.com.mx/?p=12982.

Plumwood, Valerie. *Environmental Culture: The Ecological Crisis of Reason*. New York: Routledge, 2003.

———. *Feminism and the Mastery of Nature*. New York: Routledge, 1993.

Poe, Edgar Allan. "Maelzel's Chess Player." *Southern Literary Messenger* 2 (April 1836): 318–326. https://www.eapoe.org/works/essays/maelzel.htm.

Potter, Sara. "Disturbing Muses: Gender, Technology and Resistance in Mexican Avant-Garde Cultures." PhD diss., Washington University in St. Louis, 2013.

Prandi, Mónica. "Ciencia-Ficción: Dos modos de entender el mundo. Entrevista a Jorge Volpi." *Letra Urbana* 22 (October 25, 2013). https://letraurbana.com/articulos/ciencia-ficcion-dos-modos-de-entender-el-mundo-entrevista-a-jorge-volpi/.

Pratt, Mary Louise. *Imperial Eyes: Travel Writing and Transculturation*. London: Routledge, 1992.

Priego, Natalia. "Un país en busca de su identidad: Reflexiones sobre el cientificismo de 'Los Científicos' en el México de don Porfirio." In Priego and Lozano, *Paradigmas, Culturas y Saberes*, 37–60.

Priego, Natalia, and Sonia Lozano, eds. *Paradigmas, Culturas y Saberes: La Transmisión Del Conocimiento Científico En Latinoamérica*. Frankfurt: Vervuert, 2007.

Prieto, Julia. "Doing Poetry with Science: Unthinking Knowledge in Sarduy, Perlongher, and Eielson." In Blanco and Page, *Geopolitics, Culture, and the Scientific Imaginary in Latin America*, 230–253.

Pulé, Paul M., and Martin Hultman, eds. *Men, Masculinities, and Earth*. Cham, Switzerland: Palgrave Macmillan, 2021.

Puleo, Alicia H. *Ecofeminismo. Para otro mundo posible*. Madrid: Cátedra, 2017.

Quijano, Aníbal. "Coloniality of Power and Eurocentrism in America." *International Sociology* 15, no. 2 (2000): 215–232.

———. "Coloniality of Power, Eurocentrism, and Latin America." Translated by Michael Ennis. *Nepantla: Views from the South* 1, no. 3 (2000): 533–580.

Quintana-Navarrete, Jorge. "Biopolítica y vida inorgánica: La plasmogenia de Alfonso Herrera." *Revista Hispánica Moderna* 72, no. 1 (2019): 79–95.

Raatikainen, Panu, "Gödel's Incompleteness Theorems." In *The Stanford Encyclopedia of Philosophy* (Spring 2015 ed.), edited by Edward N. Zalta. https://plato.stanford.edu/archives/spr2015/entries/goedel-incompleteness/.

Rafferty, John P. "Mary Anning." In *Encyclopedia Britannica*, May 17, 2022. https://www.britannica.com/biography/Mary-Anning/.

Rama, Ángel. *Transculturación narrativa en América Latina*. Mexico City: Siglo XXI, 1982.

Regalado López, Tomás. "El Crack vs la crítica: encuentros, mediaciones, contrastes." In Brescia and Estrada, *McCrack*, 87–101.

———. *Historia personal del Crack: Entrevistas críticas*. Valencia: Albatros, 2018.

———. "Pesar con las manos las cosas: Ignacio Padilla y el ejercicio del ensayo." *Unidiversidad. Revista de pensamiento y cultura de la Benemérita Universidad Autónoma de Puebla* 30 (January 2018): 49–56.

Requena-Pelegrí, Teresa. "Masculinities, Nature, and Vulnerability: Towards a Transcorporeal Poetics in Washington Irving and Walt Whitman." In Pulé and Hultman, *Men, Masculinities, and Earth*, 135–149.

BIBLIOGRAPHY

Reyes, Alfonso. *El deslinde.* Mexico City: Colegio de México, 1944. https://www .cervantesvirtual.com/nd/ark:/59851/bmc9p513.

Riskin, Jessica. "Machines in the Garden." *Republics of Letters* 1, no. 2 (April 2010): 16–43.

Rivas Nielsen, Niels. "Bosquejos de lo universal: La apertura del lenguaje en *Trilce, Altazor,* y *En la masmédula.*" *Alpha* 44 (July 2017): 137–151.

Rivero, Alicia. "El papel de la ciencia en la literatura hispánica moderna. Introducción." *La Torre: Revista general de la Universidad de Puerto Rico* 3, no. 9 (1998): 525–528.

———. "Heisenberg's Uncertainty Principle in Contemporary Spanish American Fiction." In Fishburn and Ortiz, *Science and the Creative Imagination in Latin America,* 129–150.

———. "La mujer cibernética en 'Salvad vuestros ojos' de Huidobro, 'Anuncio' de Arreola y *El eterno femenino* de Castellanos." *La Torre: Revista de la Universidad de Puerto Rico* 3, no. 9 (1998): 579–596.

Robles, José F. *Polemics, Literature, and Knowledge in Eighteenth-Century Mexico: A New World for the Republic of Letters.* Liverpool: Liverpool University Press, 2021.

Rodríguez, Alejandro. "La ciencia hecha poesía. Principia de Elisa Díaz Castelo." *Figuras: Revista Académica de Investigación* 2, no. 1 (November 2020–February 2021): 118–120.

Rojas Joo, Juan Armando. "The Lightning Bolt: The Allegory of Creation in Alberto Blanco's *Afterglow.*" In Martínez, *De Aztlán Al Río de La Plata,* 307–324.

———. *Posmodernidad y multiforma en la obra de dos poetas mexicanos contemporáneos: Alberto Blanco y Coral Bracho.* Madrid: Pliegos, 2018.

Rovelli, Carlo. *The Order of Time.* Translated by Erica Segre and Simon Carnell. New York: Riverhead Books, 2018.

Ruiz-Pérez, Ignacio. "Repensar la escritura: cuerpo, sexualidad y usos amorosos del siglo XXI en la poesía de Maricela Guerrero." *iMex. México Interdisciplinario. Interdisciplinary Mexico* 7, no. 13 (January 2018): 28–45.

Sánchez Prado, Ignacio M. "El giro (post)humanista. A manera de introducción." *Revista de Crítica Literaria Latinoamericana* 34, no. 68 (2008): 7–18.

———. "El mestizaje en el corazón de la utopía: La raza cósmica entre Aztlán y América Latina." *Revista Canadiense de Estudios Hispánicos* 33, no. 2 (2009): 381–404.

———, ed. *Mexican Literature as World Literature.* New York: Bloomsbury, 2021.

———. *Strategic Occidentalism: On Mexican Fiction, the Neoliberal Book Market, and the Question of World Literature.* Evanston, IL: Northwestern University Press, 2018.

Sandoval, Chela. "New Sciences: Cyborg Feminism and the Methodology of the Oppressed." In Gray, *Cyborg Handbook,* 407–422.

Santiago Ruiz, Eduardo. "La física cuántica: De la metaficción a los problemas éticos en la novela *En busca de Klingsor.*" *Hispanófila* 188 (2020): 99–114.

Shapin, Stephen. *The Scientific Revolution.* Chicago: University of Chicago Press, 1996.

Siete Días Oaxaca. "Conflicto entre Ayutla Mixes y Tamazulapam." YouTube, June 6, 2017. https://www.youtube.com/watch?v=eECthxp_ATM.

Sifuentes Espinoza, Daniel. "Alfonso Reyes y la ciencia y tecnología. Un caso: 'La pólvora en infiernitos.'" *Ciencia UANL* 18, no. 75 (2015): 15–18.

Simon, Julien J., Barbara Simerka, and Howard Mancing, eds. *Cognitive Cervantes.* Special cluster of essays of *Cervantes: Bulletin of the Cervantes Society of America* 32, no. 1 (2012).

Simson, Ingrid. "El principio de la paradoja en la literatura latinoamericana: de Jorge Luis Borges a Jorge Volpi." In Grabe, Lang, and Meyer-Minnemann, *La narración paradójica*, 105–123.

Skirius, John. *El ensayo hispanoamericano del siglo XX*. Mexico City: Fondo de Cultura Económica, 1994.

Skowronski, Ellen. "Words That Breathe: An Interview with José Manuel Marrero Henríquez." *Ecozon@* 6, no. 1 (2015): 107–117.

Snow, C. P. *Two Cultures and the Scientific Revolution*. Cambridge: Cambridge University Press, 1998.

Sobrevilla, David. "Transculturación y Heterogeneidad: Avatares de dos categorías literarias en América Latina." *Revista de Crítica Literaria Latinoamericana* 27, no. 54 (2001): 21–33.

Spencer, Herbert. *The Principles of Biology*. 1866. Project Gutenberg, 2017. https://www.gutenberg.org/ebooks/54612.

Stableford, Brian. *Science Fact and Science Fiction: An Encyclopedia*. New York: Routledge, 2006.

Stewart, Ian. *Calculating the Cosmos: How Mathematics Unveils the Universe*. New York: Basic Books, 2016.

Suárez y López-Guazo, Laura. "The Mexican Eugenics Society: Racial Selection and Improvement." In Glick, Puig-Samper, and Ruiz, *Reception of Darwinism in the Iberian World*, 143–151.

Tejeda, Emilio. "Flotar entre dos equilibrios: La poesía de Elisa Díaz Castelo." *Opción* 205 (December 2018): 104–107. http://opcion.itam.mx/?p=2682.

Trabulse, Elías. "El tránsito del hermetismo a la ciencia moderna: Alejandro Fabián, Sor Juana Inés de La Cruz y Carlos de Sigüenza y Góngora (1667–1690)." *Calíope: Journal of the Society for Renaissance & Baroque Hispanic Poetry* 4, no. 1–2 (1998): 56–69.

———. "El universo científico de Sor Juana Inés de la Cruz." *Colonial Latin America Review* 4, no. 2 (1995): 41–50.

Trujillo, Julio. *El acelerador de partículas*. Mexico City: Almadía, 2017.

Túnel de la Ciencia. "Historia del Túnel de la Ciencia." 2017. http://www.tuneldelaciencia.unam.mx/home/historia-del-tunel-de-la-ciencia.

Ugarte, Ana. "Hibris literaria, eco-autismo y empatía en *La mujer que buceó dentro del corazón del mundo* de Sabina Berman." *Revista de Estudios de Género y Sexualidades* 45, no. 1 (2019): 141–160.

Ulaby, Neda. "Edison's Talking Dolls Can Now Provide the Soundtrack to Your Nightmares." *The Two-Way*, May 5, 2015. www.npr.org/sections/thetwo-way/2015/05/05/404445211/edisons-talking-dolls-can-now-provide-the-soundtrack-to-your-nightmares/.

Useche, Óscar Iván. *Founders of the Future: The Science and Industry of Spanish Modernization*. Lewisburg, PA: Bucknell University Press, 2022.

Varona, Alfonso. "Entrevista a Sabina Berman." *Latin American Theatre Review* 47, no. 1 (2013): 133–144.

Vasconcelos, José. *La raza cósmica*. 1925. Mexico City: Espasa-Calpe, 1966.

Venegas, Socorro. "Chicos superpoderosos." In Volpi, *Homenaje a Ignacio Padilla*, 58–62.

Venning, Thomas. "Time's Arrow: Albert Einstein's Letters to Michele Besso." Christie's, November 14, 2017. https://www.christies.com/features/Einstein-letters-to-Michele-Besso-8422-1.aspx.

BIBLIOGRAPHY

Villiers de L'Isle-Adam, Auguste. *Tomorrow's Eve*. Translated by Robert M. Adams. Urbana: University of Illinois Press, 1982.

Volpi, Jorge. *A pesar del oscuro silencio*. Mexico City: Joaquín Mortiz, 1992.

———. *El fin de la locura*. Mexico City: Seix Barral, 2003.

———. *En busca de Klingsor*. 1999. Barcelona: Seix Barral, 2002.

———, ed. *Homenaje a Ignacio Padilla: De monstruos, dobles, autómatas y quimeras*. Madrid: Páginas de Espuma, 2018.

———. *Leer la mente: El cerebro y el arte de la ficción*. Mexico City: Alfaguara, 2011.

———. *No será la tierra*. Madrid: Alfaguara, 2006.

Wheeler, Wendy. "The Biosemiotic Turn: Abduction, or, the Nature of Creative Reason in Nature and Culture." In Goodbody and Rigby, *Ecocritical Theory*, 270–282.

White, Hayden. *Metahistory: The Historical Imagination in Nineteenth-Century Europe*. Baltimore: Johns Hopkins University Press, 1973.

Whitehead, Alfred North, and Bertrand Russell. *Principia Mathematica*. Cambridge: Cambridge University Press, 1925.

Whitener, Brian. "Ontology and Crises of State and Finance in Jorge Volpi's *En busca de Klingsor*." *Journal of Latin American Cultural Studies* 24, no. 1 (2015): 47–64.

Whitman, Walt. *Leaves of Grass*. Minneapolis: Lerner, 2018.

Wilson, Edward O. *Consilience: The Unity of Knowledge*. New York: Knopf, 1998.

Wood, Gaby. *Living Dolls: A Magical History of the Quest for Mechanical Life*. London: Faber and Faber, 2002.

Wylie, Lesley. *The Poetics of Plants in Spanish American Literature*. Pittsburgh: University of Pittsburgh Press, 2020.

Zalta, Edward N., ed. *The Stanford Encyclopedia of Philosophy*. Winter 2021 ed. https://plato.stanford.edu/.

Zamora, Jorge. "*En busca de Klingsor* y *Frankenstein* aspectos de intertexto y misoginia." *Revista de Literatura Mexicana Contemporánea* 30 (2006): 33–42.

Zamora-Zapata, Carlos. "Crítica contextual: *El corazón del instante* de Alberto Blanco: Ensayo de un método." PhD diss., University of Kentucky, 2014.

Zapata, Isabel. *Alberca vacía. Empty Pool*. Translated by Robin Myers. Mexico City: Argonáutica, 2019.

———. "*Principia*, de Elisa Díaz Castelo: Instrucciones para dejar las cosas intactas." *Revista de la Universidad de México* 840 (September 2018): 140–143.

Index

"¿Abedul y el abeto? El" [The Birch and the Fir] (Guerrero), 116–17
abiogenesis, 150
Acelerador de partículas, El [*The Particle Accelerator*] (Trujillo), 166
"Acta de defunción" [Death Certificate] (Díaz Castelo), 151
actor-network theory, 15
Agamben, Giorgio, 82
agency, 15, 16, 21, 64, 84; as enactment, 43; intra-active nature of, 49, 65; scale and, 61; stochastic element in history and, 49, 65
#AguaParaAyutlaYa campaign, 109
Aguilar, Yásnaya, 109–10, 125
Alaimo, Stacy, 145
"Alberca vacía" [Empty Pool] (Díaz Castelo), 157–59
Alberca vacía [*Empty Pool*] (Zapata, 2019), 195n79
Albertus Magnus, 70
allegory, 43–44
Alonso, Carlos, 7
"Anapoyesis" (Elizondo), 11–12
Anderson, Warwick, 170n23
androcentrism, 71, 75, 80–84
Androide y otras quimeras, El [*The Android and Other Chimeras*] (Padilla, 2008), 19, 68–69, 164; "Las entrañas del Turco" (The Bowels of the Turk), 80–84; "Las furias de Menlo Park" (The Furies of Menlo Park), 73–78; on history of modern Promethean projects, 70–71; on science and human/nature duality,

71–80; "Las tres Alicias" (The Three Alices), 82
androids, 19, 68, 69, 70, 73. *See also* automatons; cyborgs
animals, 68, 94, 111, 116, 184n43; biological altruism in, 103; demands of consumption and death of, 97
Anning, Mary, 78–80, 182n59
Antebi, Susan, 119, 187n65
Antes de nacer [*Before Being Born*] (Blanco, 1983), 23, 24, 44, 46, 165; circularity of, 24, 30; dialectical monism in, 27; metaphor of collage in, 28; quantum jump in, 29–30
Anthropocene, 2, 19, 20, 84, 98, 107
anthropocentrism, 13, 25, 71, 90, 95; moral foundations of, 96; neoliberal capitalism and, 85, 90
A pesar del oscuro silencio [*In Spite of the Dark Silence*] (Volpi, 1992), 10, 60
Ardi (fossil hominin), 149
Ardipithecus ramidus (hominin species), 149
Aridjis, Homero, 112
Arp, Hans, 72
Arreola, Juan José, 72
assemblage, 15, 98–99, 140, 176n61
Asúa, Miguel de, 5
atomic bomb, 47, 57, 58
Australopithecus afarensis (hominin species), 149
autism spectrum, 91–92, 94
Autobiography of Charles Darwin, The (Darwin), 104

213

INDEX

automatons: chess-playing "Turk," 70, 80–84; of Descartes, 67–68; gendered, 166; women's and nonnormative subjects' marginalization and, 69, 70, 73–78. *See also* androids; cyborgs

autopoiesis, 16–17, 19, 21, 110, 115–18; embodied consciousness and, 141, 145; life and the flow of, 129–32; self as node in branching network and, 157; subjectivity and, 137–38

Ávalos Molina, Etna Verónica, 92

Aveni, Anthony, 34

Ayutla, natural spring in, 109–10

Ayuujk Mixe language, 109, 125

Azuela, Arturo, 11

Bains, Paul, 116

Bakhtin, Mikhail, 55, 153, 195n63

Barad, Karen, 16, 17, 24, 32, 118; on agency as enactment, 43; agential "cuts," 65, 176n61; on ethics, 107; on intra-actions, 159; on material-discursive nature of reality, 126–27; on reflection versus diffraction, 163; theory of agential realism, 29, 65

Barnum, P. T., 81

Barreda, Gabino, 9

Barrera-Osorio, Antonio, 5

Beautiful Mind, A (film), 105

becoming, 16, 41, 65, 124, 132; (intra-) activity of, 29; autopoietic, 17; chemistry and processes of, 44–46; perpetual, 10, 13, 28

Beethoven, Ludwig van, 91

Beltrán, Rosa, 73

Benjamin, Walter, 81

Bennett, Jane, 15, 16, 97, 103, 175n65; on embodied consciousness, 140; on evolution and humans, 151

Berman, Sabina, 19, 84, 85–86, 120, 132, 164; ants/anthill motif in works of, 185n54; on constitutive nature of discourse, 102; Darwinian ethical turn of, 106–7, 118; newspaper columns of, 104–5, 182n2; on "schizophrenia" of internal contradictions, 95; television programs of, 184n2; on tuna fishing industry in Mexico, 90–91

Besso, Michele, 133

Bierce, Ambrose, 81

Big Bang cosmogony, 33–34, 135, 152

biology, 12, 136, 164

biopolitics, 2, 6, 10

Bixler, Jacqueline, 85, 86

Blanco, Alberto, 18, 23, 66, 84, 132, 159, 164; on chemistry and processes of becoming, 44–46; dialectical monism of, 32, 36, 59; Eastern philosophy and, 25, 26, 46; entanglement of material and human in poetry of, 25–27; Generación del '68 and, 25; intra-actions in writing of, 36–44; Principle of Complementarity and, 27–29; science-art interconnectivity and, 24

Blanco, María del Pilar, 5

Blanco [White] (Paz), 25

Bohr, Niels, 16, 37, 169n5; on knowledge-making practices, 29, 38; Principle of Complementarity, 24, 27, 36

Bollington, Lucy, 14

Bonaparte, Napoleon, 80

Boom literature, Latin American, 50, 51

Borges, Jorge Luis, 6, 33, 46, 50, 154; blurred distinction between the real and fictional, 73; as literary model in Latin America, 51

Born, Max, 179n52

Bortolotto, María, 91–92

Bracho, Coral, 25

Braidotti, Rosi, 13

brain, as machine, 44, 177n79

Broglie, Louis de, 27

Brown, Dan, 100

Brown, J. Andrew, 72, 73

Buddhism, 25, 34, 40

Buffett, Warren, 105

Bulnes, José, 17

Cabrera-Infante, Guillermo, 2, 50

"Canto a no yo" [Song to Not Myself] (Blanco), 40–43, 46, 159

Canto a un dios mineral [Song to a Material God] (Cuesta, 1942), 10

Cantú Toscano, Mario, 165

capitalism, 72, 79, 86, 90; ecological catastrophe and, 105; end of, 106–7; ethics and, 101; interconnectivity and, 97; language of empire and, 119; mass extinction and, 90; Model of Scarcity and, 105, 106

Capitullari de villis (Charlemagne), 120

Capobianco, Michael, 8

Capra, Fritjof, 26

Carpenter, Victoria, 4, 6

Carroll, Lewis (Charles Dodgson), 82

Cassidy, David, 48

Castellanos, Rosario, 72

Castoriadis, Cornelius, 170n12

Catalá, Rafael, 2, 6
causality, 3, 18, 49; chains of events, 57; in *En busca de Klingsor*, 47, 56
chance, 18, 47, 117, 129, 132; in *En busca de Klingsor*, 49, 54, 56, 57, 59–66, 164; indeterminacy and, 60; as pure category of the present, 61
chaos, 54, 58, 59, 164
Chapa, Teresa, 25, 30
Charlemagne, 120
Chávez Robinson, Irma, 25
chemistry, 12, 44–46, 164
chronotope, 153, 192n63
Cien años de soledad [*One Hundred Years of Solitude*] (García Márquez), 82, 182n68
ciencia ficción (science fiction), 2
ciencia-fusión (science-fusion), 2, 3, 7, 46, 65; autopoiesis and, 16; destabilizing effects of scientific concepts, 21; entanglement of material and human in, 12–17; hybridity and, 15; intra-active universe and, 166; paradox and complementarity deployed by, 161; perception of time in, 10; post-Cartesian intra-relationality and, 104; scientific-literary fusions in contemporary Mexico, 17–21
cienciapoesía, 2
climate change, 20, 109
cognition, 116, 121, 151–54, 166
cognitive linguistics, 13, 27
collage, 28
complementarity, 24, 27, 36, 46, 113, 132, 135, 161
connectivity, 18, 19, 86, 166
Conquest, the, 8
consciousness, embodied, 134, 140, 141, 154
Contemporáneo poets, 10, 50
Coole, Diana, 184n38
Copernicus, 5, 85
Corazón del instante, El [*The Heart of the Instant*] (Blanco, 1998), 31
Cornejo-Polar, Antonio, 171n35
Corriente alterna [*Alternating Current*] (Paz, 1967), 11
Cosmological Principle, 34
Cottingham, John, 186n43
Crack authors, 19, 48, 50, 68, 69, 178n11; "Crack Manifesto," 50, 184n70
"Credo" [Creed] (Díaz Castelo), 136–37, 138, 140, 141, 142, 145, 159
Crowe, Russell, 105
Cuerpo expuesto, El (Beltrán), 73

Cuesta, Jorge, 10
cybernetics, 72
cyborgs, 72, 73, 83. *See also* androids; automatons
Cyborg Manifesto (Haraway), 72

Dalton, David, 6, 73, 82
Daly, Tara, 16
dark matter, 111, 134, 155, 156, 195n71
Darwin, Charles, 9, 19, 79, 86, 89, 103; autism and, 91; fictional theological autobiography of, 99–104; paradigms disrupted by, 85; "positive laws" of nature and, 103–4, 105, 188n91; "survival of the fittest" phrase and, 88, 185n11
Darwinism, 7, 9, 85, 86, 88, 103, 188n71
"Datos" [Data] (Guerrero), 118
Da Vinci Code, The (Brown), 100
Dawkins, Richard, 103
Day, Stuart, 86
death, 20, 47, 133–34; in *El androide y otras quimeras*, 74, 76, 77, 80; in *El dios de Darwin*, 99; in *La mujer que buceó dentro del corazón del mundo*, 97, 98, 99; in *Principia*, 134, 136, 139, 140, 148, 150, 151, 157; in *El sueño de toda célula*, 112, 127
d'Eaubonne, Françoise, 107
decoloniality, 14
DeLanda, Manuel, 15
"De las Redes Sociales a la Red Cósmica del Universo" [From Social Networks to the Cosmic Network of the Universe] (exhibition), 1–2
"De la voz" [On Voice] (Guerrero), 113–14
Deleuze, Gilles, 15, 106, 113, 177n77, 190n18
Deniz, Gerardo, 11, 25, 65, 150
Descartes, René, 94–96; automaton fable involving, 67–68, 74; *cogito ergo sum* declaration, 92–93, 186n34
Descent of Man, The (Darwin, 1871), 19, 85, 101
Deslinde, El [*The Boundary*] (Reyes, 1944), 10
deterritorialization, 119, 121, 129
dialectics, Hegelian, 175n21
dialogism, Bakhtinian, 175n21
Díaz, Porfirio, 9
Díaz Castelo, Elisa, 20, 132, 134, 165, 192n5
DiCaglio, Joshua, 53, 55
Dios de Darwin, El [*Darwin's God*] (Berman, 2014), 19, 85, 105, 185n70, 186n82; clash of scientific and religious narratives in, 99–102; science of morality rooted in nature, 102–4

Discourse on Method (Descartes), 68, 92
DNA (deoxyribonucleic acid), 11, 23, 175n46; double-helix structure of, 24, 27, 165–66; as metaphor, 30
Domínguez Michael, Christopher, 25
Don Quixote de la Mancha, 17
dualisms, 2, 13, 27, 72, 96, 132, 147; Cartesian mind/body split, 68, 93, 146; human/animal, 94; human/nature duality, 19, 85, 93, 107; nature/nurture, 146

ecocriticism, 71, 112, 130
ecofeminism, 93, 107
Edison, Thomas, 70, 74, 75, 81; failure of project to make lifelike dolls, 77, 78; view of women as perfectible machines, 76
Einstein, Albert, 3, 27, 35, 52, 53, 59, 127, 190n3; autism and, 91; letter to Besso family, 133–34, 192n3; rupture and chaos represented by theories of, 58; on time as illusion, 133. *See also* relativity
electromagnetic force, 34, 36, 142, 145, 155
electrons, 3, 27, 29, 60, 84, 179n52, 193n31
Elizondo, Salvador, 11
Emerson, Ralph Waldo, 95
Emmelhainz, Irmgard, 89–90
empiricism, 5, 101, 113, 115, 136, 157
En busca de Klingsor [*In Search of Klingsor*] (Volpi), 2, 69, 100, 164, 173n64, 173n83; chaos and chance narrated in, 59–66; Heisenberg and, 47–48; idea of scale in, 18, 19, 49, 53, 55–59, 62; origins of, 48; plot, 49; scientific/literary analogues in, 51–55; Uncertainty Principle as motif, 49–50, 52, 63, 179n19
energy, 11, 28, 44, 137, 143, 154, 161; atomic weapons and, 47; of the Big Bang, 11; entangled, 40, 46; flows of, 24, 30, 118, 124, 151; intra-actions and, 43; monistic dualities and, 8; one with matter, 32; quantum jump and, 29
En la masmédula [*In the Moremarrow*] (Girondo, 1954), 119
Enlightenment, 9, 52, 71, 84, 179n19; Darwin and, 96; nature/culture dualism and, 93
entanglement, of material and human, 1, 3, 20, 21, 23, 163, 165–66; agency and, 16; in Blanco's poetry, 18, 24, 25–27, 29; in Díaz Castelo's poetry, 132, 148, 156
"Entrañas del Turco, Las" [The Bowels of the Turk] (Padilla), 80–84

Entre Villa y una mujer desnuda [*Between Villa and a Naked Woman*] (Berman, 1993), 86
epistemology, 14, 29, 49, 55, 83, 111–12, 162
Erinyes (goddesses of vengeance), 78
Escalante, Evodio, 25, 27
"Escoliosis" [Scoliosis] (Díaz Castelo), 138–41, 145
Escribir en el aire (Cornejo-Polar, 1994), 171n35
"Esto otro que también me habita (y no es el alma o no necesariamente)" [This Other Stuff That Also Dwells in Me (and It Is Not the Soul or Not Necessarily)] (Díaz Castelo), 146–48, 159–60, 194n44
essay, as "centaur of the genres," 10
ethics, 12, 19, 47, 59, 84, 165; Darwinian, 86–87, 106–7, 188n91; knowledge-making practices and, 65; language and, 126–27. *See also* morality
Eurocentrism, 13
Eve future, L' [*Tomorrow's Eve*] (Villiers de L'Isle-Adam, 1886), 70, 74
extractivism, 20, 21, 110, 112, 122; denunciation of, 124; Enlightenment epistemologies and, 84; human cost of, 127; in language, 121; pain of, 119; person/property dichotomy and, 105; resistances of life against, 130

Faerie Queene, The (Spenser), 158
Farnsworth, May, 91–92
Feliz nuevo siglo doktor Freud [*Happy New Century Doktor Freud*] (Berman, 2002), 86
feminism, 72
Feminism or Death (d'Eaubonne), 107
Fernández Granados, Jorge, 161, 163
Ferrando, Francesca, 14
Fin de la locura, El [*The End of Madness*] (Volpi, 2003), 48–49
"Fin del capitalismo, El" [The End of Capitalism] (Berman), 106
Fishburn, Evelyn, 6
Fornoff, Carolyn, 112
For the Love of Enzymes: The Odyssey of a Biochemist (A. Kornberg), 44
Franken, Clemens, 64
Frankenstein, Victor (fictional character), 77
Franklin, Benjamin, 80
Freud, Sigmund, 190n8
Friis, Ronald, 25, 32, 42, 175n21

INDEX

Frost, Samantha, 186n38
Fuertes Trigal, Siridia, 71, 73
"Furias de Menlo Park, Las" [The Furies of Menlo Park] (Padilla), 73–78
fusion, as metaphor, 2, 20, 161, 162, 163; nuclear, 28, 161

galaxies, 2, 46, 156
Galicia Lechuga, David, 8
Galindo Ulloa, Javier, 24
game theory, 61
García Márquez, Gabriel, 79, 82, 184n68
gender, 71–73, 82, 86, 92
genealogies, 121
Generación del '68 (Generation of '68), 25
general relativity, 34, 160
genetics, 24, 30, 44, 103
"Geometría descriptiva" [Descriptive Geometry] (Díaz Castelo), 134
Ginway, Elizabeth M., 72
Girondo, Oliverio, 119
Gödel, Kurt, 52, 63
Goebel, Robert, 50
Golem [Golem] (Cantú Toscano), 165
golems, Jewish legends of, 70, 77
Gómez-Barris. Macarena, 112, 119, 124
Gómez Gray, Alana, 92
González, Aníbal, 51
Gordo, la pájara y el narco, El [The Fat Guy, the Thieving Woman, and the Narco] (Berman, 1994), 88
Gordon, José, 3–4, 12, 17
Gorgon/Medusa (mythological creature), 162–63
Grandin, Temple, 94
gravity, 34, 134, 136, 155, 160
Greene, Brian, 36, 176n46, 180n52
Gregory the Great, Saint, 77
Gruber, David R., 13
Guadalupe ("river of wolves"), virgin/mother figure of, 129, 150, 192n73
Guadalupe, Luis Juan, 109
Guattari, Félix, 15, 106, 113, 177n77
Guerrero, Luis, 165
Guerrero, Maricela, 10, 19–20, 73, 107, 129, 164; polysemy used by, 120; reterritorialization of language by, 110
Gutiérrez, Alonso, 8

Hamilton, William, 103
Haraway, Donna, 72, 102
Hardt, Michael, 119
Heffes, Gisela, 71, 112
Heidegger, Martin, 57, 61

Heisenberg, Werner, 36, 37; atomic weapons and, 47; in *En busca de Klingsor*, 47–48, 59; Uncertainty Principle, 36, 40, 49–50, 52, 63, 161–62
Heisenberg's Microscope (thought experiment), 36–37, 46
Hekster, Olivier, 61, 65
hermeticism, 9
Herrera, Alfonso, 9
Herrera Corral, Gerardo, 4
Hesiod, 78
heterogeneity, 5, 7–9, 12–14, 124, 164, 171n35
"Hidrocarburos" [Hydrocarbons] (Guerrero), 122–24
Hill, Julia Butterfly, 125
Hiroshima, atomic bombing of, 47
historiography, 2, 12, 61, 65
history, 53, 62, 66, 86; deterministic view of, 18, 49; nineteenth-century linear view of, 58; textuality and access to, 55
Hitchens, Christopher, 188n82
Hitler, Adolf, 49, 53–54, 55, 57; Faustian moral bargain offered by, 59; rise of, 58
Hoeg, Jerry, 4, 5, 170n12, 188n71
"Hombre, El" [Man] (Blanco), 43–44
Hoyos, Héctor, 16, 121
Huchín Sosa, Eduardo, 92
Huerta, David, 25
Huidobro, Vicente, 72
humanism, 7, 12, 13, 14, 19, 86–87, 165
Humphrey, Nicholas, 140
Hutcheon,. Linda, 55, 100
hybridity, 7, 15, 73, 171n35

identity, 14, 31, 106, 148, 194n44; cultural, 112; cyborgs and, 72, 73, 83; destabilization of, 21; embodied consciousness and, 82; Mexican post-Revolutionary, 7; relational understanding of, 56
Incompleteness Theorem, of Gödel, 52, 63, 178n16
Inconcebible universo, El [The Inconceivable Universe] (Gordon), 3
indeterminacy, 45, 58, 60, 132, 164
inflationary cosmogony, 34, 176n46
Insúa Cereceda, Mariela, 62–63
interconnectivity, 1, 3, 40, 86, 99; assemblage as model of, 15; autopoiesis and, 116, 157, 164; language and, 111, 120; language of science and, 122; metaphors and, 13; between science, literature, and culture, 3–7; of science and the spiritual, 26
intertextuality, 86, 99, 104, 156

intra-actions, 16–18, 24, 36–44, 134, 166; flow of mind and, 154–60; life as intra-active process, 45
"Introducciones" [Introductions] (Guerrero), 125–27

Jaimes, Héctor, 184n70
Jane Eyre (C. Brontë), 183n59
Janzen, Rebecca, 119
Jaramillo Agudelo, Darío, 146, 148, 160, 194n44
Johnson, Mark, 12–13

Kempelen, Wolfgang von, 70, 80, 81, 82
kin selection, 103
knowledge, 2, 3, 12, 50, 110; artistic, 3; autopoiesis and, 121; destruction of ecosystems and, 20; experiences of embodied mind and, 137; knowledge-making practices, 29, 38, 65, 162; limits of, 63, 64, 66, 153, 165; poetry and, 114; spread through linguistic apparatuses, 5; transculturated, 17; transposed within human culture, 162
Kornberg, Arthur, 44, 45, 177n79
Kornberg, Roger, 44, 45
Koselleck, Reinhart, 61

Laboratory Life: The Construction of Scientific Facts (Latour and Woolgar), 169n10
Lakoff, George, 12–13
language, 20, 86, 93, 102, 169n5; anthropocentrism and, 96; autism and, 94; deterritorialization of, 111; as mediator of reality, 4; reclaiming of, 125–27; representation and reality in relation to, 101; reterritorialization of, 110
Large Hadron Collider, 4
Larsen, Kevin S., 188n71
Latin America, 7, 9, 51; ecological devastation in, 112; humanism in, 13; "two cultures" in, 5, 6
Latour, Bruno, 5, 169–170n10
Leaves of Grass (Whitman), 176n65
Lecciones [Lessons] (Blanco), 31
Leer la mente [Reading the Mind] (Volpi), 48
"Lengua del imperio, La" [The Language of Empire] (Guerrero), 120
literary studies, 153, 163
Living Dolls (Wood), 70
Livingston, Ira, 145–46, 157, 195n78
logocentrism, 90, 107

López Labourdette, Adriana, 51
Lo volátil y las fauces [Flying Beings and Jaws] (Padilla, 2018), 69
Lucas, George, 70
Lucy (fossil hominin), 149
Lütz, Heinrich von, 63
Lyotard, Jean-François, 101

Mack, Katie, 34
magical realism, 50
male gaze, 11
Mallarmé, Stéphane, 11
Mancing, Howard, 140
Mapas [Maps] (Blanco), 31
Marcuse, Herbert, 72
Marrero Henríquez, José Manuel, 130
Martí, José, 6
Marún, Giaconda, 63
Marx, Karl, 190n8
mass extinction, 20, 90
Matemáticas para la felicidad y otras fábulas [Mathematics for Happiness and Other Fables] (Berman, 2017), 19, 85, 87, 104, 105
materialism, new, 15, 21, 98, 176n65
materiality, 24, 29, 46, 98, 165, 166; Cartesian duality and, 95; divide between discursivity and, 36; monism and, 33
"Materia oscura" [Dark Matter] (Díaz Castelo), 155–57, 158
mathematics, 12, 32, 49, 178n16
Mathews, Freya, 93–94, 96
matter (materia), 2, 17, 20, 166; distribution in universe, 34; flows of, 24, 28, 30; interconnectivity and, 12, 43, 137, 157, 159; intra-actions and, 12, 15, 25, 42, 43; life and, 150, 151; mechanistic understanding of, 46, 84; mind and, 44, 93; in one with energy, 32; relational nature of, 39; theory of everything and, 3. *See also* entanglement, of material and human
Maturana, Humberto, 115, 126–27, 129; on autopoiesis, 16–17; on cognition, 156; on "structural couplings," 17, 116, 141, 153, 157
mechanization, 69, 74, 78, 81
Medicine, Power, and the Authoritarian Regime in Hispanic Literature (Pérez), 6
medicine/medical studies, 6, 67, 136
Meditaciones [Meditations] (Blanco, 2022), 44
Meléndez, Gloria, 8
Meléndez, Priscilla, 187n54

INDEX

memory, 134, 136, 143, 154, 156, 158
Mendel, Gregor, 9
Merchant, Carolyn, 71, 72, 78–79
Merchant, Paul, 14
mestizaje (miscegenation), 7, 9, 25
Mestizo Modernity: Race, Technology, and the Body in Postrevolutionary Mexico (Dalton), 6–7
metaphors, 24, 26, 36, 51, 66, 139; anthropomorphic, 117; autism and incomprehensibility of, 96, 98; of complementarity, 28; conceptual processes in, 12–13, 27; connectivity and, 27; of entanglement, 3; of hybridity, 171n35; lightning as, 43; nature's switching of, 30; of nuclear fusion, 161; transposition of scientific concepts through, 53, 59, 115
metaphysics, 2, 8, 10
Mexican Revolution, 10
Mexico: in colonial and viceregal periods, 8; *Guerra contra el narcotráfico* (War on Narcotrafficking), 88; literature and science in, 7–12
Mexico City, 1, 14; metro system, 1–2, 169n3; Monumento de la Raza (Monument of the People/Race), 7–8; Túnel de la ciencia [Tunnel of Science] museum, 1, 3, 7, 156
microorganisms, 147, 148, 191n46
Micropedia [Micropedia] (Padilla), 68, 69, 84
"Miedo" [Fear] (Guerrero), 127
Mignolo, Walter, 14, 15, 111, 190n8
modernism, 6, 75
modernity, 5, 6–7, 119
Molière (Berman, 2000), 86
monism, 33, 147; dialectical, 27, 32, 36, 59; Mayan numerals and, 34
Monsiváis, Carlos, 2, 169n3
Morales Gamboa, Fernando, 179n19
morality, 47, 52, 100; Darwinism and, 85, 86, 88–90; Judeo-Christian, 19, 85, 103; natural world and, 86, 105; unmoored in world of indeterminacy, 59. *See also* ethics
Moraña, Mabel, 14, 105–6
more-than-human world/universe, 2, 21, 24, 91, 133; ecosystem degradation and, 85; embodied consciousness and, 145; ethics and, 18; humanity reoriented within, 12, 14; indigenous languages and cosmovisions, 125, 129; interconnectivity and, 13, 105; language of, 118; relational separation from the human, 95

Moscona, Myriam, 136
Mujer que buceó dentro del corazón del mundo, La [*Me, Who Dove into the Heart of the World*] (Berman, 2010), 19, 85, 86, 101, 104; Berman's Darwinian ethical turn and, 106–7; reflections on Descartes and Darwin in, 90–96; transmutations and connectivities in, 97–99, 187n59
Music of Life, The: Biology beyond Genes (Noble), 30, 45
Myers, Robin, 112, 114
mysticism, 25, 26

Nagasaki, atomic bombing of, 47
Narco negocia con Dios, El [*The Narco Makes Deals with God*] (Berman, 2012), 19, 85, 88–90, 104
Nash, John, 105–6
natural philosophy, 8, 9
natural selection, 102–3, 104, 185n11. *See also* Darwin, Charles
nature-culture divide, 2, 5, 16; capitalism and, 87; human/nature duality, 71–80; logic of colonization and, 93; man/woman divide and, 186n38; Nature as separate ontological entity to exploit, 119–20; nature stripped of divine quality, 68; subjugation of nature, 69
necropolitics, 21, 88–89, 127
Negri, Antonio, 119
neoliberalism, 19, 86, 88, 105, 112
Newton, Isaac, 34–36, 64, 136, 137, 160
Nezahualcoyotl, 8
Nobel Prize, 44, 105
Noble, Denis, 30, 45
Nociones de biología [*Notes on Biology*] (Herrera, 1904), 9
No será la tierra [*Season of Ash*] (Volpi, 2006), 49
nostalgia, 113, 151
nuclear forces, strong and weak, 34
nuclear fusion, 28, 161
Números imaginarios [*Imaginary Numbers*] (Guerrero), 165

objectivism, 13, 32, 36
objectivity, 43, 146
Observer Effect, 36, 37, 39, 64, 65, 161, 162
"Oda a los ancestros" [Ode to the Ancestors] (Díaz Castelo), 149–51
Olbers's Paradox, 151–52, 154
Oldenziel, Ruth, 75
Ometeotol (godlike male-female unity), 8

On the Origin of Species (Darwin, 1859), 19, 85, 86, 103, 185n11, 188n71; Berman's use as intertext, 101

Oparin-Haldane hypothesis, 150

Ortiz, Eduardo, 6

Outes-León, Brais, 7

oxygen cycle, 130

Pacheco, José Emilio, 4, 11, 33, 112

Padilla, Ignacio, 120, 132, 164, 166; Crack generation of authors and, 18–19, 48; on legend of Descartes's mechanical automaton, 67–68

Page, Joanna, 5

Palou, Pedro Ángel, 69

Paracelsus, 70

Pardo, Ballester, 121

Pardo Porto, Bruno, 69

Parrilla Sotomayor, Eduardo, 100

particles, subatomic, 34, 36, 38; behavior as waves, 60; "collapse" of wave function, 64, 181n67; as probabilistic wave function, 63

"Partidas" [Beginnings] (Guerrero), 131–32

Paz, Octavio, 10, 11, 25, 89, 150, 174n21

Paz Soldán, Edmundo, 80

Peceras [Fishbowls] (Guerrero, 2013), 111

Pérez, Oscar A., 6

Pérez-Reverte, Arturo, 100

Philosophiae Naturalis Principia Mathematica (Newton, 1687), 136, 160

philosophy, 7, 27, 38, 68

philosophy of history, 55

photosynthesis, 116, 129

Physica speculatio (Gutiérrez, 1557), 8

physics, 11, 12, 36, 49, 136, 164; classical, 49, 61, 64, 66; human experience and, 51–52; Newtonian, 60, 84

Piedra de Sol [Sunstone] (Paz), 150

Planck, Max, 27

plasmogenia (plasmogeny), 9–10

Pliny, 5

Plumwood, Valerie, 87, 93

Poe, Edgar Allan, 80–81

"Poema de Tristán" (Deniz), 11

"Poemas de amor, 1" [Poems of Love, 1] (Jaramillo Agudelo), 146, 148, 160

poetry, 2, 27, 36, 124, 169n5; communicative capacity of, 39; complementarity with science, 30, 135; Mesoamerican, 8; metapoetry, 46, 66; "planetary poetics," 112; poetics of empathy, 25; similarities with science, 11; of Sor Juana, 8–9

polysemy, 114, 150

positivism, Comtean, 9

post-Boom literature, 50

posthumanism, 7, 12–14, 21, 73, 106

postmodernism, 55, 101–2

poststructuralism, 29

Potter, Sara, 73

power, colonial matrix of, 111, 190n8

Pratt, Mary Louise, 5, 120

"Preguntas" [Questions] (Guerrero), 124

Primero sueño [First Dream] (Sor Juana, 1692), 8

Principia (Díaz Castelo, 2018), 20, 134, 135, 190n5; "Acta de defunción" (Death Certificate), 151; "Alberca vacía" (Empty Pool), 157–59; "Credo" (Creed), 136–37, 138, 140, 141, 142, 145, 159; as dialogue with Newton, 136; embodied cognition in spacetime, 151–54; embodied experience in space, 142–48; "Escoliosis" (Scoliosis), 138–41, 145; "Esto otro que también me habita" (This Other Stuff That Also Dwells in Me), 146–48, 159–60, 194n44; experience of embodied mind in, 137–42; human mind-body in deep time, 149–51; intra-actions and flow of mind in, 154–60; knowledge and the emotive in, 136; materiality of presence and absence in, 137; "Materia oscura" (Dark Matter), 155–57, 158; "Oda a los ancestros" (Ode to the Ancestors), 149–51; "Primogénita" (First-born), 152; "Puntos de Lagrange" (Lagrange Points), 154; "Radiografías" (X-rays), 142–46, 159; "Sobre la luz que no vemos y otras formas de desaparecer" (Of the Light That We Do Not See and Other Ways to Disappear), 151–54; "Zona habitable" (Habitable Zone), 154

Principia Mathematica (Russell and Whitehead), 32

"Principio de incertidumbre" [Uncertainty Principle] (Fernández Granados), 161–63

Principle of Complementarity, 24, 27, 36

probabilistic systems, 60, 61, 62, 66

probability waves, 180n52

"Prodigiosa tarde de Baltazar, La" [Balthazar's Marvelous Afternoon] (García Márquez), 79

Proyecto Manhattan [Manhattan Project] (Díaz Castelo, 2021), 135

Puleo, Alicia, 186n38

"Pulmones" [Lungs] (Guerrero), 115–16

INDEX

"Puntos de Lagrange" [Lagrange Points]
(Díaz Castelo), 154
Putin, Vladimir, 105

quantum jump/leap, 29, 175n31
quantum mechanics, 3, 26, 34, 84, 133,
169n5; Copenhagen Interpretation of,
36, 38; in *En busca de Klingsor*, 49, 57, 66
Quijano, Aníbal, 14, 120, 190n8
"Química" [Chemistry] (Blanco), 44–45, 46
Quintana-Navarrete, Jorge, 10

Raatikainen, Panu, 177n16
race, 6, 7, 73,
racism, 7
Racknitz, Joseph, 81
"Radiografías" [X-rays] (Díaz Castelo),
142–44, 159
Raíz cuadrada del cielo, La [*The Square
Root of Heaven*] (Blanco, 2016), 18, 40;
"Declaración de principios" (Declara-
tion of Principles), 31–32, 43; "El
hombre" (Man), 43–44; poetic epigraph
to, 164; "Primera lección de geometría"
(First Lesson of Geometry), 32–34;
"Teoría de conjuntos" (Set Theory),
39–40, 43, 144; "Teoría de la incertidum-
bre" [Theory of Uncertainty], 36–39;
"Teoría de Newton" [Newton's Theory],
18, 34–35
Raza cósmica, La [*The Cosmic Race*]
(Vasconcelos, 1925), 7, 9
readers, as participants in act of creation,
24, 27
Real y Pontificia Universidad de México
(Royal and Pontifical University of
Mexico), 9
redshift (Doppler effect), 152, 194n56
Regalado López, Tomás, 50
Reino de lo no lineal, El [*The Realm of the
Nonlinear*] (Díaz Castelo, 2020), 134,
190n5
Relámpagos paralelos [*Parallel Lightning
Flashes*] (Blanco), 40–41
relativity, 52, 152, 153, 194n63; general
relativity, 34, 160; special relativity, 59;
world as events rather than things, 154
religion, 12, 25, 26, 27, 95; Abrahamic
monotheism, 103; clash with science,
101; Darwin and, 100
Republic of Letters, 9
Requena-Pelegrí, Teresa, 176n65
"Respirar" [Breath] (Guerrero), 129–30
reterritorialization, 110, 121

Reyes, Alfonso, 10, 11, 13
Riskin, Jessica, 71
Rivero, Alicia, 6, 72
Robles, José Francisco, 9
Rodríguez, Alejandro, 135
Rojas, Max, 150
Rojas Joo, Juan Armando, 25, 33
"Romanza de la niña y el pterodáctilo"
[Ballad of the Girl and the Pterodactyl]
(Padilla), 78–80
Rovelli, Carlo, 152, 154, 158
"Ruinas circulares, Las" [The Circular
Ruins] (Borges), 82
Ruiz-Pérez, Ignacio, 111
Russell, Bertrand, 32

Sánchez Prado, Ignacio, 9, 13, 14, 173n83
Sandoval, Chela, 73
Santiago Ruiz, Eduardo, 65
Sarduy, Severo, 6
Schrödinger, Erwin, 27, 58, 59, 60
Schrödinger's Cat, 40
science: clash with religion, 101;
commodification in name of, 78–80;
history and, 61; literature and, 4, 160,
161, 163; magic and, 51; as metanarrative, 101; permeable boundaries of, 4;
poetry and, 11, 30, 135; reductionist
claims and, 44–45; scientific method,
115; subjugation of nonnormative
subjects and, 69; transition from
natural philosophy to, 8, 9
science–art relationship, 3–4, 46;
entanglement of material and human
in, 24; heterogeneity and, 8; language
and, 11; rhizomatic multiplicity of
connections, 6; Snow's "two cultures,"
4, 5, 6
science fiction, 2, 70, 73
science studies, 29
Scientific Revolution, 5, 19, 69, 120, 164;
human relation to natural world and, 71,
78; mechanization of nature and, 78;
nature/culture dualism and, 93
"Segunda teoría del caos" [Second Theory
of Chaos] (Blanco), 59–60
Selfish Gene, The (Dawkins, 1976), 103
Se llaman nebulosas [*They're Called
Nebulae*] (Guerrero, 2010), 111
"Señor muy viejo con unas alas enormes,
Un" [A Very Old Man with Enormous
Wings] (García Márquez), 82
set theory, 39–40, 175n58, 176n61
sexism, 56

sexuality, 86
Shapin, Stephen, 78
"Si" [If] (Trujillo), 166
Sifuentes Espinoza, Daniel, 10
Sigüenza y Góngora, Carlos, 8
Skirius, John, 10
Snow, C. P., 4, 6
"Sobre la luz que no vemos y otras formas de desaparecer" [Of the Light That We Do Not See and Other Ways to Disappear] (Díaz Castelo), 151–54
social Darwinism, 7, 89, 185n11
"Social Imaginary," 4, 5, 170n12
"Song of Myself" (Whitman), 40–41, 160
Sor Juana, 8–9, 11
Spain, 5, 8, 192n73
Spanish language, 6
special relativity, 59, 165
Spencer, Herbert, 185n11
Spenser, Edmund, 158
Stableford, George, 70
string theory, 34
structural couplings, 17, 126, 128–29, 147, 153; defined, 116; embodied conscious-ness and, 141, 145–46
Suárez y López-Guazo, Laura, 9
subject-object relationship, 2, 15, 25, 38
subjectivism, 13, 32, 36
subjectivity, 14, 17, 20, 146, 158; automata and, 80; autopoiesis and, 137–38; destabilization of, 21, 38; interconnected nature of 95, 134, 137; limits of, 165; material reality and, 29, 43, 159; monistic, 42
Sueño de toda célula, El [The Dream of Every Cell] (Guerrero, 2018), 10, 19–20, 73, 107, 164, 165; "¿El abedul y el abeto?" (The Birch and the Fir), 116–17; autopoiesis concept in, 110, 115–18, 129–32; "Datos" (Data), 118; "De la voz" (On Voice), 113–14; fear confronted and embraced, 127–28; "Hidrocarburos" (Hydrocarbons), 122–24; "Introduccio-nes" (Introductions), 125–27; language of empire in, 118–24; language reclaimed in, 125–27; "La lengua del imperio" (The Language of Empire), 120; "Miedo" (Fear), 127; nurturing of life in, 128–29; "Partidas" (Beginnings), 131–32; "Preguntas" (Questions), 124; "Pulmones" (Lungs), 115–16; "Respirar" (Breath), 129–30; science, language, and care in, 111–15
sunyata (Buddhist concept), 34

Tabla de Flandes, La (Pérez-Reverte), 100
Taoism, 27
Tao of Physics, The (Capra), 26
technology, 6, 70, 75, 80, 81, 164
Tejeda, Emilio, 135–36
"Teoría de conjuntos" [Set Theory] (Blanco), 39–40, 43, 144
"Teoría de la gravedad" [Theory of Gravity] (Blanco), 160
"Teoría de la incertidumbre" [Theory of Uncertainty] (Blanco), 36–39
"Teoría de Newton" [Newton's Theory] (Blanco), 18, 34–35
Teorías [Theories] (Blanco), 31
"territorialization," 15
theater, 2, 88, 165
theory of everything, 3, 34, 179n19
"Theses on the Philosophy of History" (Benjamin), 81
Thousand Plateaus, A (Deleuze and Guattari), 15, 177n77
Through the Looking-Glass (Carroll), 82
time, 2, 20, 28; abolition of, 10; cyclical time in Aztec tradition, 150; four-dimensional universe and, 33; human mind-body in deep time, 149–51
transculturation, 2, 14, 17, 122, 171n35
"Tres Alicias, Las" [The Three Alices] (Padilla), 82
Trujillo, Julio, 166
Túnel de la ciencia [Tunnel of Science] museum (Mexico City), 1, 3, 7, 156

Ugarte, Ana, 92
Uncertainty Principle, 36, 40, 49–50, 63, 161–62, 179n19
unified field theory, 35
universe, observable, 41

"vanguardia blanca" (white avant-garde), 25
Varela, Francisco, 16, 115, 126–27; on cognition, 156; on love and social life, 129; on "structural couplings," 17, 116, 141, 153, 157
Vasconcelos, José, 7, 9, 11, 13, 171n35
Vavilov, Nikolai, 125
Velásquez, Lucila, 6
Venegas, Julieta, 109
Venegas, Socorro, 79
Venn diagrams, 176n58
Vida íntima de los encendedores, La [The Private Life of Lighters] (Padilla), 67, 77, 82, 182n68

INDEX

Villeda, Karen, 112
Villiers de L'Isle-Adam, Auguste, 70, 74
Villoro, Juan, 109
Volpi, Jorge, 2, 10, 47–48, 66, 77, 84, 132, 166; Crack generation of authors and, 48, 68; language of European colonial knowledge coopted by, 173n83; on parallel of police and scientific investigations, 54; on science and literature, 4; on writing of *En busca de Klingsor*, 51
Von Neumann, John, 61

Walsh, Catherine, 111
War and Peace (Tolstoy), 56
Wheeler, Wendy, 30
White, Hayden, 49, 55, 180n59
Whitehead, Alfred North, 32
Whitman, Walt, 40–41, 160, 176n65
Wilson, Edward, 4
women: automata and, 73–78; in *En busca de Klingsor*, 57; female cyborgs, 73; nature and materiality associated with, 72; subjugation of, 19, 69
Wood, Gaby, 70, 74, 76, 81, 82
Woolgar, Steve, 169n10
World War I, 58
World War II, 58
Wylie, Lesley, 112

X-rays, 143, 147, 149, 193n31

Yellowstone National Park, rerelease of wolves into, 125
yin–yang complementarity, 27, 36

Zamora-Zapata, Carlos, 32
Zamora, Jorge, 57
Zapata, Isabel, 112, 136, 157, 195n79
Zea, Leopoldo, 13
Zen Buddhism, 25, 175n21
Žižek, Slavoj, 88
"Zona habitable" [Habitable Zone] (Díaz Castelo), 154

About the Author

BRIAN T. CHANDLER is a professor of Spanish at the University of North Carolina Wilmington. His research on contemporary Latin American narrative, theater, and poetry has been published in edited volumes and journals such as *Romance Quarterly, Latin American Literary Review, Hispania,* and *Chasqui.*

Printed and bound by CPI Group (UK) Ltd, Croydon, CR0 4YY
01/12/2024

14602660-0003